PRAISE FOR
BOYS KEEP SWINGING

"Wow! So brutally honest and such a really addictive read."

ELTON JOHN

"On the stage, Jake Shears is a triumphant explosion of unembar-
rassed carnality and charm. On the page, he's very much the same.
Boys Keep Swinging is one courageous joyride of a memoir. It should
be illegal for rock stars to write so beautifully."

ARMISTEAD MAUPIN

"*Boys Keep Swinging* goes beyond the origin story behind some of my
favorite music. . . . A wild, sexy, emotional ride through underground
New York at the millennium. From the fringes to the top, it's a tale
that speaks to the outsider in all of us."

ANDY COHEN

"Jake Shears puts it all on the line. He draws you in and you can't look
away. *Boys Keep Swinging* is the book everyone will be reading and
talking about."

SANDRA BERNHARD

"This is a beautiful, fascinating memoir by a beautiful guy who has
lived a fascinating life—and he has the insights and receipts to prove
it. Wonderful!"

DAN SAVAGE

"[Shears] writes fluidly and often affectingly, giving shape to his peri-
patetic, never-dull life. . . . Readers will be captivated."

BOOKLIST

"Fun and compulsively readable, precisely the kind of book one would expect from someone who sang about getting his mama jacked up on cheap champagne . . . *Boys Keep Swinging* is no ghostwritten autobiography; Shears studied creative writing at Eugene Lang College in New York. But what he has written is splendid: a star-studded memoir, a cultural history of gay millennial New York, and an origin story for one of the most important pop acts of the 2000s."

LAMBDA LITERARY

"[Chronicles] not just the ups and downs of rock stardom but a saucy slice of downtown New York in the aughts."

THE NEW YORK TIMES

"Entertaining and honest."

NEW YORK POST

"A thoroughly endearing portrait . . . an exhilarating yet poignant account of one boy taking flight. And [Shears] is just as clever a narrator as he is a lyricist, keenly sketching the gay bars and nightclubs that fostered the electroclash scene in which the band spawned. *Boys Keep Swinging* is an absolute joy, even for those who don't feel like dancing."

SHELF AWARENESS
(STARRED REVIEW)

"Scissor Sisters front man Jake Shears shows a whole new side of himself in this candid account. He sensitively reveals his lifelong struggle with self-acceptance while also detailing New York's queer scene with salacious ease."

ENTERTAINMENT WEEKLY

"Well-crafted and entertaining."

THE ADVOCATE

BOYS KEEP SWINGING

A MEMOIR

JAKE SHEARS

ATRIA PAPERBACK

New York   London   Toronto   Sydney   New Delhi

ATRIA
PAPERBACK

An Imprint of Simon & Schuster, Inc.
1230 Avenue of the Americas
New York, NY 10020

First Atria Paperback edition January 2019

ATRIA PAPERBACK and colophon are trademarks of Simon & Schuster, Inc.

For information about special discounts for bulk purchases, please contact Simon & Schuster Special Sales at 1-866-506-1949 or business@simonandschuster.com.

The Simon & Schuster Speakers Bureau can bring authors to your live event. For more information or to book an event, contact the Simon & Schuster Speakers Bureau at 1-866-248-3049 or visit our website at www.simonspeakers.com.

Interior design by Amy Trombat

Manufactured in the United States of America

10 9 8 7 6 5 4 3 2 1

The Library of Congress has cataloged the hardcover edition as follows:
Names: Shears, Jake, author.
Title: Boys keep swinging / Jake Shears.
Description: First Atria books hardcover edition. | New York : Atria Books, 2018.
Identifiers: LCCN 2017038858 (print) | LCCN 2017039837 (ebook) | ISBN 9781501140143 (ebook) | ISBN 9781501140129 (hardcover) | ISBN 9781501140136 (pbk.)
Subjects: LCSH: Shears, Jake. | Singers—United States—Biography.
Classification: LCC ML420.S5352 (ebook) | LCC ML420.S5352 A3 2018 (print) | DDC 782.42164092 [B] —dc23
LC record available at https://lccn.loc.gov/2017038858

ISBN 978-1-5011-4012-9
ISBN 978-1-5011-4013-6 (pbk)
ISBN 978-1-5011-4014-3 (ebook)

For my rocks, Kelly and Mark

And my rolls, Josh and Brody

PART 1

YOUTH

1

I WAS BORN A SHOWMAN. FOR YEARS, EVEN MY BIRTH played out in my head as a grand entrance. I assumed my mother's giant stomach had exploded in some public place, followed by a balloon drop, confetti cannons, and people celebrating in the streets. It would have been a mess, a gory birthday party, with a lot of cleanup involved, not to mention my poor mother would have had to have been put back together.

I haunted all corners of my house, like a jazzy poltergeist with swinging hips and splayed hands. I terrorized my sister's unsuspecting girlfriends. My favorite catchphrase, ironically, was "I looooooove women!" I was desperate for their revulsion. *Ew, your brother is like . . . so gross.* But then I would ratchet up the charm, a perfect little gentleman. *Aw, he's so sweet. Where'd you get those blue eyes, huh?*

In kindergarten, I told flat-out lies. I confessed that I was *very* sick, bathing in the concern of my classmates—and especially that of their mothers. God, sympathy was satisfying. One afternoon, my mom picked me up from school and my teacher said she hoped I would get better soon. My jig was up. "You can't try to make people believe things that aren't true," my mom said afterward.

But human pity was preferable to the distant regard my stuffed animals offered. They lined my bedroom shelves and did not bother to applaud my one-man shows, which I performed against the wooden footboard of my bed. No matter how loud I sang they just stared back. Tough crowd.

My imagination was wild and irrational. The first time my mom took me to the doctor for my blood to be drawn, for some unknown reason I thought everyone would be wearing Victorian garb, that I'd be auctioned off to the highest bidder in some antiquated display. I was so sad, thumbing through a booger-ridden Mr. Happy book in the waiting room, thinking it would be the last time I saw my mother. I was relieved that there ended up being no auction, but the drab gray room into which they led me, where two ladies told me I'd feel something like a beesting, still wasn't half as cool as the Dickensian scenario I had imagined. Unsurprisingly, I cried.

My sisters would get their hair done at a beauty parlor that had a huge painting on its front window of a woman with giant, Medusa-like locks. "Is that what you're gonna look like?" I remember asking just before they shut the backseat car door in my face. I was disappointed when they finally emerged from the salon, not with giant, freaky hairdos that could barely fit into the car but with simple, feathered blowouts. If only it had been my salon, they would have looked like super-vixens with ashen bushfires encircling their painted faces.

Maybe that was why when I was asked what I wanted to be when I grew up, the first thing I could think of was a "hairdresser." I loved going to the barber with my dad, feeling like a big boy riding in the front seat. My first haircuts were from a vampy woman outside the Phoenix suburbs by way of sleepy desert side roads. She had long black hair and smoked as she cut, a cigarette clamped between her lips while I sucked on my binky.

Later, my regular barber spot was in the entryway of a Smitty's grocery store. When I sat in the chair, a very tan, wrinkled man would ask me if I wanted "the G.I. Joe or the Mr. T?" Duh, the Mr. T: He had a Mohawk. My dad, as if he believed the barber were serious, tapped his shoulder and said, "Just a regular cut is fine." I was crestfallen when we left. My hair looked like it always did.

One day in a Stride Rite shoe store, an older, masculine woman wearing a polyester pantsuit found out I couldn't tie my own shoes. She showed me the bunny-rabbit-ear method, making two loops and twisting them around each other. Suddenly I could tie them myself. I walked out of the store with a pair of lace-up Hot Wheels sneakers that she *swore* would make me run faster. On the playground, when I put them to test, it was total baloney. I ran no faster than I had in my old Velcro-fastened shoes.

It seemed that everywhere I went, someone was up-selling a total dud. Whether it was some toy slime creature that didn't secrete like it had in the commercial, or Michael Jackson not *actually* performing in *Captain EO* at Disneyland—it was just a 3-D movie of him that played all day long—the world was full of exaggerations. I felt gullible, and often embarrassed at my expectations of real magic. Sometimes I thought people could read my overeager thoughts, and it humiliated me.

I didn't understand that what I saw on TV wasn't real. I stood paralyzed one Saturday afternoon, a dirty Cabbage Patch Kid dangling from my hand, as Gene Siskel and Roger Ebert reviewed Pink Floyd's *The Wall*. They showed a clip of schoolkids walking into a meat grinder and getting turned into sausage. Where was that grinder, and what would cause me to fall into it? The image was now branded on my psyche, but *so was that song.* I needed to hear it again. I found my mom in her bedroom and did the best rendition I could, hoping she'd be familiar with it. What did *"We don't need no education"* mean?

Soon after, she took me to a plush multiplex to see the musical *Annie.* I'd been singing "Tomorrow" to the secretary in my dad's office, to my friend's mom, to anyone who would listen. The movie theater had gigantic glass windows in the front, and inside, red and orange velvet curtains and patterned carpets that stank of butter. Every theater door was a mystery; each one marked a new universe. But I was certain we would walk into the wrong theater and see something just as horrible as those kids falling into the meat grinder.

Another time, my mother took me and my sisters to see *Ghostbusters*. As soon as the first specter popped out at the five-minute mark, the fabric of my reality unraveled even further. I dragged my mom into the theater lobby and, of course, cried. We went shopping in the adjoining mall while my sisters finished the film, and I watched as my mom flicked through a rack of leggings, the thin material in her fingers just like the scrim between our world and dimensions unknown. I was so scared that some hideous creature from hell would burst from behind the ruffle-neck maroon blouses and create total chaos.

One single detail could now send me into an obsessive state of fear. There was a shot of someone's hand in a bottling plant at the beginning of *Silkwood*: It seemed a harbinger of doom. The video for "Don't Come Around Here No More" played behind my eyelids when they closed, Tom Petty scooping up Alice in Wonderland's insides as if they were a cake. I couldn't sleep alone. I'd wake up in the middle of the night, pad into the hallway, and just stand there. The house was alive and breathing. I crept into my parents' bed on my mom's side. With a gentle hand she'd lead me back to my room and wait until I fell asleep. But sometimes she'd just give up and let me sleep next to her. That habit continued almost through high school.

Still, I couldn't leave well enough alone and was fascinated by what scared me. I would make my sisters give a play-by-play of *Aliens* or *Gremlins*. They were patient and skilled at breaking down the movies into acts, turning blockbuster thrillers into bedtime stories. I could browse forever in our video store. The VHS boxes were graphic and scary, and I hovered near their lewd cardboard cases until I was made to retreat to the children's section, where I supposedly belonged. How I resented the woman at the counter. She always suggested I take home boring animal movies, or family westerns. I felt obligated and rented them to be polite, not wanting to hurt her feelings. At home, *Phar Lap* or *The Golden Seal* played while I sat alone and watched, bored. I hated the movies she recommended; there was never anything even resembling a Muppet, and the horses always died at the end.

My nightmares were tempered by dreams of men. I thought of them holding me kindly. I wanted to fall asleep in their arms. While watching *The Muppet Show* with my sisters one evening, I turned to them and said that I was going to marry the episode's guest host, Christopher Reeve. I imagined he would make a perfect husband, and wouldn't it be great to be able to wrap my arms around his shoulders? My sisters were gentle but firm: Boys didn't marry boys. My face flushed. It was the first time I remember feeling ashamed.

At the cusp of the '80s, Mesa, Arizona, was where the suburbs of Phoenix slowly transitioned into desert. It was a haven of RV parks, a simmering mass of gravel lawns and parking lots, pockmarked with newly constructed strip malls and chain grocery stores. New businesses seemed exciting only until the last of the grand-opening balloons popped, the dust wearing the sheen of the signs to scratched plastic.

My family lived in a ranch-style house that my father had built in the '60s. It sat on a square piece of land surrounded by orange groves and a cotton field, which was sometimes also a watermelon patch. The house was as Spielbergian middle-class as they came: yellow-patterned linoleum in the kitchen and foamy-looking olive-green shag carpeting in the bedrooms. Any hint of ostentation resided in the antiques my father had bought from an estate sale of some wealthy old-maid aunts of his. The Oriental rugs and oil paintings in their ornate frames made no sense next to our '70s wallpaper and corduroy bedspreads, but from my low height, they were treasures from some other world, far from the baking desert.

The popped top of my dad's first Coors punctuated his days of hard work. My mom passed me the silver can, which I would deliver to him just in time for the *CBS Evening News* with Dan Rather. I'd lie at my dad's side, content in the shadow of his satisfaction. He had done well for us, and if there were any stresses of not having enough money, I wasn't aware of it. I would play with friends down the road, families with way too many kids in run-down houses sprinkled with cat pee. I never considered us rich, but to my friends nearby, my family probably seemed it.

Both of my parents came from modest means, so there was very little extravagance other than Dad's love for transportation and machinery. His main passion was planes, and he built boats and rejiggered old cars with his bare hands. Whatever money was spent on our leisure, it was accompanied by his own elbow grease and ambitious imagination.

He was born Archibald Borders Sellards all the way back in 1928, just before the Depression, in California, just outside Los Angeles, which he remembered as a swath of orange groves divided by dirt roads. He did his best in school, but no matter how hard he tried, he couldn't learn to read. Turns out this was because he and his uncle had painted a whole house with lead paint when my dad was eight. Every day he'd be covered, colors running down his arms. No one realized at the time how badly it impaired vital learning skills. I always wondered growing up why my dad couldn't spell very well.

He dropped out of school in the seventh grade, opting instead to try and make money for his family's survival. He took work filing down horseshoes. For a dime apiece, the cook at his old school's cafeteria bought dead rabbits he'd shot. When he was twelve, he left with a circus, touring around California, his main task running the generator that powered all the lights in the tent. The circus traveled with one elephant, a chimpanzee, ring horses, and dancing girls. My dad drove trucks between gigs, having no license. It made him a careful driver for the rest of his life.

It was all grueling, endless work—hard on a grown man, much less a thirteen-year-old with only the clothes on his back. One night, spilled battery acid ate through his pants, which he had to keep wearing until he found another pair. Eventually he graduated to spraying insecticide on lemon trees, riding on top of trucks, his head floating above the groves as he showered them in chemicals. He persevered month after month, and waited for any free afternoon that he could go observe the sky. He'd loiter at the airport, just to be in proximity to his real passion: airplanes.

In 1943, the Rosemead airport, east of Los Angeles, was the perfect spot to get a job, small but active enough where he could be close to the planes and begin learning how to fly. The fifteen dollars a week he made gassing planes and starting propellers wasn't half as valuable as the thirty minutes of flying lessons he'd get every Sunday. He then moved on to the tiny Palm Springs airport, where all of Hollywood came through, arriving to their desert getaways. Dad served and observed the famous and the rich, most of them friendly, but they must have seemed as if they came from another planet. Howard Hughes would land his four-engine with his entourage. My father would unload their luggage, exchange pleasantries, and watch them take off in a fleet of limos or in Hughes's '37 Packard.

My father flew solo for the first time on his sixteenth birthday, the earliest he could get a pilot's license. He then moved to Phoenix, which at the time had a population of only forty thousand. The government was unloading airplanes for real cheap from the war. My father teamed up with some buddies and they pooled together enough capital to start buying the planes that the government was dumping. Engines were inexpensive, so he used everything he'd learned and rebuilt the planes himself. From 1963 to 1986 they ran Globe Air with a fleet of bombers and brave pilots, fighting fires and crop-dusting with DDT. It was dangerous and sad work. They lost upward of fifteen men over the years, all friends working for my father.

One of those guys, Bill Clark, had done a job up in Alaska, and his plane disappeared there months before he was to be married to Freida Jean Rector. She was a bubbly and hip young thing with a thick North Carolina drawl who had driven cross-country to Arizona from the Smoky Mountains to be with him. She wore miniskirts, smoked slender cigarettes, and sparkled with Southern charm. Now, her fiancé gone with no explanation. I imagine her for weeks after, smoking, her eyes dull, making pots of coffee, crying into the phone with her hope wilting. There wasn't much closure; Bill's family never had a funeral for him. Grieving, with her future uncertain, Freida got a job with Globe Air as a secretary.

There, she met my handsome father, twenty years her senior, with two small girls and a teenage boy from previous marriages to women that he's told me were a disaster. Being the first in Arizona to attempt firefighting by air had led to financial problems and a reliance on alcohol as self-medication that weren't conducive to good marriages. He's said to me, grinning: "You can't blame those ladies for everything, just most of it."

Hoping that the third time would be the charm, Archibald and Freida eloped to the Little White Chapel in Vegas, no one else there but themselves. In the photograph, my mom sported a graceful updo, my father overgrown muttonchops, both of them with huge smiles on their faces. They've been happily married ever since.

I've never liked the saying "Everything happens for a reason." But what if that reason is yourself? Is it wrong that I'm thankful that my mom's fiancé, the first love of her life, never returned from that fateful flight? I sometimes think of this alternate person that would have existed instead of me, a dream brother. I picture someone with my flaws and oddities ironed out, striding with ease through his normal, quiet life.

Windi and Sheryl, my sisters from my dad's second marriage, were nine and ten years older than I was, respectively, so by the time I was in kindergarten, their braces had come off to display sets of blinding white teeth. They were beautiful girls, with faces framed by coiffed brown hair out of a Nagel painting. I'd watch them get ready for a school dance, tucking and untucking the fronts of their shirts, trying their best to mimic the styles they saw on MTV, which was beamed into our home courtesy of the new miracle of cable.

They knew I would believe anything and filled my head with false stories designed to fuel the flames of my anxiety. For example, they'd tell me I'd been found on the side of the road as a baby because some woman was trying to give me away. Or Windi told me that if I got hair spray in my face, my eyes would turn blue and I'd die in a matter of minutes. Once I got some in my eyes and my screams ricocheted around the house; I thought I had mere moments left to live. Meanwhile, it never occurred to me that my eyes were already blue.

My brother, Avery, was out of the house by then. He was twenty years older and got married as soon as he returned from a Mormon mission he had taken to the Philippines. My friends all had complex and brutal relationships with their brothers. Maybe because my father was older, I felt jealous and sad that I didn't have a brother closer to my age.

My father was fifty when I was born and I became conscious of his age when I was six. There was a Wednesday-evening church group that I attended, and one night everyone brought their fathers. I was initially excited, but when we arrived, all the other dads were so much younger. No one else had a father near as old as mine. I tried to send him home.

We rode to and from his work on the airstrip, me in the back of his blue Datsun 280Z, crouched behind him in a kind of trunk with no seats, much less a seat belt. I had to lie flat, with my face propped up in my hands as he explained to me concepts that seemed abstract, like how an instrument wasn't just something that made music. "See that phone booth?" He pointed as we drove by. "A telephone is an instrument too." He thought about the world in a way that I had a hard time finding interesting. I didn't share his fascination with machines and cars and boats.

His face was serious. The lines of his rugged complexion, the result of years in the desert without sunscreen, pointed to a perpetual scowl. His observations came across in few words, but he had a big laugh on the occasions when it appeared. You could spot his distinct loping gait from across an airfield, hands greasy, the tattoos on his arms from boyhood blurred beyond recognition. All the same, we were buddies, and I loved spending time around his workshops and playing inside the old parked bombers.

He must have been perplexed when I suddenly vanished on weekend afternoons, choosing to be inside the house reading rather than tinkering with him on projects. I wonder if my aversion to dirt and disinterest was disappointing, as it slowly dawned on him that his son wasn't forming in his image?

When he dragged me to my first day of Little League, I blubbered and begged not to play. His face was stony as he pulled me out of the car, and kicking and crying onto the field. In the end, I knew it would hurt his pride too much if I didn't even give it a try. Yet no one had even thought to teach me the basic rules of the game. What could anyone do but laugh at my ineptitude in the outfield? I stared at the sky and ran from the ball. It always plunked on the ground yards away from me, like a dead shooting star, its flame long extinguished.

I was obsessed with books and got the hang of reading from Laura Ingalls Wilder's innocuous prairie tales, the *Wizard of Oz* books, and Raggedy Ann and Andy's psychedelic journeys. To challenge me, my first-grade teacher gave me a copy of *A Wrinkle in Time*, and I attacked it with a puzzled vigor. I couldn't figure out what the hell was going on, but I was determined to read it anyway. I wanted to read everything.

I'd lurk around the stacks in the public library for as long as my mom would let me. The peaty smell of books and their filmy, lacquered library covers incited a Pavlovian response, to browse and thumb, inspect and comb through bookshelves I'd already looked through many times. I parked myself at the desk of any librarian who was working, adamant that we would be friends.

While I was learning to read, I realized I could also tell myself more intricate stories with my toys. I was frequently on the floor of my room, flat on my stomach, surrounded by countless He-Man figures and castles. I amassed the little bulging chunks of plastic as if they were tender prophecies: steroid-fueled bodybuilders I could hold in my hands, just as I might one day hold the real thing in the flesh. The dramas that unfolded weren't those of action cartoons but of relationships and tragedy, backstabbing and sacrifices. While I should have moved on to BB guns and remote control cars, I remained in my room talking to myself with misproportioned male dolls.

I simply loved a good story, and found I was able to write my own. My first one was written on a small spiral notepad, and it was about Garfield in a haunted house. We started getting our first creative writing assignments in school. Other kids would scrawl out a couple mangled sentences and I would keep adding on to mine, stretching the narrative into something much longer than I had even expected. I always ended up asking for extra paper.

By the time I was in second grade, I'd been placed in a separate advanced reading class taught by the school librarian. She wore long prairie skirts, had an air of sophistication, and seemed interested in what I had to say. I liked the way she didn't talk to me like I was a little kid.

My second-grade teacher, Ms. Brown, was in her late twenties, attractive, with a bob haircut and black-framed glasses. When my parents went out of town on a business trip to Taiwan, they asked Ms. Brown to watch me for some extra cash. Our usual babysitter, Dorothy Reed, a shrill, prune-like woman with gray straw hair and polyester housecoats (my sisters hated her, and hated me for loving her), wasn't available, and my parents thought there was nothing strange at all about asking my teacher to watch me at my own house. My sisters at that point could take care of themselves, so it was Ms. Brown's duty to make sure I was fed, wearing my pajamas, and in bed by nine.

The household took on a more magical, conspiratorial atmosphere when Ms. Brown was there. I don't recall telling anyone at school what was happening; it was like a strange, glamorous secret.

The two whole weeks we lived together were like breaking a favorite toy to inspect its insides and see how it worked. Here was Ms. Brown making me oatmeal for breakfast. Here was Ms. Brown blow-drying her hair in a black nightshirt. It was like living with a celebrity.

At night we'd lie in our pajamas on my parents' king-size bed in front of the TV, me on my back with a stack of pillows under my head. She'd be propped up on her elbows grading papers with a red marker while we watched *Moonlighting*. We had our own private life, an invisible rope that tied us together, and it filled me with a subtle superior coolness.

How strange it was to be in class, watching Ms. Brown teach us cursive, when just the night before I had snuck out of my room when I was supposed to be sleeping. Silent, I crouched on all fours and crept down the hall. Her boyfriend, Sheldon, had stopped by, with his thick dark hair, wearing a coat and tie, wielding a coconut cream pie from Marie Callender's. "Oh, Sheldon," she said, staring into his eyes, just before he kissed her lips. This was pretty juicy stuff.

My parents came back, scholastic life returned to normal, and I felt dejected: Ms. Brown acted like nothing had ever happened between us. I would angle for any kind of private aside when I could, desperate to see the friend with whom I had shared those nights in my house. She was liberal with her praise of my school performance, but I never again got to see that side of her. I was now on the lookout for adult women to connect with, mostly just friends' moms in their kitchens, who were amused that I wanted to talk to them rather than play with their kid. It was a specific kind of attention that I wanted from them, an informed validation of my idiosyncratic self. It was the beginning of a pattern that would have a tremendous effect on my life.

We took a vacation the following summer. Instead of my dad piloting the family in his little Cessna airplane (which he did occasionally), we decided to drive our motor home to Canada for Expo '86—but the behemoth broke down just north of Seattle and we never made it. Out of commission for a whole week, we unloaded the Nissan Maxima that my dad had had the foresight to stick on a trailer behind us, on the off chance we felt like cruising around in a smaller car. It was the kind of ingenuity that never escaped him. He was a man who believed in inconvenient convenience.

That was how we found San Juan Island, a tranquil, tucked-away rock in Washington State about five miles across the water from Vancouver. The island's town, Friday Harbor, was idyllic, affordable, and charming to a family that had been living in a desert sprawl all their lives. We were smitten with the landscape of forests, beaches, and moss-covered rocks. Taking the two-hour ferry ride from the mainland, gliding over the calm ocean, was like being in a placid purgatory.

The island was isolated but active enough not to feel sleepy, especially in the summer, when the tourists on their bicycles poured out of the ferry like spilled club soda on a fancy rug: The vacationers were a temporary wet spot, but one that was cleaned up and had disappeared completely by fall. Friday Harbor had just one main street with two grocery stores, a courthouse, a diner, a movie theater, and some tacky souvenir shops. In the off season, only about three thousand people lived there. It seemed like everyone knew each other.

We found twenty acres on the water. The first time we saw the house, the beauty appeared staged: Deer leaped, pods of orcas puffed by, a lighthouse foghorn gently boomed in the distance. By the time we made it back to our repaired motor home, we had decided that we were leaving Arizona. Dad was in his late fifties and about to retire anyway.

As we packed up to move, I leafed through a pile of books in my parents' bedroom and came across one called something like *The Joy of a Gifted Child*. I skimmed some of it and came to the conclusion that "gifted" meant "special." But didn't every parent think they had a special kid? Now I realize "gifted" meant "gay." A code word invented to let parents down easy.

When I was seven, I had no idea I was gay, but I was effeminate, sensitive, and demanding of people's focus. My mom knew very early, as most mothers do. She lived in a state of loving preoccupation about my sexuality, trying to figure out in secret if there was anything that could be done—and if there wasn't, how to make things easier on me. She refrained from harping on my obsession with her Jane Fonda workout videos and my daily screenings of *Nine to Five*, both bastions of comfort for me. They were the opposite of my father's strange, oily world of machinery.

My mom's personality always complemented my dad's stoicism. She's like a feel-good radio station that never turns off, always able to talk to anybody, anywhere, about anything. Her mastery of breezily filling complicated silences with folksy conversation has to be seen to be believed. When she laughs she often punches you on the shoulder. Her energy and devotion to my upbringing was unflagging. She packed my lunches, cleaned my room, and always made me feel loved. To this day I've never seen my parents get in a fight.

I was spoiled, a total mama's boy. My rages when I didn't get my way could be jaw-droppers to adults. A friend of the family even nicknamed me "The Little Dictator." Since my sisters were so much older than I was, it sometimes felt as if I were an only child. And I was treated like one, getting what I wanted most of the time, whether it was toys, books, or attention. Perhaps my mom was scared I would break, so she tiptoed around me, trying to figure out how exactly to parent this "gifted" child.

She was just trying to protect me, using her instincts to cushion me from any potential pain. In line at the grocery store, I remember seeing Rock Hudson dying on the cover of the *National Enquirer*, a baroque photo of Liberace next to him with the words *AIDS* headlined in dead-end red letters. I asked my mom what *AIDS* meant, but she couldn't seem to come up with a solid answer. I have a memory of Jane Pauley on the *Today* show introducing a segment about how some scientists thought it was possible that you could get AIDS from a toilet seat. The fear of this unknown threat was palpable, even to a child. I could read between the lines of an adult's cursory glance or nervous pause when it was mentioned.

One day I asked my mom what *gay* meant. She looked at me in the rearview mirror and thankfully just said, "They're very nice people."

2

OURS WASN'T A MUSIC HOUSEHOLD EXACTLY, AT LEAST
of the recorded kind. The radio was never heard other than in the car
or coming from my sisters' bedrooms. I had my own turntable but my
records were mostly kids' stuff. Most of the music in the house ema-
nated from live instruments. My sisters played the cello and the harp,
and all three of us played the piano. Our teacher, Mr. Heck, ambled
into our house on Tuesdays, wearing stale polyester in a smelly cloud
of mothballs and Brylcreem. He smacked the sheet music with his
retractable pointer, keeping time while we prepared for our biannual
recitals. Windi and Sheryl practiced constantly, filling the house with
music. I found practicing to be drudgery, having a hard time counting
bars and remembering where the sharps and the flats were supposed
to go, and I had to count by hand the lines in the staff. A chord just
seemed like a tangle of notes, and deciphering them from each other
was tedious. I didn't want to rehash what someone else had already
put on the page. I wanted to make up stuff myself.

I was a better singer than I was a piano player. I took elementary
school choir from Mrs. Bell, who sported a fierce Toni Tennille hairdo.
She was lovely and kind, but I was horrified when she clapped her
hands in our faces in a rhythmic fashion and made us say, "Tah, tah,
tee-tee tah." We'd go sing at the convalescent home to cheer up the old
folks, and to entertain myself, I'd caterwaul as if I were completely

tone-deaf, or I'd attempt my third-rate Aaron Neville impersonation, which I thought was just hilarious.

It wasn't until I discovered one particular singer that I truly started to fantasize about the possibilities of performing. I had watched a bootleg VHS of *Labyrinth* repeatedly and was captivated with its songs. I would fast-forward and rewind scenes so I could memorize the lyrics sung by this man in tights and a frosted Tina Turner wig. I had no idea who he was but I was beyond intrigued. My sisters informed me that his name was David Bowie, and he was apparently a big rock star.

On a subsequent trip off-island, my mother let me buy *Let's Dance* on cassette. I picked it from a random selection of his albums. From then on, my Walkman headphones didn't leave my ears. The first half of the record, full of the singles, was immediate, but it was the darker side B that I played even more. I showed off the cassette on my desk at school, never letting the artwork out of my sight, counting the hours until I could listen again.

I lay in my dark room after bedtime, the songs softly playing on a boom box. I imagined being in front of an enraptured crowd of classmates, envisioning a stage in my school gym, somehow an endless starry sky stretched above. I wore a tuxedo, crooning in front of a dapper band with a full horn section. It was the first time I thought with true conviction: *I want to be onstage. Singing.*

I followed *Let's Dance* with Bowie's *Scary Monsters* and *Lodger*. Most of the lyrics were opaque, some of them even frightening. But I memorized every second of those albums, listening at any opportunity, sometimes choosing the music over hanging out with my friends. I knew by instinct I could never play it for them. I had no interest in trying to convince anybody of what I already knew to be brilliant.

When I finally made it onstage my fourth-grade year, it in no way measured up to my bedroom fantasy. My mom had the wise idea that the two of us were going to take tap-dancing lessons. We signed up with Bill Ament, a local instructor who had a one-room studio across from the courthouse in town. Bill was a jolly modern-tap dancer with a very large wife named Rita who wore colorful muumuus, had frizzy hair and purple lipstick, and was always sweating profusely. She sat on the sidelines in a folding chair and ran the music, interrupting Bill every ten minutes to tell him he was doing something wrong. They made a fun team.

I was no tap-dancing prodigy, but I could certainly remember a sequence and was thankful that this wasn't an outdoor sport. Tom was the only other boy in my class. Though we both wore glasses, he had a permanently runny nose and was unable to keep proper time. I couldn't help but feel superior. But superiority was all relative. For me, as the new kid in town, it wasn't a great look to be publicly learning dances to "Don't Worry, Be Happy" and "The Surrey with the Fringe on Top."

We worked through the spring for the show, which we were to perform at the community theater—which was actually a one-room movie house with the screen taken out and transformed into a small stage. The show was called *Dance Happy!* and it would star all the students from Bill Ament's classes, including my mom. The number I was in was set to the theme song from the John Waters film *Hairspray*. At the end, Tom and I were to enter from the sides of the stage, clad in blue spandex tights, hopping on one foot and pretending to play a saxophone solo around a woman dressed up as a giant can of Aqua Net. My mother's number was to be even more mortifying. It would consist of her and a troupe of middle-age ladies dressed as clowns, dancing around to circus music. They would enter through the audience, throwing confetti all over everyone, Rip Taylor style.

On the day of the show, my mother and I were getting ready and she reminded me to go feed Oreo, the rabbit my sister Windi had unloaded on me about six months before. Oreo's large cage was at the end of a short trail through some trees, up the hill from our house. I made sure feeding the rabbit was the last thing I did before leaving for the show, so before going out to his cage, I spiked my hair with goopy gel and donned my tights, saving the tap shoes for the performance. (I didn't want to scuff them up on the concrete.)

I knew something was wrong as soon as I skipped halfway up the hill and approached Oreo's little pen. The air was too still. I slowed my pace and rounded the corner, not prepared for the full reveal of fresh violence. Clyde, our springer spaniel, had somehow gotten inside the cage and was sitting at attention, growling at me. Blood dripped off his wet jaws. Oreo's two little hind legs were splayed perfectly in the air, as if they were in the middle of doing a festive high kick.

I screamed like a slowly deflating balloon, whirled around with my palms in the air, and ran down the hill, blind with panic, until I tripped on a rock that sent me flying. I landed hard, skinning my chin. My mother, in her pancake clown makeup, tried to console me as I picked the gravel from my palms and cried.

I couldn't possibly perform, I thought. How could I grace the stage in such extreme mourning? "You'll just have to wait until after the show to think about it," my mother said as she wiped my face with a warm towel. "Let's just get in the car, okay?" Doing my best to pull it together during the six-mile ride to town, I was unsure if I could face an audience. What if I cried onstage? I was going to have to occupy two places in my head at once, straddling a line between spandex hair fantasy and fresh rabbit guts.

I ended up doing the plastic-saxophone hop with red eyes, my face swollen from all the tears. But the number turned out all right. In any case, Tom and I were basically forgotten by the audience as soon as they got a load of the scary mom-clowns. When they stormed the crowd, showering them in confetti, my mom got a big chunk of it stuck between two molars. Backstage, all the other clown ladies surrounded her with a flashlight, her head tilted back and her jaws open as far as they could go in a frozen clown scream. They became one single greasepaint-encrusted beast as they clucked and prodded with tweezers, finally dislodging the glimmering piece in triumph.

When we returned home, I allowed myself the space to feel sadness for my eaten pet. But I also felt accomplishment for having gone out onstage anyway, powering through, making people think that I was "dancing happy." The audience was there to be entertained. No one cared that I was having a bad day, and it was my job to not let them see it. All they saw was a really rotten number, and that was just fine.

It wasn't just pet-on-pet violence responsible for introducing me to the natural world; I now had my own interactive ocean exhibit in the front yard. At sunset in the summer, I'd clamber onto the small peninsula of giant bleached driftwood that had gathered and watch the whales swim by. It was surreal when the orcas breached, shooting out of the water and slapping themselves on their sides, sometimes so close it would startle me. I poked around the tide pools alone, both fascinated and revolted by the lesion-like anemones and mussels, freaky creatures unearthed with the receding tide. I'd always had an irrational fear of animals without backbones. Unfortunately for me, the island was also home to large banana slugs that could grow to be almost a foot long.

As soon as other kids found out about my slug phobia, they would chase me down the beach, flinging them, cackling at my girly screams. Some mornings I would run into the kitchen and have a meltdown after having pulled up my blinds: The giant slugs liked to climb up my bedroom windows, as if begging to be let in. My father, eating his breakfast at the table, would frown, unamused by the heights of my hysteria.

I had a new friend named Ryan Smith, who didn't seem to care about my squeamish, girly proclivities. He was a kind child, and had befriended me on my first day of fourth grade. Outdoorsy and hilarious, he was the second-youngest of a peaceful Catholic family who ran an apple orchard and lived in a log cabin they'd built themselves. It was a playground in the woods almost from another time. We'd stage talent shows in the summer and ice-skate in the winter when the pond froze over. They made cider, had dogs, and didn't watch TV except perhaps an old movie during the weekends on their sputtering VCR.

Spending the night on a Saturday could be dicey. I'd end up getting dragged to Mass the next morning, an exercise in profound boredom. Sometimes I wished I could partake in Communion so I could at least eat something. Father O'Neill made up for the snoozy Sundays with his eclectic family-friendly VHS collection, which he had in his house that adjoined the church. It was mostly stuff from the '60s and '70s. I got my first great education in film from those tapes. Ryan and I would go over and watch Vincent Price mince around in *The Abominable Dr. Phibes* or Madeline Kahn chew the scenery in *What's Up, Doc?*

When we were at my house, Ryan and I became video game fanatics, staying up all night with wide, glazed eyes, staring at the huge pixels of my brand-new Nintendo I'd received for my eighth birthday. Occasionally we still played with my He-Man collection, but we knew we were getting too old for such things: It wasn't as cool to pretend.

I was in between selves, not a little kid anymore. Impatient, I longed to experience culture with more mature themes. I wanted to go to the movie house, no matter what was playing. Every Friday, as we drove down Main Street, I pressed my nose to the car window and tried to make out what was on the theater's faded marquee. They'd stick a computer printout of the title and two showtimes behind the scratched Plexiglas.

A friend of mine and his mom who had cosmopolitan taste took me to see my first R-rated film, *Working Girl*. At the opening shot of New York and the Statue of Liberty, my heart soared while Carly Simon wailed "Let the River Run." I too could be privy to stories about the complications of adults. As the credits rolled, I realized that so many of the movies that I'd been watching before this had been absolute swill. That Bobcat Goldthwait movie with the talking horse? Garbage! *Ernest Goes to Camp*? Baby stuff! When I heard people actually saying *fuck* out loud, or glimpsed a man's bare ass and thrusting hips, I felt an inexplicable pang, a desire to be older, to one day inhabit the roles that I saw played on the screen.

I became a true movie hound. In the sixth grade, as I was leaving the theater, a classmate's mother spotted me and approached me with a curious look. "Funny seeing you at *Crimes and Misdemeanors*," she said.

I was working my way through meatier books now. My sister Sheryl had left a dog-chewed paperback of Stephen King's *Tommyknockers* lying around. I would squirrel it away behind the couch in the den and read for hours, possessed by its horrific imagery. I had already learned to be careful: A girl in my class had caught me reading *If There Be Thorns* by V. C. Andrews in the school library. She seized it and chucked it away from me, turned to one of her girlfriends, and said disgustedly, "Oh my God, he's a fucking gay."

3

MY NEWFOUND DISCERNING TASTES WERE SATIATED
when my parents went off-island. They often left one of my sisters
in charge. Windi would immediately have six-packs and sullen boyfriends strewn around the house like dirty socks. In exchange for
keeping my mouth shut, I'd be allowed to watch the Playboy channel,
which for me, in 1987, was the pinnacle of entertainment.

The Playboy channel was my heaven. I didn't find it sexually ap-
pealing, but I was blown away by the upscale-trash aesthetic. The living
centerfolds were a nonstop breast parade, champagne streams of women
with perfectly feathered hair, framed overhead shots of freshly tanned
bodies in David Hockney–blue swimming pools. They were the epitome
of decadent glamour, preening with their arching backs and oversize
sunglasses, wet tits in the air, licking their glistening candy-apple lips.
There was never a woman in the pool without her high heels on.

I got the courage one day to confide in Joseph Alred, a jock-boy with
a flattop haircut from the mythical fifth grade above me. Thinking we
were friends, I told him that I'd been watching Playboy at home when my
folks were gone. Within seconds, he turned on me and threatened that if
I didn't give him money, he was going to tell my parents. The thought of
my mom and dad finding out suddenly made what was so colorful and
inspiring seem dirty. I felt the bloodless sink of shame and fear and gave
Joseph a little bit of cash every week for the rest of the school year.

If Joseph Alred was treating me like a puny nerd, it wasn't for my lack of trying to be one. I was thrilled when my vision went bad, since I had always wanted to wear glasses. Thinking I was projecting refinement instead of weakness, I would wear garish button-up shirts and sometimes a tie, and I begged my mom to buy me a briefcase in which I carried notebooks full of my meandering, unfinished stories. I tried to share one with my favorite icy librarian and was a little hurt when she refused to read it. "You can't just give me notebook pages," she said. "You need to type this stuff out."

Adults were the stimulation I was looking for, or at least they understood what I wanted to talk about. The lady at the used-book store allowed me to loiter by the register and gab with her between customers. The clerks at the drugstore humored me in my musings almost daily, as I talked a blue streak about celebrity gossip and current events. I was a funny kid and loved making people laugh, using shock value if nothing else did the trick. My friends' mothers were still a special target. Some moms kept me at arm's length, which I simply viewed as a challenge to my wooing powers. Others seemed to enjoy my company as I recounted the blow-by-blow of Jim and Tammy Faye Bakker's *PTL Club* scandal, or when Zsa Zsa Gabor slapped a police officer in Beverly Hills. My dad was especially mystified by my Zsa Zsa fascination. He called her a phony. I didn't care what she was, I just wanted to order her exercise video for senior citizens.

My sixth-grade teacher, Sheila Dyer, was an earthy, feminist hippie. She had long brown hair and glasses, and didn't shave her armpits, to the horror of the class. Sometimes she and I would stay in the classroom at lunch, where our private asides made me laugh so hard I'd snort milk out of my nose. If it was feigned interest, she had me fooled. My elaborate journal entries and stories merited her critical but thoughtful feedback. For Halloween, just because I knew it would crack Ms. Dyer up, I dressed as Geraldo Rivera with a broken nose (he had been fortuitously smacked by a flying chair on his own show while hosting a panel of KKK members). I wonder now if she felt a little sorry for me. I had morphed into an awkward-looking boy in pink glasses with a shrill giggle and campy gestures. Yes, my mother let me pick out pink glasses.

There was occasional tension between Ms. Dyer and me. The boundaries would blur and I'd go too far by drawing unflattering cartoons of her boyfriend, or telling her she was old. I knew I could make her mad, but our tiffs remained private. Neither of us wanted the bother of exposing our exclusive relationship. A precious thing, at least to me. I felt that, more than anyone else, she understood my unsettled fascinations. Our friendship was the first time I really got a taste of what it would feel like to be autonomous, a grown-up. It made me care less what other kids thought of me: Her approval was all that mattered. I guess she was my first muse.

Those late elementary school years were plagued by my sisters' getting into trouble. When we moved to the island, they were sent to spend the last two years of their secondary education at a boarding school in Tacoma. Windi got expelled for sneaking out and drinking while underage and returned to the island to finish out her senior year. I'd now sit in my bedroom, frightened of the mascara-streaked battles that raged in the kitchen between her and my once-jubilant mom. The phone would ring in the middle of the night: Windi wouldn't be coming home. "We're here if you need us," I'd hear my dad say. He sounded resigned.

I couldn't piece together what exactly was going on, but the unease bled into my school hours. Two lowlifes in my class, Matt McCutcheon and Darren Lawson, approached me one day at lunchtime. "Your sister is a whore," they said. With half of a sandwich hanging out of my mouth, I felt sick, knowing what they meant, but not sure what they were talking about. I was too frightened to fight back. Matt would shove me or call me a pussy given any opportunity. For years I fantasized about his death. A decade later, when he drove off a cliff and actually died, I was both surprised and not surprised that I felt nothing.

Windi soon vanished from our lives. She moved in with her townie boyfriend before the school year was over. He was a stranger, and I hated him. Sometimes, from the car, I would spot Windi in town, walking with him down a side street, wearing a fleece-lined denim jacket and smoking. I felt so lonely seeing her like that, unable to understand why she had left. The division of our family seemed pointless.

My other sister, Sheryl, now at college, started struggling as well. My parents became preoccupied with her antics and assumed that both my sisters were alcoholics. In retrospect, I don't think it was alcoholism, just unhappiness. We had moved to this serene island, envisioning a peaceful and easy life surrounded by beauty. But it was out of our grasp. The bones we needed to hold each other had fractured, and when we attempted to reset them, they broke again. Why couldn't our lives be more like those of Ryan Smith's family, with their mellow evenings and log cabin?

Those years were a blur of rehab centers and counselors' offices offisland, to which I'd be dragged along. They were depressing, sterile places, followed by nights in nearby motels, where I shared a double room with my parents. One time we got on the 6 a.m. ferry, picked up Windi from rehab midday, and had a dismal Thanksgiving lunch at Denny's.

On these bleak trips I stayed preoccupied with books. I'd shut myself in the bathroom with Piers Anthony and a hot bath. Writers like William Sleator and John Saul helped me pass the hours in the backseat of the car, waiting for a therapy session to end. I'd sit outside on the late-night ferry, seeing nothing but blackness, with only the sound of the engine and lapping water.

As distracted as my parents became, I never felt ignored. My mother would come into my room and embrace me after some scorched-earth battle, tell me she was sorry and that she loved me. At the time it felt like my family was really fucked-up. But really we were just normal people. I think everyone was trying to do their best.

4

SOMEWHERE AROUND AGE TWELVE, MY FEATURES
started running—dripping—off my face. No hair under the pits yet,
but my eyes were drifting wider, my brow getting heavier, my face all
follicles and pores. As bad as my vision was, I was blessed, by way of
my glasses, with a new kind of mutant sight and attention to detail.
The crooks of boys' arms, the hollow of a collarbone, the thickness of
some flexed calves were all magnified to me, would make me perspire
new kinds of oils. And when I glanced at my reflection, I knew there
was no way around it: I wasn't lookin' as cute no more.

The next few years we jumped around, a lot. Back and forth from
Arizona to the island, at the mercy of my father's whims. He had
started designing and building amphibious boats, so called because
they could be operated on both land and water. At the end of the
sixth grade, my parents told me we were moving back to Mesa. My
sister Windi, having reconciled with the family, was going to follow us
down and get a job and her own apartment. I was going to miss my
lunchtime ruminations with Ms. Dyer and sneaking hard cider with
Ryan Smith, but I would be back on the island in the summers.

Mesa had grown into what seemed like a metropolis, but maybe that
was just because we'd been living on a remote island for the last three
years. It was all Blockbuster video stores and heavily air-conditioned
frozen yogurt shops with that chalky smell of rainbow sprinkles. We

moved into a one-story house in a cul-de-sac with a dusty backyard, where the nearby public schools were much larger than what I was used to. To be a new kid among thousands was scary, so my mom and I found a modest junior high called Redeemer Christian School.

We were Christians—at least, my mom was—but we had never been super-religious. My dad was not a churchgoer, and my mom's pluck took precedence over any hellfire-and-brimstone talk. A Christian junior high seemed less stressful; its small size was inviting. I figured the inevitable junior high drama might be more manageable with only twenty-five kids in each grade.

There was a tepid dress code: Girls had to wear skirts and guys collared shirts. The boys got around this by wearing T-shirts with logos, then donning a collared short-sleeved shirt over them. I was mortified by PE. We had to play basketball as either shirts or skins. I was embarrassed to take mine off since I was so small and skinny.

Classes were what I imagine homeschooling to be like. First thing in the morning, we had Bible study, which was mostly combing through the savagery of the Old Testament, slaughtered babies and lambs, locusts, people being stoned to death. All of our textbooks were Christian-based, and unintentionally hilarious. There was a poster on the wall with a caveman standing next to a brontosaurus that read, MAN AND DINOSAURS: LIVING IN HARMONY.

Evolution and secular entertainment were generally frowned upon, but above all else, homosexuality was the greatest transgression. AIDS was a punishment, described often. We had all kinds of conversations in class about how gay people liked to do horrible and disgusting things, like defecate and pee on one another, spread disease, and recruit children. Still, it didn't feel like something to revolt against. After all, I didn't totally realize yet that they were talking about me. I would just try my best to make sense of it and agree—*yeah, gays were super gross. Ew.*

At Redeemer, there was a certain social hierarchy. I knew I was thought of as a nerd by the other kids, mostly because of how I looked and because of my love for books. But I was still cooler and more world-wise than some of the sheltered Christian kids on the periphery. The ones from the strictest families were on the bottom rung, unable to contribute to any conversations on secular culture. I liked straddling this line of not being the most popular, but not being a reject, either.

I wasn't shy, often piping up just for a laugh and relishing it when eyes and ears were on me. I felt urges to jump up on my desk at school and shake my arms and sing. I wanted to put on costumes, wail into paper-towel rolls, and stomp my feet. Energetic and hyper, I ran around at lunchtime, harassing kids with performative shit-stirring. One day a girl a year older, in the eighth grade, broke down in front of one of the teachers and cried. She pointed at me, her face crinkling into a sob. "He's terrible, can't you see?" As if she were the only one to recognize that I was a monster. "He's just so . . . . so happy!"

Once a week, we had an art class taught by a glamorous twenty-six-year-old woman named Jennifer Lebert. I could tell she was perfect woman-friend material and latched onto her right away. It was only a matter of time before my parents went out of town, and of course I nominated Jennifer and her husband, Mat, to stay at my house and look after me. Jennifer and I became close, and though she was a devout Christian, her outlook never felt judgmental or stifling to me. She was one of the cool ones. We both were enamored with the movies and always had tons to gossip about, and she introduced me to her favorite bands—OMD, the Psychedelic Furs, and the Cure.

Jennifer and Mat worked multiple jobs. In the daytime he sold mobile homes in Mesa. At night he worked in a themed restaurant called Bobby McGee's, where he waited tables and had to dress up like a quack doctor named Mel Practice, or Dracula. They were also salespeople for Amway, which seemed to me to be a pyramid scheme that hawked everything from toothpaste to vacuum cleaners to their friends and neighbors.

When I was with Jennifer, we talked about pop culture and went places I could never just go with a friend my own age. The world around us felt a little looser: We ate at drive-thrus and riffled through record store bins, saw horror movies at the dollar theater, drank Big Gulps, had sleepovers, and stayed up late watching warbly VHS tapes.

I dreamed about having real guy friends, but such a thing seemed impossible. I thought I wanted a brother. I already had a half brother, of course, but he was twenty years older and we didn't have much in common. Sometimes Jennifer's husband, Mat, would try to take me out to do manly things, like attend an air show or go golfing. But it was obvious that I was distracted, bored, and wishing I were elsewhere.

One evening my mom took me to Fiesta Mall and I wandered into a B. Dalton Bookseller. I was browsing around in the horror section when a young man in his early twenties appeared beside me and asked me about the book I was looking at, a pulpy Dean Koontz paperback. We began talking writers, about whom we loved and the books we hadn't read yet. He picked one I recommended, *Curfew* by Phil Rickman, and thanked me. I watched from the other side of the store as he bought it and left.

During the car ride home with my mom, I was imbued with a brand-new sadness. Bereft, I knew I'd never see that guy again. Here was a grown man who was interested in the things I had to say, and familiar with the writers I rattled off. Now he was gone, never to be seen again. I watched the church parking lots and fast-food joints fly by. A wave of grief passed through me. It might have been the first time I felt my heart break.

After convincing my mom to let my cousin Jackie Sue perm the front of my hair, I started the eighth grade in style. The new paisley button-ups that my mom let me buy in the women's department at an outlet mall made me feel chic. The pictures tell another story, however: I had pimples and braces. My face looked like a splitting nucleus. On top of that, I had flat, pigeon-toed feet that pointed like an arrow when I walked.

It was at video arcades, or the mall—where the cooler boys tore through in overalls (one strap hanging down at the waist), maneuvering in packs, loud and vicious—that I truly realized what a girly freak I was.

We had just one of those cool types in my class—only one. His name was Austin. Cocky and boisterous, he had thick, dark hair, and his lips were twisted in a perpetual yet sexy sneer. Austin always bragged about his skateboarding and sexual exploits. In PE, I would gawk at his meaty, gorilla-hairy legs. He was a full year older than everyone in the class and wasn't a boy like the rest of us, not anymore. At school he could be callous and cruel toward me. But on weekends he slept over at my place, where we would lie on my waterbed and talk into the night about girls and sex, seducing each other with language. These nights were agonizing bliss. As it grew later, I'd begin to tremble. We never kissed, never even tried. That would have been too gay. But everything from the neck down was fair game.

At school, we held this knowledge, this dangerous secret over each other. He'd be a jerk most days but knew he could never go too far. It kept me up at night: Would he dare say anything? We kept fooling around until the very end of the school year. I knew once the semester ended that I wasn't going to see him anymore. Our final night together was almost romantic; I remember already feeling nostalgic for it before it was done. The affair was over, but I think we'd both had fun. I'm sure today he's probably got a wife and kids; I was just someone to get off with.

My desires at the time, however, were confusing. When I was by myself, the words *I'm gay* would flash in my head, accompanied by a sharp bolt of anxiety. I would push the notion away, telling myself it was something I could deal with later. Gay people were not cool, supposedly pooped on each other, and all had AIDS, not a desirable scenario from any angle. It didn't help when my sister would play me

Andrew Dice Clay tapes, with their jokes about dead fags hanging off trees, AIDS spreading among the queers like mildew. I would do my best to pretend I thought it was funny, while on the inside it was scaring me to death.

At the dinner table, my mother capitalized on my queenery. She would beg me to do my impersonation of Lady Miss Kier from Deee-Lite in front of dinner guests. I obliged, in my pretend pink faux-fur shrug, pouting and pacing. "How do you say . . . delicious?" Sultry and alien. "How do you say de-lovely . . . delectable, divine?" I mimicked her steps on our living room floor. "How do you say . . . DE GROOVY?!" My hands up in a Y, palms to the sky. This was the shit.

I would wait until no one else was home and play Deee-Lite's "Power of Love" at full volume, twirling through the house, gripping the couch when the room wouldn't stop spinning. I found a photograph in a magazine of Lady Miss Kier and Kate Pierson of the B-52's, standing together at a PETA rally. There was so much flair in that tiny, crinkled photograph! I'd gaze at it and fantasize about writing the two women letters. Maybe, just maybe, they would meet up with me for lunch sometime.

I'd hang up Budweiser posters that my sisters' guy friends had given me: They were trying kindly in their own ways to butch me up. I thought that if I just looked at more girls in bikinis, the correct desires would form within. But no matter how long their legs were, how inviting their breasts, nothing in me wanted to fuck them.

This was pre-internet, so I had to get creative with masturbation, jerking off in the bathroom to International Male catalogues. I pored over every chestnut-haired Adonis with his Supercuts hairdo and perfect square jaw. I'd concentrate on two guys standing next to each other, in swim shorts or underwear, and rip off little pieces of toilet paper to lay on top of them. If I did it just right, I could make it look like they were standing naked next to each other, only covered by clouds of Charmin. I would then lie on my back and finish off with an intense longing—praying for some big man with broad shoulders and a pelt of hair on his chest to appear in the doorway and scoop me up. My mother had to have wondered why every day she would find tiny pieces of toilet paper scattered around the bathroom floor.

My discoveries weren't just with regard to sex. There was a new girl in my class that year named Rachel, and she was dialed in. The first day of class, she came in shaking rice out of her hair because the night before she'd been at a showing of *The Rocky Horror Picture Show*. Later, she explained to me what "alternative" music was and that I could hear it on this AM station, KUKQ.

The day she told me, I played it in the dark as I was falling asleep. Maybe I thought my subconscious mind would sponge up the songs, so hungry was I for input that would move me. But just as I started to doze, a song came on that made me sit up, causing my waterbed to make tiny waves. I cocked my ear to the speakers, afraid to move, to miss anything. I couldn't tell if the singer was a man or a woman; the voice was aggressive and hallucinatory. It was "This Is Not a Love Song" by Public Image Limited.

Violent Femmes, Red Hot Chili Peppers, Big Audio Dynamite, REM—I discovered so many bands. My first real concert was Siouxsie and the Banshees. The anticipation and release of that performance were almost like what I knew sex to be. Each discovery was leading to another. At the Siouxsie concert I asked a guy standing next to me what the preshow music was. He told me it was a new album by Nine Inch Nails called *Pretty Hate Machine*. I saved up all my money for cassettes and when I couldn't afford something, Rachel, who seemed to know everything good, would just dub me a copy of, say, Jane's Addiction's *Ritual de lo Habitual*.

My parents gave me quite a bit of freedom. They intuited that I wasn't interested in trouble. I wasn't seeking out friends who had access to booze or drugs. I was looking to experience as much movies and music as my free time and allowance allowed. But my mother drew the line at *The Rocky Horror Picture Show*. The film was enjoying its fifteenth anniversary and had just been released on video. I wanted so badly to go see it live at the theater on Mill Avenue on a Saturday night, but my mom was steadfast in her suppression, reasoning that there were "heavy themes" that she didn't think I was "ready for yet." She was being ridiculous, and I was going to see that damn movie.

Windi, who was living nearby us in Arizona at that point, let me rent it when my parents were out of town, just like old times. I lapped it up, every shot, song, outfit, hip shake. *Rocky Horror* was like an invitation to the rest of my life. I'd found the message in a bottle, a sly telegram from my future letting me know that there were people out there like me.

Both my art teacher Jennifer and Windi got pregnant at the same time that year. Windi was going to be a single mom, to the chagrin of my parents. I found out the night before Valentine's Day. I sat at my desk the next morning chewing on candy hearts, a pall over me. I was worried for her, about how she was going to support herself and raise a baby at the same time.

Jennifer was ecstatic about having a baby, but halfway into her pregnancy there were complications. These visits to doctors were kept under wraps, but finally she told me that the baby would die as soon as she was born. Jennifer decided to carry her to full term. It felt different being around her: Our lives carried on, but it was impossible not to feel an immense sadness. There was no way I could comprehend her and Mat's private pain. But her chipper optimism was unremitting as she exhibited bravery to an extent I had never seen.

It was an accident, but I managed to scare Windi into labor. After entering her apartment one day and realizing she was asleep, I stood close over her face and stared at her, my nose inches from her own, thinking I was being funny. When she opened her eyes and screamed, her water broke. It was such a joyous moment, she really couldn't get mad. My nephew, Caleb, was born within hours.

5

SAN JUAN ISLAND SEEMED SO MUCH SMALLER UPON our return, my father having finished his business in Arizona. At first, I thought it could be a new start, an opportunity to brand myself as someone a bit cooler than I'd been. But high school soured on me like a glass of old milk. The rot was subtle, at first. I could feel it in a small shoulder shove in the hall from an aloof stoner, or a word bomb (*"—fucking girl—"*) tossed from a car window. I was officially being clocked for what I was: a queer.

In the hallway three guys tackled me and wrote the word FAG in black Sharpie on my forehead. I didn't fight back. There were three of them and one of me; I just went limp like a rag doll and let them do it, revolted with myself for not putting up a struggle. Even after I washed off all traces of it, I still saw the word on my forehead when I looked in the mirror.

There were certain things I tried to improve my standing at school. I threw a party at my house when my parents were gone. I befriended the louche, laid-back girls in the grades ahead of me and tried pot with them for the first time. I thought that if a few of the *right* people liked me, maybe they could influence how the rest of them felt about me, too.

There was a boy named Curtis that I had grown up with in elementary school. We weren't that close but would find ourselves hanging out together alone. Our conversations about sex turned into effortless blow jobs. One night, he stole his dad's car and parked it up at the road, walked down our long driveway, and snuck in my window to fool around. I didn't feel the strange guilt I had when kissing girls or the jittery tumult of hooking up with Austin from junior high. On the couple occasions that I tried anything with girls, it felt like I had just done something really gross, like making out with my mom or my sister.

My clothes were getting incrementally louder. My hair—sometimes colored with markers—grew longer. I pierced my left ear, trying to show that I was different. I looked for anything that made a statement. For instance, I thought it was a great idea to wear a knit purse on my head as a hat.

I was still friends with Ryan Smith, whose family owned the apple orchard, but we bickered frequently. Every week we would get into a fight about something inconsequential. He thought I was getting strange and could see through my need for attention. In turn, I thought Ryan was being too square. Still, our connection was strong, and when we hung out, more often than not, our differences would fall away.

We were both cast in the school musical of *Narnia* that year. And our roles were magnified mirrors of who we were becoming. Ryan was cast as Edmund, a proper, well-spoken, and well-mannered young man. I, on the other hand, played a monstrous henchman of Fenris Ulf, the snow queen's bloodthirsty right-hand wolf. I wore giant boots and leather, my long hair lank and stringy, my nails painted black.

I started shoplifting cassettes from the drugstore, suddenly deft at the sleight of hand. There were a couple close calls, but thankfully I never got caught. It gave me a huge rush, to walk out of a store, not having paid for something. It was not an unpleasant feeling, the way it made my heart race and the blood throb in my temples.

My most daring and dangerous heist was unplanned. My mom and I were in a mall off-island. I was perusing the magazine rack at a Waldenbooks when I saw a *Playgirl* peeking out on the top shelf. Without waiting to think twice, as if it were nothing, I reached up and pulled it out, holding it discreetly to my side. After walking to a more conspicuous part of the store, I slipped the magazine into one of my shopping bags and walked casually out. The layers of illicit action gave me a sudden, slight boner, which I covered with my bags. I couldn't believe such contraband was in my possession: a treasure that—if found by anyone—there would be no way to disavow. Its discovery would automatically brand me a thief *and* a homo.

The *Playgirl* lived under my waterbed that whole year, deep in a cubbyhole only I was able to crawl into. No longer would I tear up toilet paper to place on International Male underwear models. I had complete access to images of grown men with engorged dicks and thatched chests. If any object had fulfilled its reason for existence, pulled its weight, it was that magazine. I got off on it every day.

That summer, I was cast as Baby John in a depressing community theater production of *West Side Story*. The director couldn't pull a band together in time for opening night, so we sang to recorded instrumentals. The costumes were reinterpreted as glam-punk disasters that looked terrible on the cast of mostly thirty- and forty-somethings. The play got an abysmal, borderline scandalous review in the local paper. The piece singled me out as the one decent thing in it, but they were probably just being nice because I was fourteen years old and the youngest person in the cast.

It was a weekday afternoon and I was in the theater rehearsing when an ambulance screamed by outside—not a sound you normally heard in Friday Harbor. They were responding to an accident that had happened near my house on the west side of the island. A boy had fallen down a cliffside while rock climbing. It was Ryan Smith. My memory has blocked out who told me or where I was when I found out. But it was as if I'd entered some parallel reality, an uncanny feeling that *yesterday* was continuing on as it was supposed to, somewhere else.

The next morning I shuffled into work at my summer job in a consignment clothing shop. I was numb, seeing everything as though peering through thick, warped glass. I went through the motions, totally checked out. My thousands of memories played faster than I could keep up, erratic jump cuts mixed with visualizations of my friend falling down the cliffside, over and over. I could see Ryan's parents and siblings in that big log cabin they all shared so closely, now just shells of themselves.

I went to the service, but skipped the burial. I don't now recall if it's actually real, but I have a memory of driving past the cemetery afterward while the burial was happening. I refused to watch Ryan go into the ground. The few times in life I've experienced intense grief, I've had a delayed reaction, been unable to cry. Weeks later, my sister Sheryl insisted that I cut my long hair off for her upcoming wedding. At last, this caused me to have a complete meltdown.

Jennifer and Mat came up to the island a few weeks later for a vacation. They were like family now, and we'd kept in constant contact the past year. They appeared to me as an EXIT sign, a way I could get off the island: My surroundings looked like nothing if not a beautiful prison.

Above all else, I needed access to music. Unlike when I was in Arizona, on the island I had to make extensive plans just to order a CD or see a concert. If it was a school night, my mom would take me and a friend, boarding the ferry as soon as classes ended. After seeing Faith No More, or Nirvana, or Jesus Jones, we'd make the drive back to the ferry and sleep in the car for a few hours before the 6 a.m. boat. I would arrive at school on time, bleary-eyed but reveling in the afterglow of whatever performance we'd seen.

My mom was doing her best to make sure I wasn't missing out on anything. But it still wasn't enough. I had to find more people like me. The *Playgirl* under my bed had fostered new wants, fueling my drive for sex—with guys. The voice in my head that had previously been sidestepping the truth had begun declaring itself. I was gay. Maybe my mom knew there'd be an emptiness in my life, now that one of my closest friends had died. Or maybe it was just out of a deep generosity, but after much deliberation, and talks with Jennifer and Mat, my parents let me go: I left my home and moved back to Arizona, where the Leberts would become my legal guardians while I attended a public school. I didn't pause to calculate what this meant. I just wanted out of that place.

I knew I had to get rid of the *Playgirl*. But I couldn't just leave it under my bed or throw it in the garbage for somebody to find. I took it down to the beach and jerked off one last time over the tan men. I doubled over and gasped on my knees, coming on the ancient beach rocks. Primordial ooze. Pulling up my shorts, I stacked some driftwood kindling underneath the well-worn and crinkled pages. The ocean was flat and still when I burned the magazine. It slowly caught fire and disappeared, pieces floating upward in the air.

6

CHILDHOOD WAS OFFICIALLY OVER. MY OLD SKIN WAS
sloughing off quicker than I could make a new one. This other self
was growing outward from the inside, started tilting my head at certain angles, making my hands fall limp. Moving states didn't make it
easier to fit in—in fact, the opposite was true. But I still found plenty
of fellow misfits in the vicinity.

Like stray dogs, we hung out in my friend Josh's backyard. It was
pretty gross: Dirt and dead grass, Coke cans and candy bar wrappers
were littered around a long-dead trampoline. We sat on rusty lawn
chairs and smoked cigarettes so cheap they disintegrated after three
hits. Courtney would stand, half swaying to the handbag house that
blared from a weary boom box, the speakers shot, the CDs always
skipping. As the Arizona sun cooked everything in sight, we found
shelter in the shade of the house's fragile roof.

Atticus, a ropy blond boy with a penchant for backward base-
ball caps, demonstrated a recent dance-floor sandwich. The previous
weekend, he'd been at Preston's, a gay club in Phoenix that would let
minors in after 2 a.m. Between swigs of beer he droned on: ". . . And
the lights, they have, like, three strobes. I can totally get us in."

Josh, with his math-teacher glasses and long, straight hair, was
quiet but bemused as he rolled joints. His weed kit was a metal Band-
Aid box with the *a* and the *n* replaced by a *u*, so it read BUD-AID, the

gear splayed before him on a warped particleboard card table. I never saw him take off his black leather jacket, even in the heat. "Maybe my dad would let me drive his car," he said, brushing a lock of greasy hair behind his left ear. "He's let me drive it before."

"You can't just drive a car, dummy. Trust me. You don't even know how," Courtney said. She was the oldest of us, pushing seventeen, and still didn't have her license. She was too tweaked out most of the time to be driving, anyway. Preoccupied, always rearranging the contents of her lunch box, looking for God knows what, its insides smelling like rose oil. Courtney turned around and now stared at the stucco wall ferociously.

"But my dad's cool," Josh said. "He lets me do whatever I want." The back window of the house looking into the kitchen was just clear enough that we could see the broad figure of his father puttering around. A few weeks before, we had gotten ripped from bong hits while watching *Cat People*. Josh told me under his breath that his father had molested him and his sister for years. I never asked what happened to his mom.

His dad stuck his head out of the kitchen door and made everyone jump: "Everything all right today, guys?" His voice was serene. We all nodded our heads in unison. He didn't seem to mind us smoking pot and drinking beer. As he receded into the darkness of the house, I thought, *What a fucking creep.*

I walked home some days in the silent dry heat and passed tract houses, their gravel yards dotted with cactuses. No one down here really walked anywhere; it was too hot. I wondered if people noticed me out the front windows of their houses. I scratched at the fishnets on my arms and tugged at my mustard-plaid, pleated wool skirt. Sometimes Courtney walked back this way with me, but more often than not I left her behind in whoever's backyard. Usually the next time I'd see her, she'd have been awake for a couple days, large black sunglasses hiding her Ping-Pong–ball eyes. A meth vampire. If she wasn't in school, she was usually hiding from the daylight in her darkened, air-conditioned bedroom, posters and photos overlapping on top of each other. When I wasn't with her, I imagined the blurry, secret things she did. The fun she was having that I was not. I didn't judge people who did crystal; I just figured they were doing what they wanted. All the tweakers I knew seemed stable enough. Courtney could get overly dramatic and excited by something as tiny as a toothpick, but I just thought she was enthusiastic. She never offered me drugs. And I don't think I would have taken them if she had. I was perfectly happy with the rush I got from my generic GPC Light cigarettes. They were only two bucks at 7-Eleven—that is, if you could find someone over eighteen to buy them for you. I carried them around in a repurposed old binocular case, adorned with a Sisters of Mercy sticker.

Jennifer would be home with her newborn daughter, Emily, perched on her bosom as she stirred pasta.

Our conversations were blank with denial:

"Hi—how was your day?" Her cheer was always genuine, and I was grateful for it.

"Fine," I lied, feeling a small jet of fear.

"Dinner'll be ready in ten. Your mom just called."

"What'd she say?"

"Wants you to call her, we talked for a half hour. I told her your grades. Your math is terrible, but she says it's fine if you want to go to the concert." I had been begging to see Concrete Blonde at an all-ages club. "I can probably take you, but maybe we can get Courtney's mom to pick you guys up—Mat and I have class."

"Class" meant an Amway motivational seminar. Jennifer and Mat's shelves were filled with hundreds of cassette tapes on salesmanship with titles like "Be a Comfortable Shoe" and "Jesus Wants you Rich." The clipped pictures of sports cars and golf courses taped to the fridge were supposed exercises in manifestation. Often when she and Mat went to Amway meetings, I'd attend a Christian youth group called Young Life. It was something to do, and I found the familiar devotional songs relaxing, despite being at odds with their subject matter.

At the end of every school day I'd walk into my makeshift bedroom, drop my stained backpack on the floor, and begin to disassemble my look, starting first by unstrapping my heavy leather bondage belt, taking five pounds off my frame as it fell to the carpet. I wore fishnet stockings on my arms and cut holes in the feet for my fingers, my head placed through a rip in the crotch, but to get to them I'd first have to pull off the too-large Skinny Puppy or Ministry T-shirt, emblazoned with demonic-looking serpents or a blurred grimy angel, over my head. I was desperate to advertise the bands that I loved, and logos always took precedence over shirt size.

Music was a primary way to identify myself, and going to concerts felt like permanently searing a band in my own history, like a tattoo. My favorite moment of a show was the anticipation of the headliner coming to the stage, the crowd slowly swelling, each minute feeling like an eternity. Since I'd been back in Arizona, I'd already seen Nine Inch Nails twice on their tour for *Downward Spiral*, as well as KMFDM and My Life with the Thrill Kill Kult.

I was a vile vision: Spindly and spotty, my features roamed as if they were still trying to find a home on my face. My blue eyes were too big, and my long brown mop of hair was sprayed to look like a tumbleweed. Angry, cyst-like nodules covered my skin. Braces with purple rubber bands were glued to my teeth and made my gums puffy, cranking my whole face to an elevated degree of busted. The braces were to be taken off soon, and I dreamed of what it would feel like running my tongue over smooth teeth. If I thought of this in front of the mirror, I could see a glimmer of another, more handsome boy blooming underneath this one. But my acne had been so explosive, I'd convinced Jennifer to let me start taking Accutane. We found some sketchy doctor in a dilapidated office to give me a prescription. Every day I took an orange pill from a blister pack decorated with a logo of a pregnant woman with a red slash through her: Apparently it would deform your baby if you got pregnant while taking it. Later it was found to have a pretty big side effect: teenage depression and, therefore, suicide. I often wonder if those pills had anything to do with the fact that I made myself a walking bull's-eye wherever I went, subconsciously putting myself in harm's way.

Once the stockings were off my torso, they left red crosshatched indentations on my skin. Now, there was just a plaid skirt or overly baggy black shorts and boots. My skirt was too small for me, so I had to button it above my hips. It was constricting, but it was the only skirt I had.

I had bought some rainbow-colored metallic "freedom rings" that I wore on a chain around my neck. They were supposed to be an outward symbol of your own gay pride. A way to be visible and out in your everyday life, kind of like a bumper sticker. It was exhilarating to wear them at first. They were my refusal to apologize. But I soon had an allergic reaction to the cheap metal chain and developed a rash. I kept wearing them, though the rash persisted. They started eating into my neck, making it a gooey, raw mess of exposed flesh. *It figures*, I thought, finally deciding to just hang them off my backpack. But those freedom rings really did a number on me: The scabs were gross and took a long time to heal.

It was freedom I had been looking for that year, away from my parents, and to a degree, I'd found it. Jennifer didn't put up too much of a fuss regarding what I wore, and she didn't ask too many questions. But that autonomy had opened up a whole other brand of trouble. I wasn't actually ready to come out to her and Mat, or to my parents. But I was ready to start telling *somebody*. And I realized the weirder I dressed, the more attention I got. Even if it was mostly negative, it was still attention. When I clomped through the school quad in my creepers and chains, everyone stared. Then soon they started to yell. Eventually they started getting in my face and chasing me. I felt like a fucked-up rock star. But at least everyone knew who I was.

The first person I came out to was a girl at school named Liz. She had a dry sense of humor and wore flowing dresses with embroidered flowers on them. She was one of the few people at school who made an attempt to get to know me. We'd eat Taco Bell burritos in the courtyard at lunchtime, make wry observations about the popular kids, and discuss our love of Bowie.

Despite my new friend, an unbearable loneliness crept its way through my excitement of being in a new environment. One night I listened to the radio in my room, anxiety chewing through my center, feeling homesick for my folks. Was this larger alienation worth trading in the beauty of the rocky beaches and bluffs, the peaceful harbor and the deep whistle of the ferry horn? My mom and dad?

I called Liz, and after a few minutes of stammering, I told her as my tear ducts turned to floodgates: "I think I'm gay," I said. "Actually no, I *know* I'm gay." The grief I felt in that moment was awful; it was like someone had died. Even though the words were uttered into the phone, hearing them out of my own mouth finally made it real, defined me as something new. Overwhelmed and sobbing, I felt trapped by my age, exhausted by my desires.

Liz must not have known what to say and handed the phone to her stepdad. He listened to me cry and consoled me for what seemed like an hour. Though he sounded like he was probably not well versed in the gay experience, his voice was strong and deep as he did his best, telling me that everything would be all right. I could even have kids if I wanted to someday, he said. It was perfectly fine if I was a gay person. Her stepdad, whom I'd never met or spoken to, was a momentary angel; I needed to hear those things from anybody, especially a man.

Soon after, Liz stopped meeting me in the courtyard at lunch. She called one evening and told me she was pregnant and was leaving school altogether. I've never seen her since.

From then on, when asked if I was a fag at school, I would just stare straight ahead and not answer, or mutter a *Yeah? So fuckin' what*, which transformed my outlandish looks into provocations, which in turn gave me tunnel vision, which in itself became a strategy. I learned to see my surroundings in the periphery.

Every day when I got home, I took off the thrift-store armor, never saying a word to Jennifer or my mom about what was really happening at school: the disgusted looks from classmates, the menacing stares, passing laughter escalating into shouts. Aggressive, ugly boys swarmed around me like wasps. Objects were tossed at my head when a teacher's back was turned. I was scared to walk across the sprawling campus, never knowing who could be standing around the corner. I learned not to use my locker; they were housed in cage-like structures, perfect for getting cornered in. At lunchtime, I walked all the way across the empty playing field to stand behind a fence, puffing away on a cigarette until the school bell rang.

The classrooms were a cold hell. Air-conditioned and windowless, they lay deep within hulking stucco walls. Before one lunch period, Mrs. Connelly, my biology teacher, found my hiding spot—between two filing cabinets in a back office.

"What are you doing here?" She was small-framed and composed. I was fond of her because she was friendly with me. I did well in her class.

"I'm waiting until the halls clear out," I said.

"Why are you doing that?"

"These guys wait outside. I don't even know who they are."

"For what?"

They followed and yelled at me in the hall, like they wanted to kill me. It scared the shit out of me when they got in my face. *You fucking fudge-packing faggot.*

"Oh, for crying out loud." She shook her head. "This is nonsense." Mrs. Connelly reached her hand out and pulled me from my foxhole, led me back through the classroom, and walked me to the door. I was scared to even look to see if they were out there. "Listen, I'm going to stand out here and keep an eye out. Every day. It's not right." She kept her promise. Similarly, I found allies in a couple of my teachers.

I had a literature teacher who looked like Robert Altman. He read us Langston Hughes and encouraged me to write. One day after passing back an assignment, he told me I was the only one in class who could properly write a story. Sometimes he looked at me funny, like he was seeing something that surprised him. At the end of the year, I was the last to leave the room and he called after me to stay for a minute. "Special burdens are given to special people," he said. I bristled as I walked out of that class for the final time. I didn't have a burden, I was just gay. But I now understand it as one of the kindest things anyone has ever said to me.

But sometimes the teachers were traitors. They could seem benevolent, like they wanted to help, but would lead me by the hand straight back into the mouth of the beast: the principal's office. My algebra teacher, with his huge, brushy mustache, pretended that he couldn't see when a boy started throwing pencils at me or knocking chairs into my desk. It was almost as if the teacher was scared of appearing weak by acknowledging the abuse. The day I finally turned around and told my torturer to "fucking stop," the kid got out of his chair and heaved his whole desk at me. We were both sent to the principal's office.

The cocky shit sat with a creepy grin on his face, staring at me as the principal trotted out his warmed-over wise-man act. "Now, uh, Jason, is it?" He looked like Dr. Phil. "Why do you think this is happening? I understand it's developed into a problem?"

I said that obviously this kid didn't like the fact that I was gay.

"How would he know this?" he said. Why was I being grilled, as this asshole just sat there, smiling at me? The principal sighed. "We all have our differences, other viewpoints, et cetera." *Blah blah blah.* "There's all kinds of people in the world. But just stop for a minute and think—would this be happening if you could just leave that stuff at home?" He eyed my clothes. "If you kept your private life to yourself, would these incidents be happening?"

"I see guys and girls here holding hands all day long. What about that?" I had a lump in my throat. "Is that their private life?"

"That's the world we live in, Jacob," he said, patting my back and standing up. The discussion was over. I'd made a huge mistake in outing myself. It was a brazen miscalculation in a bid for freedom and attention, an irrevocable move. I had been careless, strolling out of the closet just to turn around to see that the door had disappeared. There was no way now to hide in plain sight.

7

THE EDGE WAS A PHONE LINE FOR LONELY AND BORED people all over Phoenix, and the number was passed to me by Atticus, who apparently went to my school, though I never saw him there. Atticus claimed to be bisexual and I didn't know him very well, but he and Josh and I had a clumsy three-way late one night in Josh's basement that was kind of sweet and lackadaisical. Atticus was always talking about the Edge. "I think you'll be into it," he said, scribbling down the memorized number onto a scrap of paper.

It was kind of a prehistoric chat room, where all kinds of folks left strings of messages for one another. The main menu option was a general discussion zone where you could ask people's opinions, have arguments, talk smack about other callers, or just ramble. Every day you listened to the compiled messages from the day before, then had the option to leave a response to what you'd just heard, or to start a new discussion.

Often the messages would sound something like this:

Hey, this is Mama Ho. And I just want to give a shout-out to all my hos tonight. Especially Dr. Lou, who wanted to know why men had nipples. Well, I'm not a man, but—have you not had your nipples licked?

—BEEP—

What's up, guys, this is Pay Phone Goddess and I just want to say to Shy Girl, you shut your fucking mouth. What the fuck you have to say, bitch? Got shit with me, you come and say it to my face. Otherwise, shut your fucking hole, you stupid whore.

—BEEP—

Hey, this is Deja. I'm just kicking back after a long day, watching some Sally Jessy Raphael. *Uh, I need to talk about the hair. Just for a minute? Has anyone noticed it hasn't moved since 1985? Also, is it just me, or is Jenny Jones suddenly trying to look like Björk? Anyone?*

My name on the Edge was Barbie's Nightmare, and upon signing up, I obtained my own voice-mail box where I could receive private messages from other callers. I waited impatiently for the update every afternoon, before which the system was offline. Usually I had to redial repeatedly to get through, as there could only be three people using the line at one time. Every night I listened to people's squabbles, sex fantasies, and pontifications.

Everyone on the Edge had their own distinct timbre and syntax; I imagined what they looked like from how they sounded. Kaskha I envisioned to be a swinging office lady from the '70s with feathered hair and a polyester pantsuit. Nightshade orated soft-core sex fantasies and had a very deep, intoxicating voice. Later I found out he was quadriplegic. Someone who went by the name of Deja (see above) caught my attention. She wasn't as negative as some of the others could be, and made me laugh. I left her a poem in her voice-mail box one day. "If only I could just shrink you down and put you on a shelf in my bedroom," she said in her response. We exchanged numbers and began speaking on the phone. Her real name was Mary Hanlon.

Mary and I began talking every day. I'd tell her what was going on at school, and she'd regale me with lukewarm adventures about her high school friends, with whom she still hung out. Her stories could be mundane, but were told with a dry and laconic sense of humor. She was twenty-one and had skipped college, but worked a nine-to-five job and for the most part seemed to keep to herself. After a few weeks of talking, we decided to meet in person. She lived about an hour away, but we orchestrated a date to an Italian restaurant called Fuzi.

"There's something I haven't told you about me," she said the day before we were to meet up. She sounded nervous. "And seriously, if you don't want to hang out, I totally understand."

"Did you just get out of prison?" I couldn't possibly imagine what she was talking about.

"No." She paused. "I'm really, really big. Like—obese big. I didn't say anything because I had no idea we would be talking so much, or that we'd end up actually meeting each other. But yeah." Her laugh was brimming with pain. "I'm a biggie."

It bummed me out that she thought I would care. The age gap between us was so wide, I was just flattered to be chatting. She was a smart, adult woman who wanted to hang out with me. My favorite.

We went to movies and restaurants every weekend, drove through the suburban sprawl, and listened to alternative music in her car. She got nervous sometimes about leaving her house and being made fun of. In shops, and at the mall, I could tell how uncomfortable she was in public. Everyone stared. Waitresses were rude. Retail clerks were dismissive of us—that is, if we weren't downright ignored. I witnessed firsthand how horrible people could be, and I didn't blame her for not wanting to leave the safety of her home.

We began going to hangouts where people from the Edge would get together and meet in person, at a park or at Randy's, the system operator's house. Mary and I knew we were just as odd and mismatched as everybody else, but we marveled at the strange combinations of folks that the Edge attracted. There were vampy ladies, unhygienic introverts, square professionals, bored housewives, teenage queers, potheads, hookers, and musicians.

Randy, who ran the whole operation from a spare bedroom, had some kind of day job and lived in downtown Phoenix. He was an attractive gay guy with an easygoing personality, and loved having his denizens hang out all night at his house. A slew of us often slept on the couch and the floor. I would lie to Jennifer and tell her that I was staying with a friend from school. She'd want to talk to my "friend's" mom, so I convinced some lady who lived in Randy's garage to call Jennifer and pretend to play the part. It always worked, but I was nervous about being found out. I stayed away from any booze or drugs, which would have made getting caught a lot more complicated.

There was something paternal about Randy. Whenever I needed some extra attention, or guidance at the end of a bad day, he would always be available to talk. I felt safe around him, and he treated me like I wasn't just fifteen but someone with formed opinions and ideas. He'd confide in me about a crush on some guy he was having or share gossip about drama from the Edge. A couple years later, when I tried to track him down to say hi, I found out he was in prison. Apparently he'd been busted for having sex with underage guys. I didn't hear any details of the story, but it made me feel hurt and betrayed. He had genuinely seemed like a nice guy and was a good friend. The sour aftertaste was accompanied by relief. There were so many situations and nights when he could have potentially taken advantage of me.

I eventually made it to Preston's, the gay bar in Phoenix that Atticus had been raving about for months. It was hideous and delicious, a brass-and-glass affair with a chintzy dance floor to boot. Mary drove the two of us there, but sometimes she'd be too tired to go in and would just sleep in the car while I danced. Afterward, we'd hang out in the parking lot, listening to tweakers' souped-up car stereos. I discovered tons of new music from the various party kids with their processed hair and elaborate shoes.

It's a miracle I never got into any trouble. Older guys came up to me, yanked on my bondage belts, and asked me, "What is this? What are you all about?" I'd brush strands of my long green bangs behind my ear and smile. Always polite, I'd manage to steer myself away to a safer spot. Some Sunday mornings, I'd open my eyes to see acquaintances smoking rocks out of glass pipes, trying to wake up enough to drive me home. I never tried those drugs, never got assaulted. But other than Mary, this was not a crowd any mother would want her teenage son to be hanging out with.

I balanced my secretive Phoenix weekends with the Christian Young Life youth group that met on Wednesdays. The meetings took place in family living rooms, where we sang songs about Jesus while Desi, the head pastor, played guitar. I didn't dress so flamboyantly at Young Life. It was a place where at least for a few hours I was happy to blend in. The meetings had about thirty kids from various high schools. Ironically, I felt comfortable and welcomed there. One night, I came out to one of the assistant youth pastors in a Taco Bell as we slurped on sodas. He seemed puzzled and didn't say much. In the following months, the former warmth turned into distance, and we never really spoke about it again to each other, which hurt.

I thought I had succeeded in keeping track of all the moving parts of my life. But it was sloppiness, primarily, that caused the threads to unravel. My mother came down for a weekend visit, and independence had made me cocky. I took her to Mill Avenue for a wander with Randy and a couple other people from the Edge: this teenage queer, Fro-baby; Randy's creepy roommate who looked like Buffalo Bill; and this girl who kept saying she was feeling sick and thought she might be pregnant. When we got home, my mom was shell-shocked.

"Jason, who are those people?" She ran her hands through her blond hair, something she did when she was anxious. "How do you know them?"

"They're just friends that I met down here."

"They're nice enough, but . . ." She winced. "Why are you hanging out with them? There's something . . ." *Gay* was the word she couldn't quite bring herself to say.

"They're nice people, Mom. I hang out with all kinds of them."

"*All kinds* is right." She put her hand on her forehead. "Jennifer found a pack of cigarettes in your . . . purse." She pronounced *cigarettes* spitting the consonants. She looked in her lap for a moment, then raised her finger and jabbed it in the air. "If you think for one second you're going to get away with the same crap your sisters did, you've got another thing coming, buddy." She could feel that I had slipped out of her reach.

"You're fifteen years old! And you're my son. And you're *smoking?*" She folded her arms and shook her head, looked at me like I was someone she didn't recognize. It made me hate myself. The last thing I wanted to do was hurt my mom. Yes, I had started smoking, but had I done anything *really* wrong? As far as I was concerned, I'd been very responsible. She was quiet when she left for Washington the next day. I don't blame her now for being worried. She should have been.

Meanwhile, school got worse. My friend Courtney was caught with crystal meth in her lunch box and whisked away to rehab. Her bubbly personality had kept me afloat at school, and she had been one of my only friends there. Now, she'd left me alone with the wolves. Most of my teachers, knowing the danger I was in and the potential for violence, allowed me to finish all my exams early and skip the last two days of school. I screamed, "FUCK YOU!" to all the kids leaving for the day, leaning out a friend's car window, both hands flipping the bird as I rode out of the parking lot the final time.

The week after school ended, I went to a weeklong Young Life retreat that my youth group had been pushing us all year to attend. The camp was cheesy, full of peppy cheer and solemn talks about God. Desi, the youth pastor, oversaw my cabin and would lead discussions with our group every night. My sexuality was discussed heavily yet always between the lines. There was a lot of talk about "wanting to change." Group leaders pulled me aside for small conversations, saying, "There is something you could do about it, if you really want to." I was flattered by their regard. Everyone could see how miserable I had been and wanted to help. I still feel they were just being kind.

I'd take walks by myself and contemplate how my sexuality had not only been a burden; it had made my life a fucking drag. Being gay had gotten me into this mess, not knowing where or who I was supposed to be. Exhaustion was permeating my bones. I was sick of defending myself, tired of fighting. I didn't have much to lose. On the last day of camp, I prayed with Desi, asked Christ to save me from my sins, and pledged to walk in His footsteps.

My time in Arizona ended at a river deep in the desert. I wore a white robe. Courtney, now sober, watched from the river's edge in her cat-eye sunglasses. She witnessed the spectacle, looking a bit perplexed.

"This is Jason Sellards," Desi said to the air and our audience of one. "And he comes today to be baptized into Christ. Now repeat after me: I believe that Jesus is the Christ."

"I believe that Jesus is the Christ."

"The son of the Living God, and my Lord and Savior."

"The son of the Living God, and my Lord and Savior."

"In the name of the Father, the Son, and the Holy Spirit." Desi pushed me back into the water and immediately lifted my head out. "You are born again." He laughed, delighted.

8

MY SALVATION LASTED ABOUT FIVE MINUTES. NOT THAT I really tried too hard. I waited a few days to start being attracted to women, but it never happened. I felt like a gullible kid again, thinking there was some magic solution to my issues, believing the claims of the commercials. It had sounded too good to be true, but the notice that I'd received from my youth pastor and camp counselors had been too tempting to pass up.

I went back to the island that summer to live with my parents, still gay and definitely not about to start back at the island high school. I would have rather dropped out, and I think my mom knew it. I had faith I could find a school that wasn't on the island but was close enough to please my parents. I knew they had put money aside for my education, so I convinced my mom to let me attend the Northwest School, a college-prep school in Seattle. The venerable, well-kept old schoolhouse was perfect. I'd be living in their boardinghouse, and it didn't hurt that it was located on Capitol Hill, Seattle's gayest neighborhood—a fact that must have throbbed in my mom's mind like a migraine. But she was so impressed with the rigorous classes and no-nonsense faculty that the benefits must have outweighed her reservations. Besides, I had never actually been in any real trouble, other than getting caught with a pack of cheap smokes. And on top of that, I reminded her when I needed to that I had "found" Jesus.

It didn't take long for me to acclimate. The students at Northwest were mature, laid-back coffee drinkers, creative and hip. My sexuality was a nonissue among teachers, who all went by their first names. I focused on the work. It was stringent and unsparing. Papers were due by the multitudes and subject to critique in conferences. My essays were picked apart until sometimes it felt like there was nothing left of substance. But I was learning to be a better writer.

The city was thrumming with great local bands, writers' talks at bookstores, a lively café culture. I was dumbfounded by my luck: Seattle was still enjoying its newfound heyday in 1995. I spent most of my time doing my schoolwork in Bauhaus, a cavernous gray coffee shop down the street from the dorm, smoking vanilla cigarettes and chugging bottles of Jolt cola, plowing through novels and bullshitting for hours with vampires, bleached-blond lesbians with candy-colored barrettes, ambiguous effete guys, and musicians. The curfew at the dorms was 8 p.m. on weekdays; I never stayed out late unless I had specific permission.

I had a sampler keyboard, on loan from my sister Windi, that could play only four notes at once, but it made me happy to noodle on it. I could play music whenever I wanted. Not that I was particularly good, but I could construct melodies over bass notes or simple chords. I'd lose hours jotting down words in a notebook and singing them back to myself.

And now as I plunked away on the keyboard in my room, unfocused, I was convinced that my luck had run out. I had stretched the freedom I had earned to a breaking point. Not only did my parents not know for sure I was gay, but I was spending time with Pete, a salty, thirty-three-year-old deadbeat guitar player. My brazen and loose lips were to blame for the dorm's suspecting a questionable relationship. Ethically, they knew it would be problematic to "out" me to my parents. But if they gleaned any details of this non–parental approved "friend," they would have no choice.

"Jason, I'm really at a loss," the head resident advisor had just said, sitting across from me calmly. "I don't know what's going on, but if it's something inappropriate, your parents need to know. If you aren't willing to tell them, don't think for a second that I won't. Can you see it from my perspective?"

I stared out the window, dog-paddling for the right response. At least she wasn't talking to me like a child. "Give me until next week," I said. "I promise I'll figure it out."

I slowly ascended the stairs to my room, then closed the door and took a deep breath of its smell—burnt paint from a radiator, acrid but comforting. I turned the radio on. It was 8 o'clock, and Dan Savage's local advice show was starting. I listened to it every Thursday night. Savage's filthy and funny sex column in the local weekly, *The Stranger*, was my bible. I began calling his show. Almost every week I explained my predicament live on the air. I was out at school, yet my parents were still in the dark. If they found out, they could pull me back home, extinguishing my independence.

I made my way to the dorm pay phone and put a couple quarters in the slot. Busy. I tried again. "*Savage Love Live,*" the studio assistant answered.

"Hey, it's Jason." After a couple minutes of listening to the show on hold, I was patched through, a disorienting moment as the show was on a ten-second delay.

"We have Jason on Capitol Hill on the line. . . ." To Dan's credit, he was never exasperated with my frequent calls. "Jason, how's it going?"

"Everything's all right—well, not really. . . ." I paused to disentangle my jumbled thoughts.

"What's 'not really'?"

"I think I'm screwed." My throat tightened. *God, please don't let me cry.* "The school just told me I have to come out to my parents."

"I don't think the school can do that, as far as I know."

"They found out I'm hanging with this guy. They think he's too old for me."

"How old is he?"

"Thirty-three."

"Okay—first of all, that's insane. What the hell is he doing with you? You just turned sixteen."

"But he's really sweet. It's no big deal. He's taught me how to play the guitar."

"I don't care if he's taught you Mandarin. He has no business hanging out with a sixteen-year-old." I could hear Dan was frustrated. "My main concern is that your folks could find out about everything, including this asshole you're seeing—*which has got to stop*—and throw you into shock therapy."

"They'd probably just bring me back home with them."

"And how could you *blame* them seeing that you're dating a *thirty-three-year-old*? Listen, I think your parents already know you're gay, first of all. If you don't think they're going to put you in the gay-teen slammer, I don't see why you shouldn't just say something at this point. But get rid of this creep first." I clinked the receiver into the cradle and rested my head on the edge of the phone. There was homework waiting for me in my room, but I knew it would be hard to concentrate.

Being in an accepting environment had made me more comfortable with my eccentricities. The weird clothes I insisted on wearing were now colorful and expressive, rather than worn as a defense. I bleached my hair and decorated it with barrettes like my girlfriends at school. I would assemble looks that I would feature only once, and I received compliments on them now rather than threats. I could walk between classes and take in my surroundings, socializing with whomever I wanted. I stopped looking over my shoulder.

The more adjusted I felt, the more I realized I needed to find more queer people to hang out with. It was rare to meet anybody my own age who was out. There was a teen social outreach group I joined. They

threw dance parties for young queer people, using the platform to pro-
mote condoms and safer sex. In 1995, we didn't know that the AIDS
drug cocktails were about to change the landscape. So many people
were still dying. One guy my own age I was acquainted with suddenly
disappeared. It turned out he had been hospitalized and passed away.

I might have accepted my sexuality, but I was terrified of sex, all
too aware of what the consequences could be if I slipped up. I'd met
a handful of people who were HIV positive: people my age from
the outreach program, as well as Robert, an adult volunteer. Sometimes I'd walk down the street and see gay men who were visibly sick.
Though I was incredibly safe and I wasn't having full-on intercourse, I
began the ritual of getting tested every three months. Even if I'd done
nothing but jerk off to the porn mags my café buddies would buy
me on the sly, I would still get tested. It was about a two-mile walk
to the free clinic, thirty minutes of sadness and stomach butterflies.
The full week it took before the results came back were distraction
at its worst. I'd manage to convince myself that some freak accident
had happened, and I would test positive. Maybe I had gotten it from
jerking a guy off, or a blow job, or maybe I'd be the first to have an
Immaculate Seroconversion. I'd sob in the school bathrooms in front
of my girlfriends, convinced I had HIV.

The queer youth dance parties I helped throw were an exciting
way I could meet other young people. But unfortunately the criteria
weren't strict enough at the door, because that's where I had met Pete,
who, being thirty-three, shouldn't have been there. He was handsome,
charming, didn't seem to have a job, but had been in a few bands.
We'd sit cross-legged in his apartment on rainy weekend afternoons.
"Can you show me how to play guitar?" I asked. He taught me five
chords and let me borrow an acoustic, which I spent hours practicing
on every day.

Pete's apartment was piled high with dog-eared books by the Beat
poets, photos of Bowie and Chet Baker. The place was the size of a
bunny hutch and grimy in the corners. The bedsheets were usually a

couple days past their expiration date, and his hand-rolled cigarette butts were piled high in the ashtray, a trail of smoke always flowing out of his right hand, which was connected to an arm covered in homemade Germs tattoos and track marks. He kept an address book on the side of his couch that I would occasionally flip through and see names of the likes of Iggy Pop, Duff McKagan, and Joan Jett, all people he was acquainted or had played guitar with over the years. He introduced me to records by Lou Reed, the Birthday Party, and the Flaming Lips. Then there was Wayne County, a ferocious punk staple from someplace called Max's Kansas City in New York. Apparently Wayne had transitioned to a female and was now called Jayne County.

I ate it all up.

Some days Pete and I just watched TV. He must have been on government assistance, because he spent his days not doing much. He'd wake up at noon, stroll to the library or sit with an espresso on the street. He had played guitar in a string of bands, his current one fronted by his girlfriend. Sometimes she'd be sitting on the couch when I came over, cordial but tense. I wondered if she thought there was something going on between Pete and me. Her voice was pretty, if a little flat, and she sang in a sighing, dejected way. Most of the songs seemed to be about being in love with a junkie. Pete was the closest thing I'd ever met to a rock star. And though his life had become a little boring and sad, there seemed to be so much possibility in that music. In that address book.

I started my own band. It consisted of me and Mike McCracken, this senior from my school, on drums. Some guy named Ian played guitar. He was stocky, bisexual, the same age as me, and smelled like a goat. I met him in the Bauhaus café one night, after asking what the big X's on the back of his hands meant. He was "straight edge," he told me, meaning he didn't drink or do any drugs. Sometimes after rehearsals we would go for walks and make out.

We were called My Favorite Band, and our songs were written with the only five chords Pete had taught me. The song titles such as

"My Chair" and "I Had Sex with Your Sister" were the least offensive. I loved nothing more than to shock people with disgusting lyrics and was now in the habit of saying anything for attention. We played a total of three shows: two at my school and one at the Puss-Puss Cafe, which was run by Kim Warnick from the Fastbacks. I had given her a demo cassette we had made on a four-track. I'm not sure if she listened to it, but she let us play. It didn't occur to me we weren't very good. I just got a kick out of looking at an audience looking back at me. It was like a mirror, reflecting a hundred eyes that weren't yours.

I knocked and opened Pete's screen door. He was draped listlessly on the sofa, with one leg up. I sat down, my hands in my lap, and told him that the school knew about us now.

He didn't move his head but cocked an eyebrow and frowned. "Us—what? What'd they say?"

"Uh, they're not happy about it? They want me to tell my parents I'm gay?"

He waved his hand and croaked. "What's that got to do with me? Look, it's just your folks. Don't worry about it. You're a good kid. Smart." He squinted his eyes and sucked on his cigarette, pinched between his thumb and index finger, his peroxide-bleached pompadour looking less than fresh. He swung his legs around and sat up to look me in the face. "Look—you know I like you. You're sweet. We've made out a couple times. I gave you a mixtape. But I'm not—I've never been—your boyfriend." He scanned my face. "Have you been telling people I'm your boyfriend?" I didn't answer. "Shit." He stood up and looked at the cherry of his smoke, like someone would stare at a fire. "We haven't even fucked. Don't make this more trouble than it's worth."

That night Pete took me to see Pearl Jam at the Moore Theatre downtown. I got permission from the dorm to have a late curfew, but I didn't mention that I was going with him.

It was a homecoming show. Eddie Vedder had Neil Young onstage for part of the set. I wasn't the biggest Pearl Jam fan, but the electricity in the room was undeniable. After they finished, we went backstage and I felt like I had caught my foot in some door I'd been dreaming of. For the first time, I was among living and breathing musicians. Whatever tiny piece of music history was occurring, I was getting to see it with my own eyes and ears.

Perched in a smoky booth with a couple of the women from 7 Year Bitch, I listened to them, astonished that I could be a witness to their barbed banter and gossip. Neil Young sauntered around as the band greeted their friends. Pete introduced me to Stone Gossard from Pearl Jam, who seemed kind. I talked to him about my school; he was an alum.

I arrived back at the dorm. Everyone had already gone to bed, and the halls were quiet. As I brushed my teeth, I watched myself in the mirror. My face was starting to settle. It wasn't as embryonic, my acne had calmed, and my eyes had a sparkle that I hadn't seen in years. But that night, I felt another new desire. I wanted to be a part of everything I had just seen, the energy of the show and the excitement I had witnessed afterward. What if I was a rock star myself one day? What if I was able to conjure in others that frenzied trance that occurred when a band was slaying? As I padded back to my room, I couldn't feel the carpet beneath my bare feet.

Mary came to visit me and I took a bus to pick her up at the airport. She walked off the plane in a beige-and-black-striped dress, a louder look than usual. It was her first time in Seattle, and she was immediately taken with its gloomy beauty.

She'd booked a room down the street from my school at the Sheraton, and I'd gotten permission to stay with her for the weekend. It felt as if we were actually adults together, riffling through the minibar and pretending to shop in stores that would never carry Mary's size. I noticed when we wandered around downtown, Mary had started to limp and couldn't be on her feet for too long before having to sit. We parked ourselves one afternoon in the Four Seasons hotel lobby and nicked a half-smoked cigar out of an ashtray. I lit it with the Zippo that Pete had given me for Christmas, and we attempted to smoke it. We went and saw *The Adventures of Priscilla, Queen of the Desert*. Mary liked to sit two seats away whenever we saw movies. At night we got drunk and made each other blow booze out our noses from laughing. Chattering and cackling, we were a team. All our musings were hilarious, to ourselves at least. She loved Seattle so much, she talked about moving there.

"I don't see why you couldn't," I said. But the thought of her moving to another state seemed like a long shot.

"It's not a super-easy city for biggies," she said. "I probably wouldn't have a car."

"Maybe you're not always going to be so big."

"Oh, please."

"Anything's possible."

Mary rolled her eyes. "If you're Gwyneth."

For spring break, my mom and dad wanted some family time, so we flew to Las Vegas. I had never been, and as I wandered through the vast casino of the MGM Grand hotel, I was unable to even pause and have a look because I was underage. I thought, *What are we supposed to do here as a family?* I had no one to hang out with, and while my mom and dad played slots on the floor, I roamed around the hotel, desperate for something to do.

It was a huge fixed-perspective *Wizard of Oz* diorama in the front lobby that changed everything. It depicted Dorothy and her crew, skipping down the yellow brick road, their lifelike faces filled with frozen wonder. I marveled at the detail, circling it slowly as if it were some sort of holy shrine. The Emerald City tower's glistening phalluses seemed like they had been put there just for me, filling me with a queer reverence. The jangling sounds of the slot machines faded as I squared off with Dorothy. The room dimmed, her ruby slippers a gentle blur in my unfocused gaze. It must have been the boredom of the trip, or maybe I just felt like, again, I wasn't getting enough attention, but standing there in front of Dorothy, I knew what I had to do, and it had to be now.

Keeping my sexuality from my family was eating away at my happiness, just as those shitty kids had feasted on me in Arizona. The layers and compartments to which I tended, the juggling of selves—it was wearing me out, rubbing all sides raw. I was sick of hiding magazines under my bed, sick of sneaking boys in through the window, sick of announcing in the school hallway anytime my mom came to visit, "You guys, my mom is outside and she's coming in. I'm NOT GAY. OKAY?" I wanted to feel like a complete person, to be ashamed of nothing and apologize to no one.

That evening, the burnt smell of a curling iron and hair spray permeated the small bathroom as my mother and I put the finishing touches on our hair. She had always been so pretty. But it wasn't because of the spunky clothes she wore or her trendy hairdos. It was her smile, which made it seem as if she had two open arms extending from her face. And right then it was breaking my heart.

"Which earrings should I wear?" She displayed a conservative pearl-colored option and then a gaudy rhinestone waterfall.

"The glitzy ones. It's Vegas."

She placed the more tasteful earrings back in her bag. "The show's in an hour. I need to hustle." We were attending *EFX*, a new Michael Crawford spectacular that was playing in a theater downstairs. "How was the amusement park?"

"Pretty quiet, but there were a few good rides." I had ridden a river rapids ride alone in the park behind the hotel. Staring at the empty seats around me in a circle, I had spun under a huge downpour of a waterfall. I walked away soaked, my outlook grim. "I've had fun," I lied. "But I'll be ready to leave tomorrow."

"When we get back to Seattle, I want to talk to you about something." She adjusted her lip liner.

I froze, one hand covered in gel, coaxing my strands to stand. What was *something*? Did this mean she suspected? She looked over at me and must have known I was going to ruin any chance of us coming out of this vacation happy. *Christ, who cares?* I thought. *Here we go.*

"Is it about me being gay?" There, I had said it. Boom. The pale yellow tiles in the bathroom looked the color of sick. I felt nauseous. It was over. Out of the bag. Neon lights. Phase two. *Lady, it's official, your boy is a big fag.*

She paused, set down her brush, and extricated herself from the bathroom. I followed and sat next to her on the stiff bed. My father lay on one side, silent and watching TV.

"Is that what you meant?" I said. "Is that what you wanted to talk about?" Her eyes were seeing atrocities on an invisible horizon. "Mom, I've always been like this."

"Jason," she said, just under her breath. "Your father is trying to watch the news."

We sat through the overblown Michael Crawford show, none of us able to focus on the stage. My parents ordered a bottle of wine at the table; it was the first time I saw either of them have a drink in about ten years. Dad was quiet and went back to the room after it was finished. Mom and I walked "to get ice cream." We paced and hissed, raising our voices in front of a buzzing food court. "It's a death sentence," she said. "What did we do to make this happen?" At one point: "I'm never going to have grandchildren!"

"People do that now sometimes," I said between spoonfuls of Häagen-Dazs. "Mom, I can totally have kids."

"Over my dead body!" she shot back.

We all flew back the next day and didn't speak. On the way to drop me off at my dorm, we stopped at a gas station and my mom went inside to pay. My father faced forward as the car idled and the wipers swiped off the drizzle. "Dad? Are you okay?"

He glanced at me in the rearview mirror and gave one small shake of his head, eyes back on the windshield. "We're simply devastated, Jason."

That evening when I returned to the dorm, I had two hours to get ready for a queer-youth dance my outreach group was throwing. My warm room was a refuge from the rain, from my parents. The thought of having to turn on my charm and pass out condoms to people was enough to send me under my bedsheets until the last possible minute. As I lay there, watching the endless shower of the dark evening, I remembered that we had a guest of honor that evening: Dan Savage.

It wasn't hard to pick him out of the crowd, standing about a foot and a half taller than everyone else. He was in drag: six-inch heels and a gargantuan sprayed wig. My own purple latex minidress, despite the baby powder, was too tight and pinched my skin. All the volunteers were wearing them. It made me feel unsexy and self-conscious. I approached Dan and his boyfriend, Terry Miller, as I tugged at my hem and ripped out leg hairs in the process.

"Dan?"

"How can I help you?" he hollered, over the blaring music.

"My name is Jason." Yelling back, I felt dispirited by all of it—the crowd, the bowl of condoms in my arms, this fucking purple latex dress. But somehow I knew, in that moment, my best hope for getting through high school lay in this man's hands. There was suddenly a lump in my throat. "I've been calling in to your show? I'm the kid who was talking about coming out to my parents?"

"Hey!" His painted face lit up with recognition and he tapped my shoulder. "So that's you! Nice dress, I've never met anyone your age who's into rubber."

"The volunteers have to wear them." I raised my condom bowl. "I'm part of the team throwing this. So thank you. For coming." I was about to turn away but instead blurted, "I told my mom and dad I was gay. Last night."

Dan's face scrunched up and then didn't move.

Terry leaned over. "What'd they say?"

"My dad says they're devastated."

"Oh. Jesus. Christ." Dan looked to Terry. "What have I done?" Then back to me. "Don't tell me they're going to throw you out. Are they going to throw you out? God, this is terrible." He looked back at Terry again. "I feel terrible."

"I'm living at school at the moment, but I don't think they'll pull me out."

"Oh yeah, that's right, you're at boarding school. That could actually be a good thing, you know." His face was still twisted with concern as he wrote his number down on a piece of pink construction paper. "Look, just call me. This is my fault. Fuck. Do you think I can do anything? Wait—don't answer that yet, just call me."

A week later, Dan picked me up after school and took me to my first AIDS funeral. "It's something you need to see," he said. Over the next few months, and eventually years, then decades, Dan made himself available for coffee, took me to events, and suffered through me yammering about my problems. We discussed my baptism and theology. ("It's all bullshit.") He'd let me know when I was on point, and felt free to tell me when I was being an asshole. ("Don't ever grouse about an old guy checking you out; you're going to be old too, one day.") And he demanded I stop seeing Pete immediately. ("This is fucked-up. What is he doing? And you messed around with him? Ew! That's like me messing around with you. Fucking gross. Stop it.") He started to talk about our friendship in speeches he gave, on the importance of mentoring younger people. ("How can we begin to make some headway with equality if everyone thinks that we're trying to fuck their kids. Jason, where are you? Oh, right there. Have I ever tried to fuck you?") Hanging with Dan and Terry made me feel smarter and cool, good about myself. If these guys wanted to spend time with me, then I must have been something special. They made me feel that one day I could be as interesting as they were.

My mom and I were talking a little, but each conversation on the dorm's pay phone was heavy. She was worried someone would take advantage of me, and kept saying she was so sad, knowing all I would have to go through in my life. From my dad it was just radio silence. We were only speaking if we had to. I'm sure if I hadn't been doing so well in school, they would have yanked me out. But my grades couldn't be argued with: I was flourishing.

Dan told me it was important to tell my mother we were hanging out. "That guy scares me," she said. She'd read a profile on him in the *Seattle Times* that talked of his leftist politics and explicit sex column. I'd try to explain that he was really brilliant and kind, but she wasn't buying it. So Dan introduced his own mother to her. When she visited from Chicago he set the two of them up for lunch and she took my mom to her first Parents and Friends of Lesbians and Gays meeting.

Toward the end of the school year, I was cast as Sky Masterson in my school's production of *Guys and Dolls*. Dan and Terry came on opening night. During intermission I remember him walking down a long hallway, his arms outstretched. "Oh my God," he said. "You can really sing." He was the first person I remember ever telling me that.

9

FOR MY SENIOR YEAR, MY MOM DECIDED SHE WANTED me to spend my last year of high school with her, under the same roof. She and my father rented a two-bedroom apartment down the street from my school. My mom and I got closer, and would have lunch dates or go the movies. Dad and I were chilly; he'd watch TV, and I'd hide out in my room and make music. We did our best not to talk if we didn't have to, keeping it civil for the sake of my mom.

I often hung out at an anarchic queer-punk group house in the Central District where my friend Andy lived. He was a twenty-two-year-old blue-haired beanpole from Montana. Polite but political, he lived with a ragtag gang of brilliant and conscientious freaks. They stayed up all night in a haze of smoke listening to grrrl punk and indie pop or watching whatever VHS tapes anybody could procure. I got high on their water bong hits and was introduced to movies like *Cabaret*, *Tokyo Decadence*, and *The Forbidden Zone*, and the films of Derek Jarman. They called me "Bambi Continental" and encouraged my flair for the dramatic.

One night I jumped on the mirrored coffee table and belted *Wailing Betsy*, a one-act musical I had written for school. It was the story of Betsy Ross, the designer of the American flag, getting in a time machine and traveling to a pro-choice women's rights rally. It was a big hit in that house.

Andy was sensitive in nature but staunch in his views. His opinions frightened me at times. To grasp his politics required me to reexamine beliefs I held on monogamy, gay marriage, and social work. As foreign as the ideas were, I was open to his thoughts on what it meant to be queer and on the destructive nature of assimilation. There was a drawing taped to the fridge in his house that always stuck with me: It was two smiling white men in respectable clothes, standing in front of a picket fence. The caption read: WE'RE JUST LIKE YOU! SEXIST. RACIST. CLASSIST. I realized that just because you were gay, it didn't absolve you from enacting the prejudices and violence ingrained in mainstream society.

It wasn't only Andy exposing me to new ideas; music was bending my ear and instilling within me an itch that I wasn't quite sure how or where to scratch. Of all the concerts I saw that year, there were three that affected me the most. Thrilling and dangerous, each one was influential in its own way. Nothing could have prepared me for the queer aggression of seeing the Cramps live. Lux Interior was the maniacal front man, and I was transfixed by his unpredictable energy. He loomed over the crowd with his hair dyed black, wearing PVC pants and heels, deep-throating the mic. It was like watching someone activating their own seizures and refusing assistance.

I saw Bikini Kill play their unrelenting sugar punk manifesto party music at an all-ages show at the Sailors' Union of the Pacific. Kathleen Hanna in her joyful rage was so sure of herself and her own convictions. It freaked me out that she wouldn't let any guys get within twenty feet of the stage; she said she'd kick their asses. I went to that show alone and I stood in the back. I think at the time I understood why I wasn't welcome up front, but it didn't make me feel any less unsettled. Still, I found the anarchy cleansing.

I only got to see Bowie play once in my life. It was the Outside tour that year with Nine Inch Nails, the first of two times I'd be in the same room with him. It was like seeing the Easter Bunny for real. I thought I was dreaming as he belted "Strangers When We Meet" in a powerful wide stance, his feet rooted to the stage.

These performers went out in front of the crowds boiling over the edge, making themselves and their work the spectacle, matter-of-factly embodying a creation of their own intent. There was so much pain and energy inside me. These shows made me want to stand up in cafés and flip tables over, cackle and squeal and break things, do the fucking Charleston, feel the loss of control, and let something else, something unknown, take the wheel. It all looked like a hell of a lot of fun to me.

Being juiced up on Jolt cola and half-cocked on my own rock fantasies and personal successes at school made it easy to slip into parts of my personality that weren't so cute. I managed to betray myself and my values on occasion. The worst was when I became friends with a German exchange student in my grade named Jens. He looked like he had walked out of one of my tattered International Male catalogues with his blue eyes and cable-knit sweaters. It was a new sensation to have a straight "mate" with whom I shared common ground. My crush was undeniable, but I did my best not to lust after straight boys.

One night, with my parents out of town, Jens asked me if he could stay the night. The instant we were alone, I turned into the room and he was at my face. We started kissing. Taking a step back, I caught his eyes, skeptical. It was an unspoken question: *Do you really want to do this?* We kissed more deeply this time and began touching each other. I couldn't believe that my daydream sexual fantasy was coming to life. We pulled off our clothes, moved to the bed, gave each other head, and came, our limbs forming a knot. We looked at ourselves and laughed at the absurdity of what we'd just done. Then fell asleep in each other's arms.

He was in the shower the next morning when I called Ariel, one of my girlfriends from school. I had a network with the girls—we told each other everything. Malicious or not, we loved to gossip. "You're not going to believe who's in my shower right now," I said. I couldn't help myself. It was a conquest, and I'd triumphed. When I hung up, Jens came into the room with a white towel wrapped around his waist, smiled, and kissed me again. He had no idea I'd just sold him out.

By the end of the day on the following Monday, the entire school knew that he and I had slept together. He must have stumbled through his classes with a sinking feeling of disappointment as, one by one, every person around him suddenly saw him differently. For the rest of the year it seemed that Jens walked the halls with his head down. He couldn't look at me—or anyone, for that matter. We stopped speaking, our friendship and the possibility of any future trysts decimated.

Whether he was actually straight or not, I'd outed him. I'd played the locker-room jock, bragging about a sexual victory. And by doing that, I'd felt a kind of power I'd never had, the sensation of putting somebody in their place. No one at school would have been inclined to bully him, but he now carried the label of being gay. I might have seemed adjusted and happy with myself, but the anger from the abuse that I'd taken in Arizona was still alive and well. It was a toxic, sick victory, and I was filled with a hollow satisfaction over finally having made someone else know what it felt like to be a fag.

10

HAVING JUST CONCENTRATED ON SURVIVING HIGH school, I hadn't properly considered collegiate life, so my choice of colleges was random. I had no real idea of where I wanted to be, or what I wanted to study. Attending Occidental College in the Eagle Rock neighborhood of Los Angeles was kind of like spinning a globe and blindly setting my finger down on a spot. Some girlfriends that had graduated a year ahead of me had decided to go there, so I figured, at least I'd know some people. At Occidental, I fit in well enough, enjoyed my classes, and made friends, but I still wasn't happy with what campus gay life had to offer. The school was small and it didn't seem like there were many other homos around, so I took my car into Hollywood often, looking for any kind of trouble. I was still seventeen when I started classes, so unfortunately there weren't many options until October, when I became a legal adult, and could get into certain places.

I eventually found a club that I loved on Sunday nights called Velvet. It was fronted by this terrifying queen dripping with black mascara called Candy-Ass, whom I'd watch, enraptured. He had all kinds of sleazy looks and themes: no-nonsense businesswoman, satanic flapper, Easter Jesus. It was drag, I guess, but he did nothing to hide his hulking frame. Candy-Ass was a man, glam and scary, and seemed like he'd bite your head off if you ever talked to him. He presided over a crowd that was a grab bag of LA party weirdos. The regulars included a silver-haired cowboy, a severe burn victim, and countless Debbie Harry look-alikes. I went religiously, my eyes never leaving Candy-Ass and his floozy go-go minions. I loved how they were always the center of the room's attention.

Maybe my wistful fascination with Candy-Ass wasn't only focused on his aggressive performances, but also on his gargantuan size. I was scrawnier than ever. The cafeteria food at Occidental was putrid, so I just lived off chicken sandwiches from Burger King every night, supplemented with a pack of Camel Lights—and despite how unhealthy the sandwiches were, I didn't gain a pound. When I took my shirt off, it was ghoulish. You could count my ribs. But still, I brightened up my gaunt look with loud colors and a penchant for dumping a very fine glitter over my eyes and face.

I was unhappy with how I looked and felt less than desirable. I'd thought I was going to arrive in California, make a ton of new friends, and get laid all the time, but that was just not happening. However, there were a handful of people I liked hanging out with, and there were new drugs I began to enjoy.

I tried ecstasy, which kicked in on my way back from a club, as I drove past downtown Los Angeles. I stroked the car window saying, "Oh my God" over and over while "Water from a Vine Leaf" by William Orbit took me down a waterfall. It felt fucking heavenly.

I'd make mushroom milk shakes with my friend Abbey or we'd take acid and putter around her Renaissance castle–style house or take in her epic *Tron*-board view of the valley until sunrise. She had a pet monkey, an emu, a trampoline room, a little movie theater, and their old favorite pet goat's head taxidermied and mounted to the wall wearing a top hat. We'd be tripping really hard in the kitchen at four in the morning when her little sister, a body contortionist, would come in and start folding herself into a box in complete silence. Her whole family seemed like they stayed up all night, and I convinced myself at one point, high on LSD, that they were actual vampires.

Mary flew from Arizona to visit and we cruised around in my

Chevy Beretta, spent a day at Disneyland, and sat on my dorm room twin bed and drank beer. Our barbed conversations and jabs would sometimes turn into little fights. She was so sensitive and would get mad if I said something the wrong way, or if she perceived a slight. Still, no one could make me laugh like her. In another life, one where she wasn't so pummeled by the world, she would have done good stand-up.

On her last night with me, I took her to Velvet and she wore a funky, diagonal-striped maroon and blue dress with Lisa Loeb glasses. Mary didn't seem so self-conscious there among all the club freaks, she didn't stick out like she did other places. I had the rare sensation that we both belonged there, even if just for a night.

I wasn't going to stay in LA. It was too sprawling and I felt like a tiny fish. Who was ever going to notice me here? And what for? I had fleeting dreams of being a filmmaker, but after trying to write a short script about frat boys taking a drug called "fairy dust" that made them have sex and then kill each other, it seemed futile. I'd been making music, had scored and done the sound design for Occidental's spring play, but when I saw a Chemical Brothers concert, or listened to Daft Punk's *Homework*, music production seemed like a stretch, too. I was trying new things, but I understood that just because you gave something a shot, it didn't mean you were sealing any deals. There were other kids who would blather on and on about all the movies they would make, and I could tell it was just talk.

I've always found it creatively dangerous to spin fantasies about your work. Dreams and desire are necessary, but if you talk about your ideas too much, they can get weak, and remain unmade. There are a lot of people who equate having the thought with having implemented it. If you spill too much to the world, it can make you less excited about creating.

I had no goal, other than to find my aim. And I needed to be in a smaller place to find it. I'd get a job again in Seattle at the movie theater

I had worked at in high school. I'd hang out in cafés and smoke. I promised my mom and dad I'd go to community college and figure something out. But I was uneasy, on the verge of feeling completely lost.

A friend of mine and I decided to drive my car up from LA to Seattle. About an hour out of the city, the engine exploded. My father had to drive all the way down from Seattle and we towed the car back up the coast.

When he arrived, he didn't say much. We both knew I wouldn't be returning to a proper college the following year, and he must have thought I looked terrible, nothing but eyes and bones, probably assumed I was on drugs, with no real plan for the future. Most of our ride was in silence. The mutual disappointment was like a choking smoke, filling the air between us.

Seattle turned out to be a good move. There was plenty of culture to satisfy me, but it was compact enough for me not to feel like I was being swallowed. I tore tickets at the movie theater, studied American Sign Language at school, then got an extra job working for Sub Pop's record store in Pike Place Market, hawking all the local bands and labels to tourists.

I didn't realize how badly I needed to perform. Not by seeking it out, per se, but by finding myself onstage in strange ways. I became obsessed with Billy Idol, listening to him nonstop and bleaching my hair, wearing leather vests, perfecting my sneer in the mirror. One night it occurred to me that I could get in front of a crowd and sing his songs at the various karaoke nights around town.

I was now nineteen, still not old enough to get into bars, but I found an ID at Bimbo's Bitchin' Burrito Kitchen, this fast-food joint I'd been working at. The guy pictured on the ID obviously wasn't me. His name was David Joseph Wiktorski. He was in his early thirties and was balding. But somehow, when I was brave enough to use it, it worked. On karaoke nights, I would go to a bar by myself, nervously flash the ID with my eyes to the ground, and walk straight to the DJ booth. After picking a song, I'd keep a low profile until it was my turn, then pounce on the stage in my best imitation of a pro, as I strutted and growled through "White Wedding" or "Cradle of Love." I saw people's faces light up with surprise, both at the performance and at the fact that I was obviously underage. As soon as I set the mic down, I ran for the door, knowing I'd get thrown out immediately.

I had a friend named Jon who lived down the street from me and worked the door at 20th Century Foxes, where the clientele was a broad swath of transgender women, gender illusionists, run-of-the-mill drag queens, and men who simply liked to wear women's clothing, plus a few drifters and grifters, surly bartenders, and the occasional homeless person huddled in a dark corner. There were shows every night, and it occurred to me that I could dress in drag and have a regular place to perform. With enough makeup, a wig, and a high fur collar, who was to say that wasn't me on the ID?

My looks were assembled without a great eye for style, but I did my best with what I had, borrowing cheap dresses or fur-lined coats from girls I knew. I decided that every week I would do a different James Bond theme song and call myself Cubic Zirconia. The soaring melodies were a strange but complementary juxtaposition with the weary interior of the bar. I would have rather been actually singing, but it brought me enough adrenaline every week to get up and lip-sync.

Each time I performed, I felt a sensation not dissimilar to déjà vu: that I was in the right spot, doing something I was meant to be doing. Which was strange, because I had no real desire to dress in drag. It felt like someone else's world in that bar, but it was still a stage—a glorious ramshackle proscenium with a wonky railing around it that made it look like a wrestling ring.

The other performers were quite memorable. "Star" was a girl who seemed in some way developmentally disabled. She was very large, and wore dirty leggings and a T-shirt that was way too small so that her belly rolls hung over her waistband like melting ice cream. She always did "Proud Mary" by Tina Turner. It was a master class in confidence. She was a showgirl, and you could feel the happiness radiating as she shimmied and jiggled and stomped, her cherubic face vacillating between distorted beauty-pageant grins and dogged determination. It was effortless the way her hands shot out to collect all the dollar bills flying in from the bar patrons. To this day, that number is one of the best things I've ever seen.

Then there was "Wheelchair Betty," as people called her. No one knew her actual name, and Lordy, she was a sight. Frail and wrinkled in a gray Barbara Bush–style fright wig and a tattered, gold-sequined blouse, she sat in her wheelchair with a kind of stately poise, chain-smoking. Her eyes were crudely shadowed and sunken. She had no legs and was also deaf.

Whoever was hostessing would wheel her onto the stage and start the song, then would run in front of her to signal that the song was playing. It was always "Strike It Up" by Black Box. She'd move her mouth like a goldfish and wave her arms in a repetitive circular motion, as if she were an animatronic figure trying to explain itself out of a loop. The DJ let it run for about two minutes and then turned it off, unceremoniously. Someone would stand up and wave their arms again, indicating to her that the song was over.

I was studying ASL at the community college, so I approached her one weekend, introduced myself, and asked her what her name was.

"*D-A-R-R-E-N,*" she told me.

"Nice to meet you, my name is *J-A-S-O-N.*" I thought it was appalling they'd been calling her Wheelchair Betty this whole time.

"Get me a cigarette," she said.

"No problem," I replied, and retrieved one from my purse.

"Get me a beer." I did.

"Tell the DJ to play 'Black Box' again," she demanded. That was usually the extent of our conversations.

I really loved that little corner of the universe. It was a place for those whom the world ignored. In 1997, so much of the LGBTQ world still lived in hiding. There was something a little magical about this stage, a light in the middle of a long shadow. Star and Darren were examples of consummate performers, satisfying a need to be up in front of people, sharing themselves, however rough they were.

I was tending to a compulsion I'd had ever since I was a child harassing my sister's friends, or singing to stoners in our college dorm rooms. I needed an audience. From friendships to boyfriends or conversations at a bus stop, it was through other people that I learned about myself. I've never been good at deep examination on my own, so I take all these extreme experiences that I hold inside, spit them out, and invite others to help me understand what it all means. I never want to carry any baggage, which compels me to shake out my tragedies like a man possessed. Since I was a little kid, I just wanted to entertain people.

It's why I sometimes overshare and let out embarrassing information in formal conversations. It's why I throw myself around like a rag doll onstage, to the point of harm. The attention that I need is for the expulsion of pain, in turn transforming it into a tangible thing that people might connect with. Straw to gold, water to wine. This was never just to feel accepted; that's never been my driving force. It's a pageant on the proscenium of my heart. Performance makes me feel good, and for a moment, be a better person than I actually am.

But I suspected the karaoke and drag numbers were nothing compared to my potential. I had twenty years so far pent up and ready to throw on the table, ready to tip my hand, win or lose. If I didn't do something I was going to implode. I knew that the longer I stayed in Seattle, the harder it would be to leave. Whether or not it would chew me up, I'd heard New York City was the place that people went and fucking did something. So why not go where the gettin' was good?

PART 2

NEW YORK

11

I MOVED TO NEW YORK IN EARLY JANUARY AND THE TRIP
took a full two days. It started in Seattle, then I flew to Phoenix, where
I stayed overnight and got to see Mary. She greeted me in the brown-
ish terminal, leaning against a concrete pillar, her hair newly auburn,
holding a beige purse in front of her, trying in vain to cover her size. It
had been about six months since I'd seen her on a visit to Seattle when
she'd needed to buy two seats next to each other to sit comfortably on
the plane. Since then, she had gained even more weight. I pretended
not to notice. We made a pilgrimage to the Phoenix Denny's where all
the gays went, stayed up all night talking. She was proud of me that I'd
made the decision to move to New York. I longed to see her more.

The next day, I took a flight to the Islip airport (it was the cheapest to fly into), where I caught a train to Penn Station. At one point
we stopped suddenly on the tracks, the lights blinking out. I sat in the
dark for hours, an unremarkable tangle of frozen trees just outside the
window. A conductor sounding like she had throat cancer came on
the loudspeaker to say we were experiencing difficulties and would be
moving again shortly. *Lady*, I thought, *it sounds like you're experiencing
difficulties and need to go to the hospital.* The air in the car was getting
cold. I pulled my cheap Old Navy coat closer to my neck.

My only belongings sat near the train doors—two overstuffed suitcases and a backpack. I hadn't known what to bring but had ended up

leaving behind some of my favorite concert T-shirts in order to make room for long johns. My tattered backpack was heavy with books. I wanted to pull one out to pass the time, but it was too dark on the train to read. There was nothing to do but gaze out into the fuzzy darkness.

Two men in suits who were clearly from New York sat across from me and talked about their jobs in finance. As the hours passed, they turned to me and, making small talk, asked about where I was from. I was bored by their conversation but flattered that they seemed interested. I asked one of them if he liked taking the subway. I was surprised when he told me he hadn't taken a subway in years. I thought that everybody in New York did.

Finally the lights fluttered on and we began moving again. Everyone around me looked tired. The lights of civilization flashed at the windows, then turned jet-black as the train plunged underground. We pulled into Penn Station and I shook hands with the two men. "Good luck," they said. I wrestled with my luggage and managed to drag it onto the first escalator. There were so many people, and my suitcases were tipping over as I tried to steer them. The "good luck" those men had wished now seemed like a snarky jab.

I reached the glaring fluorescent lights of the main floor. A subtle exit sign above the throng led me to a huge set of stairs. They towered like something you'd find on a Vegas stage, only with the rhinestones sanded off. There was no way I could get my bags to the top. Panicking, I walked in circles and wrung my hands, something I do when I'm anxious. In the midst of the chaos, the thought of finding an elevator didn't cross my mind. All the other commuters, angling their paths in complicated patterns, knew where they were going. I considered asking for help, but to ask for assistance would have been embarrassing and people were walking by too fast.

I couldn't drag one bag up at a time because I assumed that if I left the other bag for a moment it could be easily stolen. Desperate, I took a breath and pulled the monoliths up, stair by stair, my heavy backpack making me feel like I could topple backward. Pausing to catch my breath, I remembered one of those stories about a mother who had so much adrenaline that she lifted a car off her baby. My forearms screamed; the climb was agonizing. If I loosened my grip, my luggage would tumble away, possibly knocking somebody behind me down like a bowling pin. I cried out as I reached the top, dropped my bags like burning pans, and shook my arms as I did a small dance of pain.

Automatic doors hissed, opening into the loud city night. Brakes screeched, and the wind whipped at my scarfless neck. The line for a cab was rows deep and the thrill of arrival was exchanged for a feeling of dread. I had stepped into a mouth of ice, the buildings its jagged teeth, and between them, I was nothing but a tiny crumb of food.

Lucy Blackburn, a college friend from Occidental in Los Angeles, now lived in a neighborhood called Gowanus in Brooklyn. But everywhere in New York could have been anywhere, for all I knew. I arrived at Lucy's modest apartment building and carried the suitcases up the stairs once again, but now I could do it one at a time. She opened the door and squealed, a beacon of warmth and familiarity. I dropped the backpack and exhaled.

"You picked a cold night," she said. "It's supposed to get, like, ten below. Hang on a sec, let me get you wine." She retreated to the kitchen but kept talking. "I was supposed to go to this play tonight, but I was like, hell no. Too cold. So how was your trip? Was it really two days to get—?" She emerged with the drinks and stopped. I was crying in my hands.

This was so stupid. I was totally fine. I laughed as I picked off tears with my fingers. I told her it had just been a long trip and slumped back on the couch. We talked, draining our glasses a few times, and I welcomed the small head rush. Lucy went to bed and left me on the couch. I kicked off my shoes and peeled away my pants, lay down, and pulled the soft blanket up to my chin. I knew right away I was going to have a hard time falling asleep.

My eyes felt like they were bugging out of my head, darting under my closed lids as they still saw visions of the city. How could I possibly sleep? I was in New York! "Tonight" from *West Side Story*, the Sharks and Jets snapping their fingers and dancing, played in my ears. I saw David Byrne in *Stop Making Sense*, doing the herky-jerky in his oversize suit, Debbie Harry pouting in front of the Manhattan skyline. Sleep was going to be impossible. Instead of trying, I stared through the dim room. On the wall was a hologram poster for the movie *Species 2*. Depending on your perspective, the image vacillated between a beautiful woman in a fetal pose and a monstrous, green alien. Waiting to be hatched.

I still hadn't graduated from college. School was a placeholder, a grace period to make sure I got in the right getaway car, spare time to figure out how I would avoid a desk job in an office. I took classes that I actually wanted to take, trying my best to avoid requirements that I had no interest in. I had five semesters left to graduate, and wanted to spend them doing the most fun thing I could think of: writing fiction. Eugene Lang College, in the West Village, was perfect, with its special focus on writing workshops. I was glad to see a lot of queer kids, but I knew school wasn't going to be the center of my social life. I was more interested in the people outside its doors.

When I left the school on my first day of orientation, I didn't really care where I ended up. I had no idea which way was north or south, but I could see the World Trade Center on certain street corners, which helped to reset my internal map. The storefronts and restaurants I passed were intimidating. I hadn't eaten since finding a breakfast sandwich in Brooklyn, and I was hungry. Block after block, I passed places selling any kind of food I'd ever want, but I had this irrational fear that I would be spotted as a tourist, so I just kept walking. I finally got up the nerve to step into an Italian eatery with tomatoes painted on the walls. I ordered the cheapest thing on the menu, minestrone soup. I must have seemed like I was from another planet, because my waitress told me I was the most polite customer she'd ever had.

I kept heading east as the masses, many done with work, jammed the sidewalks. It was getting dark. The yellow streetlights flicked on. The cold was accumulating in the dark spaces between the storefronts. The cheery rainbow-lit Indian restaurants, looking like an acid trip, jazzed up First Avenue. I passed Cafe Pick Me Up and thought it was a place where people would go to literally get picked up, like a singles bar. I was such an idiot.

That night in front of the bathroom sink at Lucy's I looked at my body in the mirror, all juts and angles. My eyes were still too big for my face. I turned and examined my flat butt and still felt like that prepubescent kid, not too long ago, praying to God for his armpit hair to start growing. It was going to take a lot to shake off this little-boy thing. I did everything I could to look older. Still, I wondered if I should take my hoop earrings with the beads out of my ears. They suddenly looked uncool.

I wasn't twenty-one yet, but had that same ID I had used in Seattle. "David Joseph Wiktorski" still looked like me about as much as Chita Rivera did. But I had all his stats, address, and astrological sign memorized in case any bouncer got wise and quizzed me. Not really having any friends yet, I'd be going out by myself. It was strange, though: When I finally did turn twenty-one, the ID just disappeared, as if it had never been there in the first place. A lot of stuff in my life happened like that. I got what I needed just as I needed it.

For example, a month before moving to New York, I met Gavin at a queer friend's boozy birthday party in Seattle. He was a lanky, corduroy-clad guy with bushy sideburns, and he always seemed to be wearing orange or olive. We discovered we'd both be moving to New

York at the same time and agreed right then and there that we'd move in together. He would find an apartment by the time I arrived.

We talked on the phone and he told me he'd discovered the perfect place, that I was going to love it. It was in a neighborhood called Crown Heights, very up-and-coming with a real community vibe, he said. The apartment was shotgun style, two bedrooms, but one of them was "makeshift," whatever that meant. Apparently there was room for a desk in the kitchen. He kept saying it was an amazing deal. It was just going to cost us 350 bucks each a month. I knew it was probably a dump, but I felt like I could handle anything.

When I went to bed on Lucy's couch again that night, it felt like I was in a little pocket, tucked away inside this giant hive. I thought of every single person, and all their dollhouse rooms, stacked atop each other like Jenga blocks, each building like a Russian nesting doll. I fell asleep thinking of bees. How wonderful it would be to have a place here, my own little hidey-hole in the hive.

The subway ride to Crown Heights took longer than I'd first expected, and when you ascended the stairs to the street you could tell you were definitely not in Manhattan anymore. The neighborhood bustled but was weary from some unseen weight: Derelict people muttered past, and cars shook from their own earsplitting bass. Between the train and our apartment there was a Laundromat that resided behind an ancient scratched window. It looked like a vortex of despair. Gavin said a place down the block had great meat pies; it was run by a family that had been in the neighborhood forever. That sounded promising, but the jars of pigs' feet in the window scared me off. I felt glares from fellow pedestrians and it made me nervous. Gavin's enthusiasm for the sketchy neighborhood always sounded like he was trying to convince himself more than he was trying to convince me.

Our apartment building was on the ironically named Park Place. Leading from the sidewalk there was a crumbling walkway that ended at an erratically painted crimson door, with splotches on it that looked as if someone had just been slashed. The first day we were there, Gavin rummaged through his murse for the keys. But we didn't need keys. I gently pushed the door and it flew inward. The doorknob was broken and the lock had been kicked in by someone. *Maybe they had just been locked out.* I tried to remain optimistic as I stepped into the dark foyer, which reeked of pee. There were various papers and debris scattered on the peeling linoleum. It resembled the inside of a defunct dishwasher, dirty plates and all.

I walked up the chipped stairs two at a time to the apartment on the third floor. It had a working lock this time, and the door hadn't been kicked in, thank Christ, but looked like it easily could have been. My heart was sinking fast. This was going to be so much worse than I imagined. I opened the door.

It was just an empty railroad apartment. Small, with the slight smell of leaking gas, but I felt a comfort in its blank potential. There was a little kitchen area with a cheery window and a bathroom on the side. Beyond it was an arid hallway, which was my "bedroom." There was no door on either threshold, but I could at least fit a twin bed and have enough room to walk past it. Beyond my hallway was Gavin's bedroom, with windows and a closing door. I couldn't argue; I mean, he found the place. And for the time being, I was stuck with it.

Soon after moving in, I thought I'd found an extra window. There was an indented square, painted the same yellowish white as the wall. I walked over, pulled the handle with a loud, wood-breaking crack, and swung it inward. A cloud of stale dust and cobwebs poured forth like something in an ancient cursed tomb. It was an old shaft. All sound disappeared into it, yet there was a soft roar emanating from its depths, like from a seashell you would find on a beach in hell. I poked my head in, looked down to see what was on the bottom, and was confronted by a whispering, endless blackness, a gateway to some dimension I'd rather not visit. Withdrawing from its maw, and shutting it with some elbow grease, I decided to just keep that thing closed.

Early mornings seemed to sand off the neighborhood's sharpest edges. It was the only time of day that seemed safe-ish. I pushed open the wrecked front door and made my entrances into the freezing air, stepping down the walkway framed by two strips of crusty, frozen dirt. My first stop was always the Jamaican pot-pie shop on the end of our block. With the most grateful smile I could muster, I received their watery coffee like a precious elixir, ignoring the first gritty swallow but appreciating its warmth.

As I passed off my crumpled dollars to the emotionless man behind the counter, I felt like he could see the green on my skin as if it were as clear as the darkness of his. I'd never felt so white in my life. Perhaps, I thought, my unease here stemmed from some kind of racism I carried, buried deep, that had now been unknowingly and unwittingly uncovered. How else could I explain it? But there was another angle that made me tense that I couldn't ignore: I was blatantly gay. There was no way I was passing for a straight guy, with my bright colors, combat boots, short bleached hair, swishy gait, and, worst of all, my voice—a voice that I had tried all my life to hammer the femininity out of, to no avail. But I had become used to walking down the street, just being myself. The thought of having to tone it down, just to get by unnoticed, rankled me. I'd done too much work to get this far and have to pack it in.

I was unprepared for the weather, stacked with layers, sweaters on top of sweaters. But I was still cold. I'd spend evenings in what was going to be my sad Laundromat for the foreseeable future. It had cracked yellow walls and corroded detergent machines. Grim-faced moms were inside, accompanied by children, screaming with glee and throwing themselves around like marshmallow pinballs.

My feelings on my current situation switched from happiness to devastation as often as I passed under store awnings, like fast-moving clouds that made the sun flicker and hide again. I longed for the familiarity of my favorite cafés in Seattle. It was so easy, being there. One day in Crown Heights, I spotted a sign for a bookstore across from the subway, but my excitement was punctured when I realized it was some kind of religious reading room, looking just as destitute and crumbling as the Laundromat a block away. There was nothing in the landscape that I recognized.

Each day as I made my way into Manhattan I felt catapulted through the intestines of the subway. I watched strange men on the platforms, yelling over the screech of wheels, their eyes aflame. I'd listen to their freaky prophecies and wonder where they laid their heads at night. One day I saw a heap of junk in the corner of a subway car I was in; riders were giving it a wide berth. At first I thought it was garbage, but then I saw the appendage of an actual human being under the layers of debris, accompanied by the smell of rotting flesh. It was frightening, I'd never seen people in such bad shape.

I discovered that the best way to brave the long ride was to do it with other people, convincing casual friends from school to get beers with me and take the train back to the Park Place apartment. I got the sense that when we arrived, they realized it wasn't much of a destination, after all. But we drank and listened to Goldie or Tricky on my desktop PC speakers, while I tried to make up for the bleak surroundings with funny stories and sometimes weed. I brought home straight guys from my classes, both of us so hungry for company we were able to talk our way through an evening, our knees drawn up to our chests on my twin bed. It was a familiar and stale sensation, some small part of me hoping they would let their knees down and kiss me. There was probably some small part of them praying I wouldn't try such a thing.

The city outside was voluminous and dark and lonely. I tried to not be scared, told myself I'd made the right decision coming to New

York. But at dusk, when I skittered from the station to my building, doing my best to stay out of the shadows, I was disquieted, looking over my shoulder while simultaneously trying not to look back.

Wonder Bar in the East Village was my first hangout. Nashom, a towering, gorgeous black man, tended bar in the long, rectangular room, which was shaped like a loaf of bread. The groovy interior was painted a green zebra-striped camouflage. I stationed myself on a stool early in the evenings and wrote in my notebook splayed on the bar, scratching away with my pen, nodding my head to the house music played by the DJ, visible through a cutout portal at the far end of the room. I ordered vodka tonics and lost myself in whatever story I was working on.

Older, drunk men sidled up to me. "Hey, there," they said with their gray suits and glassy eyes. "What are you writing?"

I'd cover the page, self-conscious, and tell them it was just a story.

"You're cute," they'd say. "A little guy, small. You know that?" I'd turn back to face the bar, flushed, not knowing how to respond, except to shrink away when their arms slithered around my shoulders. "What, you don't like me?" They'd turn to the empty air beside them. "He doesn't like me."

Nashom, the bartender, would lean in. "Can you take your drink elsewhere? You're bothering him." I'd exhale and flash a grateful grimace.

"Don't be afraid to tell those guys to fuck off," he told me once. "If you don't want somebody talking to you, you don't have to talk to them."

"I don't want to hurt anybody's feelings."

"You could break a bottle over their heads," he said. "Those motherfuckers are too drunk to feel a thing."

There'd always be a friendly, coherent man with nice eyes or a solid build who wouldn't be too intoxicated and invite me back to his place. The thought of slogging to Brooklyn so late at night wasn't as enticing as sharing a bed with a sexy stranger who lived within walking distance. Wherever we went, I still didn't have any sense of where we really were. He'd point out various restaurants and shops I'd say I'd check out. We'd enter some unmarked door with chipped paint or a smeared window, or a fancy lobby with a doorman. Sometimes it would be a closet-size apartment or an unfinished loft that looked like a handful of people lived there. He'd show me his photography portfolio, or tell me about his styling job. We'd fall on the mattress or climb to the bed by a ladder, engage in fumbling foreplay, never fucking, then, after coming, drift off, smushed up against fresh drywall or some broken nightstand. I'd creep out the next morning, gingerly climbing over a bicycle in the entryway, or we'd wake up and make breakfast. Then I'd walk to school, my backpack already with me, wondering if anyone would notice that I was wearing yesterday's clothes. I usually never saw him again.

I don't remember ever taking a trick back to Crown Heights, but I must have at some point, because I have a memory of riding the red line in the wee hours of the morning with some guy. There were two deaf men signing across from us and the guy I was with must have been staring at them, because one of the deaf guys turned to us and signed, "What's your problem? What the fuck are you looking at?"

"Sorry," I responded. "He's an idiot. I just met him an hour ago. My name is Jason. I apologize for his insensitivity. But I don't really know him." This was another one of the few times I used my year and a half of American Sign Language instruction in the real world. This exchange made it all worth it.

12

MY CLASSES CONSISTED OF SITTING AROUND A LONG
table with fellow students and an accomplished writer of some kind. I
didn't really connect with many other students. But our conversations
were intelligent enough, and the classes were constructive if you paid
attention. One of my fiction workshops was taught by Chuck Wachtel, a funny, dry novelist and poet whose books focused on blue-collar
families from his home state of New Jersey. He plied us with writers
like Isaac Babel and Raymond Carver.

The workshops were organized into weekly critiques. All the students handed in their stories at once, making enough copies for everyone to read and return the following week with their notes. The pieces
we wrote were competent, but there was a lot of lofty postmodern
meta-prose the class churned out. I just wanted to write nasty horror
stories, which I did with aplomb: genre tales full of unlikely twists and
disease. I was happy to be mean to my characters, letting grim fates be-
fall them in their innocent lives. Wachtel liked what I was writing, said
it was New Gothic. He was rumpled but had a welcoming, nurturing
presence and cared enough to inspire me. I wanted to impress him; in
turn, he introduced me to one of my favorite writers, Patrick McGrath.

My own writing was clunky, but I prided myself on its casual fun.
I got a lot of ideas from vivid dreams that jolted me out of sleep. They
terrified me, and still do, but I've always found meaning in the scares,

the details feeding my waking imagination. When I wrote my stories, they felt like an extension of these sessions in my sleep. Writing was a way I could still play with toys. But while the narratives got more complex, my characters remained plastic. Their development never transcended basic pulp. Still, it was thrilling to me that I was being allowed to do something in school that I actually had fun doing anyway.

Sometimes I read the pieces aloud to a willing friend, making them come alive with my voice. There was one story that became a favorite of mine, about an eccentric rich woman who decides little by little to begin amputating parts of her body, until she's moving around on all fours, being held up by self-engineered appendages. I'd get to the end and wonder what the fuck was wrong with me.

One blustery weeknight I arrived back in my neighborhood after dark. As I walked toward Park Place, I found myself in step with a pretty black woman in a camel trench coat. I turned to her and asked her if she generally felt safe in this neighborhood. She looked at me sideways with a half smile, took a few more steps, and said, "This neighborhood has been very good to me." I suddenly felt embarrassed to have asked.

I walked into the broken vestibule of my building feeling like I was hanging over two sides of a fence. I couldn't tell if the fear that I felt in Crown Heights was an instinctual, valuable feeling, or if it was racism bubbling up that I'd been unaware of, a residual side effect of growing up on a very white island. I entered the apartment, and I was alone. After making some canned lentil soup, I taped up a Modest Mouse poster and thumbtacked a swath of red fabric over the doorway. I stood back and was admiring my job when I heard the screams.

A child's shrill cry rose through the shaft, to the window that I still hadn't been able to close all the way since I'd first opened it. Then came the unintelligible angry sound of a woman hollering, things being thrown. The child's scream got louder, then was followed by the sound of something larger hitting a wall. Sudden silence. Like a siren, the child's wail started again, crescendoed even louder than before. I stood unmoving, frightened.

Downstairs became quiet, and in couple of hours Gavin, with his big brow and bell-bottoms, arrived home. We split a bottle of questionable red wine. He talked about how much he loved the neighborhood and our new place. I didn't mention the child abuse I'd just overheard. I was trying to stay positive, but my gut was telling me that this wasn't a very safe spot. The front door of our building had been kicked in, for God's sake.

Also, I thought we had rats. Any time I brought home groceries, I'd wake up the next morning and on the counter, cereal boxes would have been ripped open and dug into, wrappers chewed, cans overturned. Given the damage each day, I knew the size of the things must have been huge. Whatever had that much power to invade my meager food stash was not something I actually wanted to see in action.

But finally one day, I got a load of the creature in all its glory when I walked out of the bathroom, wet from having just taken a shower. The thing wasn't a rat at all, but a large, very disheveled squirrel. Whipping its head out of a loaf of bread, it jumped and stared, caught. After giving me a shady, imperceptible once-over, it dropped into an attack crouch and leaped out the open window backward. I stood dripping, shocked, and couldn't help but laugh. I could live with a squirrel.

Squirrel or not, I lasted only another couple weeks in the Crown Heights apartment. I finally got the guts to tell Gavin that it wasn't working for me and he bristled. I told him I didn't feel like I had any other choice. Living in the hallway was a bitch. I was also sketched out being gay around there. People stared. It was scary coming home after dark.

"This is how everywhere in New York used to be, Jason. People just lived with it." He could smell my guilt over leaving him and my shame at not being able to hack it. "I wish I'd have known that you couldn't swing this. Who am I supposed to get to live here now?" *Who, indeed?* I thought.

I was letting him down. A noble resolution felt out of my reach, more than I was capable of dealing with. What was I supposed to *bring* to this neighborhood? Did I need to try and pass as straight? How much of it was my own racist bullshit and how much of it was grounded in reality? I wanted to give living in Crown Heights a chance. But it wasn't a safe place at the time. For anyone, really. About three weeks after I moved out, a female college student was stabbed to death on the street, on our block.

I was writing in the school's common room one afternoon and spied a flyer with tear-off numbers on one of the bulletin boards. In black Sharpie it read, SPACIOUS LOFT SPACE IN WILLIAMSBURG.

Two days later, at seven in the morning, my breath a steady stream of steam, I met up with a handsome Frenchman with a wide nose in a café by the Bedford L stop. He introduced himself as Enzo. We made small talk and took a long stroll to South First Street between Roebling and Havemeyer, where he led me into the vestibule of a red four-story industrial building.

Now, I've always been an impressionable guy, and anyone with the right bedside manner and smoldering gaze can convince me to do or buy just about anything. It makes me a terrible shopper, a sucker for sexy salespeople. Enzo was one of those people. He touched my elbow when he spoke about how he'd found another place to live, closer to his work, but he wanted to pass this room on . . . to the right person (he looked me in the eyes).

I was half listening but gazed at his sweet lips as he told me the building had until recently been an old cake factory. To say it was a converted loft space would be like saying, "I just made this baloney sandwich into a car." In no way did it resemble a place a person might call home; aesthetically, it had more in common with a freeway underpass. Enzo gave me the walking tour.

First we shuffled through a dismal entryway covered with the dramatic patina of what was most likely layers of old lead paint. We entered a rickety rusted elevator, the kind of cage that a serial killer would stick you in, after fattening you up with some fresh, factory-made cake. "You have to make sure, no fingers," he explained, speaking over the loud motor as we ascended, miming someone poking their hands through the bars and getting their digits cut off.

We emerged from the Buffalo Bill Express into a cavernous, dusty expanse. In its center sat a decrepit couch and a coffee table covered with food debris and ash. There were two makeshift rooms on the side, made out of what looked like drywall, gaffer tape, and papier-mâché. Neither of these rooms had a door. We ambled past them without speaking. To our left were a kitchen and a bathroom—hard to tell, though, which was which. But there, I saw a toilet, a pedestal sink pushed up against the wall, and a spigot curled over a bathtub with a plastic tarp wrapped around it for a shower curtain. And here was the kitchen, a lopsided, avocado-green stove flanked by a crusty refrigerator. Just beyond the kitchen/bathroom combo was a civil, if also empty, back room. There were doorways leading to two sizable rectangular "bedrooms"—one of which could be mine for the foreseeable future.

I smelled metal shavings, reminding me of my dad's workshops with their big machines that bent and cut steel to be welded into something that would be useful: a dock for a dinghy or parts for a table. So maybe as I walked into what would be my room—nothing but an empty concrete cube, with a measly, smudged window on the end—I was able to see some kind of potential.

Enzo had a mattress on the floor and some kind of sculpture made from rocks and glass resting against one wall. There were a few candles deliberately arranged and lit. He told me that the rent was seven hundred dollars a month, which seemed steep. "It's a really special place," he added, crinkling his brow, so sincere. "Lots of creative people around." Catnip. I walked in a circle, nodding and pretending to inspect.

"Oh—one thing!" he said, as if he'd forgotten. "There's no heat back here, but I've been fine just using a few space heaters." He waved his hands as if this were nothing. "Graham—the super. He's been talking about putting some kind of heating thing in this next room." He pointed to the common room outside where we were standing. "I *think* he said he was going to do it soon." Now that he mentioned it, it was actually *freezing* in there. But as I stood in that cold, grimy box, I felt a tingle of possibility. *Look at all this room. You could shoot whole movies in here. Just think of the parties.* It was an absolute dump.

But this dump could be mine.

"I'll take it," I said, and shook Enzo's hand.

Within a week Andy, my punk friend from Seattle, helped me pack up whatever books and the couple suitcases I had in Crown Heights and we hauled it over in his car. He had been living in New York now for a couple of years, working as a nanny for a family in the Bronx. It was an overcast, rainy day, and as we pulled up to South First Street I once again questioned my decision making: The outside of my new building looked more derelict than I remembered. There was garbage strewn about and nobody really on the street.

Andy was giving me the silent treatment and not responding to much of my running commentary, remaining expressionless as I yammered on, squinting his eyes and smoking out the car window. He'd been giving me the stink-eye since I arrived in Manhattan, having had enough of my wide-eyed exuberance, and was *not* going to be my tour guide. He didn't approve of my situation. My family was paying for my education, and I was getting to live in New York on top of it. He thought I was taking it for granted, and at the same time taking *him* for granted for helping me move. I probably was.

I acted entitled sometimes, to others' attention and time. But where did you draw the line when you were trying to stay open to the possibility of what the city could give? I believed eventually I would get what I wanted, even if I didn't know what that was yet. And it would be outside help that transformed my life into a thing of real substance. No one did it alone. But some gross part of me thought that I deserved it somehow, when I really hadn't earned what was being handed to me. Nevertheless, when Andy let me off at my new place, it was the last time I would see him for a couple of years.

Williamsburg was frayed, but compared to Crown Heights, it was like the Riviera. It could actually feel festive, lots of families, Hispanic and Ukrainian, hanging in the street. Distorted mariachi music blasted from boom boxes cranked up at every hour of the day. Outside my bedroom window the jams were played on what seemed like a loop on someone's blown-out radio. On weekends, a man would drag a wagon up and down the block with a speaker that he would preach from in Spanish. There was a Hasidic neighborhood a few blocks away with the women wearing their bobbed wigs, strings of pearls, and polyester suit-dresses, pushing strollers. I thought they looked kind of chic.

My window overlooked a decrepit lot, car frames and machinery, junk. There were men out there tinkering and fixing engines. It wasn't a very pretty view but I enjoyed watching the chickens pecking around in the dirt. They seemed to have the run of the place. Every morning at sunup, a rooster crowed.

There was a musty C-Town grocery store directly across the street, a step up from the strange delis in Crown Heights, but it still felt like it was from some other dimension. C-Town seemed to carry only sugary cereal and soda, orangish meat and strange canned brands I'd never heard of. I ventured over sometimes to get a box of pasta, a can of tuna, or a jar of peanut butter. The ladies at the checkout counter didn't acknowledge me, as though some invisible ghost had just carried a box of floating oatmeal to the register.

There weren't many restaurants around: It was a pretty desolate scene for most of the walk to the Bedford stop. Then, right before you hit the subway, there was a two-block stretch just east of it that was hopping with new cafés and storefronts showing off handmade crafty purses and the like. There was quite a bit of graffiti. I saw a great stencil of Mayor Giuliani with Mickey Mouse ears and vampire teeth, and another where someone had made him look like a wild-eyed Hitler. Some wheat-pasted posters railed against the gentrification of the neighborhood: YUPPIE, GO HOME, they said. I saw a couple of response signs with a picture of a white girl in a cowboy hat and sunglasses: OH, YEAH, WE'RE THE HIPSTERS HERE TO INVADE. I passed the signs every day and wondered if I qualified as what they were talking about—another entitled white boy moving into someone else's neighborhood.

"This place is going to be just like SoHo," Graham said. He was the landlord of the Cake Factory—a masculine, broad-shouldered metal sculptor with thick black glasses. I'd have let him throw it in me, he was fucking hot, but I could tell he was also kind of a dick. The kind of straight guy who acted cool with gays but saw them on the next rung down the ladder under women. He knew I'd be a good tenant because he could sense my discomfort with his dominance; I could be easily manipulated.

My rent was due the first of every month and for some reason I was supposed to leave it in the freezer. But the entire floor was a freezer. The cold made a home in my bones, coming through the concrete floor and permeating even the furniture. There was a commercial-size heater in the very front of the loft, but the place was so big that none of the heat reached into the back space where I lived. I put my twin bed in the middle of the empty cement room and piled thick wool blankets on top of me as I slept. I surrounded myself with three searing-red space heaters that I placed strategically around the bed, and I turned them up full blast. It's a miracle I didn't burn myself alive. In the middle of the night, I woke up bathed in a fiery orange glow, a tiny pocket of warmth. When I got up to pee, my system was shocked as I plunged into the frigid air.

I started decorating. On my front and back walls, I chose a royal-blue color, on the left side a shiny metallic silver. I painted the wall outside my room a kind of robin's-egg blue with giant cheddar-orange polka dots that I made with a cardboard stencil. I hung my massage-parlor-red fabric over the window as a curtain. It looked like a sad fun house.

Next on the list was a carpet. I wanted to put it wall-to-wall so that it would warm up the room and make it feel a little cozier. I found what I needed in a remnants section in the basement of a carpet store in Manhattan. It was a stomach-churning clown-nose red.

I somehow convinced some straight boys from school—in exchange for a few six-packs of beer and a pizza—to help me bring the thing home. Even though there were four of us, it felt as heavy as a car. We had to stop every two blocks or so to catch our breath. As we carried it down the stairs and through the turnstiles using subway tokens, the attendant in the booth saw us, and rather than tell us that it was too big to take on the train, he just pointed at us and laughed. At one point I wondered if we would have to abandon it on the sidewalk. When we finally made it, everyone was still happy enough to sit and drink beers in front of the space heaters.

One of my new roommates, Leonard, was of Ukrainian descent, with a stocky build and a soft-featured face. He was cheerful but hard to read. The gigantic main room with big windows was his territory, no furnishings except a dilapidated couch and a dirty glass coffee table covered in cigarette butts, Styrofoam soda receptacles, and marijuana debris. Leonard didn't seem to read books. There weren't any on display or stacked on the cardboard-box nightstand next to his mattress on the floor.

I guess he sometimes worked as a waiter at Republic, a restaurant on Union Square, but he was usually at home smoking pot. We talked one day about his plans for the place, and he told me he was going to suspend his bed over an enclosed area of water in his bedroom. I nodded and said, "Wow, that sounds really amazing." He was kind of a tool.

One day, soon after moving in, I was on a ladder painting my walls when a weathered but handsome man in his thirties strolled into my room, finishing a loud conversation on a cell phone. He wore a ponytail and a black trench coat and carried a brown cardboard box under his arm. "Hello!" he said, dropping it and stepping forward with a manic grin, his arms outstretched. I came down from the ladder. "I've been waiting to meet you, man!" He slapped me on the back and pulled me into a huge hug. "Welcome to the pad, dude." He lit a cigarette and paced in a circle, checking my room out. "Lookin' really good in here, bud. *Really* good. I'm telling ya, this is great. Ah, what a treat that you're here. Just what this place needs. You in school?"

I nodded.

"This is gonna be so great for you, man." He grabbed my hand and shook it vigorously. "Donavan! But my parents almost named me Chase. Chase/Jason, so close, right? It's a sign, dude. Something's up. When I'm right, I'm *right*." He clapped his hands. Despite his intense energy, I was just pleased that he was friendly. If I have to live with somebody, Jesus, just let them be friendly. I asked him what was in the box.

"Ah, dude, it's this crazy bowl I just got from the Middle East. It's a doozy, gonna put it in the shop tomorrow."

"What's the shop?"

He told me he ran a stall in this antique market in SoHo. He led me to his room, cigarette crushed between his lips, and left his box sitting on the floor. He opened his door and revealed a room the exact size and shape of mine, also with a dirt-caked window at the end. It looked like a Moroccan opium den. There was a plethora of plants hanging from the ceiling and rough-edged rugs and mats on the floor. Lacquered vases rose up from behind chairs and desks, holding knick-knacks and ashtrays, a fine layer of dust over every surface. The bed on the floor was unmade, the maroon sheets having seen some kind of tussle. A scrawl on the wall in black Sharpie above the bed read, THE SEER IS UPRISING—AFRICA. He stuck a long, ornate silver pipe in my face. "Want some weed?" I took his lighter and obliged.

Donavan seemed to be thinking faster than he could speak. "So you're from Seattle? Ah, I've been there a couple times, great place. Wow, man, what a scene. You ever been to Chicago? It's just wild. Frankie Knuckles played my birthday party. My ex-wife lives there. We're still friends, you know. She's so great, you have to meet her. Was that a PlayStation I saw in your room? I played *Final Fantasy Seven* for like ninety hours. You ever been to India? Man, *that's* where you need to go. It's insane. You can live like a king for ten bucks a day. Ten bucks! A king! Hey, you want these shelves here? I'm not doing anything with them. I have too many for my stall." He gestured to a stack of glass sheets in a corner. This was perfect, because I had nothing to put my books or my turntable on.

Donavan was dialed to an intense frequency but always seemed genuinely happy to see me. His life seemed shifty, and I never quite got a grip on his story. But it sounded like there'd been some drug problems. "Heroin, man. Never touch the stuff. It's the devil." But he loved his weed, and I wondered if he wasn't on some kind of speed half the time, with his frenetic babbling. He was like a tumbling coffee mug, spilling so fast and catching itself upright after it's made a full turn.

I frequented the Hasidic warehouses that dotted the neighborhood—big, dark, sprawling caves with furniture and junk piled to the ceiling. In these hoards I found pieces, like bits of a puzzle, that might complete my room. I walked out of these damp lairs with my hands covered in a sticky film, a rusted lamp or a pleather footrest in my arms. The men who ran these places were gruff and I was too nervous to haggle with them, so I had to decide, on the spot, whether what I wanted was worth the price they tossed me.

There was this kind of office-supply shop a few blocks away, and I found an L-shaped desk for about a hundred bucks. Everything I purchased seemed to be impossibly heavy. I got a dolly and brought the desk home in two separate trips. It looked metallic and officious in my room. The size of it actually helped fill in some of the space, but as my room started to come together I thought, *There's no way in hell I'm ever gonna be able to get this shit out of here.*

I couldn't afford to buy CDs at the moment, but I did have the spare change to dig through the piles of dusty old records that sat in darkened corners of the warehouses. I swept up anything that looked interesting, paying about a dollar for each record. I found Olivia Newton-John, the Bee Gees' early albums, a scratched-up *Goodbye Yellow Brick Road* by Elton John. I took a chance on anything that looked remotely fun. There was a remarkable yet awful record from 1978 by Carolyne Bernier that I found myself playing on repeat. It had a nearly seventeen-minute-long song called "Secret Agent Love." I took the sleeve and made a spot for it on the wall. The photo was of a blond Carolyne Bernier, sporting a black chiffon blouse and a feathered hairdo. English was definitely not her first language or forte and she had some pitch issues, but whatever, it was delightful. I found a record by Tuxedo Junction, with "Chattanooga Choo Choo" on it. I knew this stuff was supposed to be terrible, but I loved it. I lay on my frigid red carpet and dreamed about "over-it"-looking women with glossy lips, half-assedly going along with the band, star filters all around their faces. My roommates and friends tried their best to be nice and hide their horror when I played these albums. It may not have been the latest or the coolest, but at least I had some damn music.

I did manage to scrape enough money together to buy a CD that had just come out: Beck's *Midnite Vultures*. I heard it in its entirety for the first time at one of Lucy's cocktail parties, staring wordlessly at the stereo, forgetting any social niceties, too wrapped up in the squonking horns and absurd lyrics. My Beck fandom had started in early high school and I had cherished each album. But this was something else, a whole world in a box, populated by shady pimps, women named Debra, screaming lesbians. The critics weren't especially fond of it, but I felt like it had been made just for me. This was somebody not just being an artist; it was the sound of somebody having a good time. That album, more than anything else, instilled a desire in me to create *something* that made people feel the same way I did each time I listened to it.

13

split not having ended our friendship. It was around this time we started going to the Cock, a bar on Twelfth Street and Avenue A. It had been there for a year or so already and I'd heard a few people praise it for being a godsend, a tribute to a bygone New York. It was apparently one of the main places to hang these days, and right away I could feel its allure. It was bringing gay sex back at the end of a decade that had made it something people feared—something that was dangerous and made people sick.

We'd usually get there early, and there weren't many people, just a few guys kicked back on the banquette, drinking. The Cock was a small room divided into three sections: the bar, which was painted black with a red-glitter countertop; a red-vinyl-banquette area next to a go-go stand in front of a curtain visible to most of the room; and, behind the curtain, a dark room. Every surface, including the lacquered bar, was covered with a muted sparkle, as if someone had wiped the whole thing down with bejeweled lube. This particular night, there was an androgynous man with upswept blond hair DJing some Iggy, Blondie, and the Runaways. Later, I'd find out that it was Miss Guy, lead singer of the Toilet Böys.

The first night I was there I saw two signs. One was very large and dominated the back of the room: NO DANCING. To the left of it there was a smaller one: WATCH YOUR WALLET.

A man who introduced himself as a music producer named Larry Tee was wandering around in thick black glasses and an oversize white shirt. He informed me that the sign was there because of something called the cabaret law. I shrugged, not having heard of it. "Means you have to have a license for people to dance. It's all Giuliani," he said. "He's been the worst mayor. It's so fucked-up. People used to be able to do whatever they wanted." He laughed. "Well, good luck. You can't stop the gays from partying."

I was shocked. No dancing? What. The. Fuck. I'd never heard of such a thing. This was a living *Footloose*, the sign like something out of *1984*. How could you tell people not to dance? Apparently the police were raiding the Cock pretty regularly, not something they normally did with straight bars. (But I guess straight people weren't having sex in the back of their establishments.) The cops would storm in, turn the music off and all the lights on, and search everybody for drugs, always making a few arrests. I'm glad I was never there for one. It would have scared the crap out of me.

As the evening got busier, men crammed up against one another, all messy hands and playful shoving. Friends would be lost to the swell, "Back in the New York Groove" playing. The air was heavy with cigarette smoke and the dancers' musk. A mammoth man would be on the bar, his banana sling cradling a bulge so big it looked like it could knock somebody out with a light *thwack*. Below him were guys reaching to touch it, sticking dollars in the elastic. He'd whip his dick out every once in a while and let somebody stick it in their mouth. I've never been big on participating in public displays of sex; I have nothing against it, though, since I'm always happy to see debauched behavior. There's something kind of sweet about people feeling free enough to do whatever they want in plain sight.

I found flyers around town for an event called Kurfew, "America's Largest YOUNG Gay Dance Party!" It supposedly catered to the under-twenty-one crowd, and seeing that I was still twenty, I thought I would give it a shot. The flyers every week had images of sleek, twinky boys preening under neon lights. It was being held at Tunnel, in the Kenny Scharf Room, which was named after and designed by the popular painter. I ventured there one night by myself, hoping to meet someone cute. It was so dark and cold outside, the prospect seemed hopeless, but I was craving some company. It was my first visit to Tunnel and I was floored: It was a black hole, a fun-house mirror of clubs within clubs. When I finally found the Kurfew party, my hopes of hooking up dimmed. It was a lot of super-young guys, many running around in body paint, which I've always thought repulsive, like covering yourself with whipped cream and strawberries.

Entering the Kenny Scharf Room was like stepping inside one of his paintings: There was fun fur everywhere, and black light that made everyone look creepy, with their eyes and teeth aglow. I milled around in the shadows, observing the scene, but eventually met a very groomed (and, more important, unpainted) guy named Michael. He told me he had just graduated from NYU and worked some kind of finance job that had been passed down from his family. He wasn't setting my sirens off, but I decided to go home with him anyway. His place was a penthouse with expensive-looking rugs and a chandelier in the foyer. We fell into bed, made out a little, and then just fell asleep. I took his number the next morning and left.

We set up a date for the following week, and he told me he wanted to take me to an off-Broadway show. No one had taken me to one before and I was excited, even though I knew I didn't care about seeing him again. We met up at a Starbucks on Astor Place, where he revealed our two tickets for *Stomp*.

Stomp? Are you fucking kidding me? I thought. *Ugh, so cheesy.* I had seen this in a touring production three years ago. My face lit up with a phony smile and I pretended to be thrilled as we filed into the theater with all the high school tourist groups. They gave it a standing ovation at the end. Out of all the shows going on in New York City, he had taken me to *Stomp*. Barf. I realized right then that just because you were from New York and had money didn't mean that you had taste. I guess I got what I deserved. We had met at Kurfew, for Christ's sake.

I began going out a lot—often by myself, since I hadn't made those kinds of friends yet. The late nights outside were silent as I stepped out of the Cake Factory into the streets for the long walk to the subway, passing by sex workers who dotted the corners, teetering on their heels. Though these streets weren't without dangers, the atmosphere wasn't as thick with tension as my previous neighborhood.

When I was out, I still felt the remains of an anger, a soft boil that came on in the gay bars and clubs. I would feel like my fifteen-year-old self again, still stuck in the hierarchy of high school. But now it was with gays. I remained gangly. My clothes were nothing fancy. I didn't have any muscle yet, even though I'd started lifting weights. From barstools I watched, fascinated, men who were bigger and hotter than I was. I was both jealous and judgmental of them. They were everything I wanted and didn't want to be.

Nothing made me feel lonelier than going to the Roxy. On Saturday nights it was heaving, all the wild-eyed butch boys and queens living for Victor Calderone's DJ sets. The heat was so thick you could barely remember that it was snowing outside. I was invisible to those men with their muscles and succinct haircuts, clipped facial hair. They looked right through me.

Barracuda was a Chelsea bar with a warmer vibe, and the bartender, Darren Dryden, was the kind of guy you would drop-kick a gerbil to sleep with. He was short and hairy, almost a little Greek-looking, stocky with a smoky, dreamy smile. I'd sit at the bar, probably seeming like a desperate child, and order my vodka tonics. Every once in a while he'd tell me it was on the house, which made me feel special, at least for a few minutes.

Sometimes I ended up at Big Cup on Eighth Avenue in Chelsea, a bright, social café. It didn't seem like there were too many of them in New York. One of the problems there was the big cups themselves. As an avid coffee drinker, I was grossed out by the extremely large mugs. I'd been spoiled by Seattle's distinct, delicious brews. It seemed as if New York hadn't quite learned yet, and it all tasted watered-down to me.

I sat in Big Cup and read books, glancing up as one handsome man after another entered. Indeed, when the door opened, everyone else looked up to see who was coming in. I was amazed at people I recognized from the porn videos I'd watched over the years. One day I saw Max Grand and was spellbound by how he moved so confidently through the room, greeting all the guys he knew. What it must have felt like being so popular, and knowing that at times everybody around you had observed you taking it six ways to Sunday.

I hadn't been watching much porn since I'd gotten to New York. I had a VCR set up with a tiny TV now in my room, but there were only two videos that I had: a Bel Ami movie called *Sauna Paradiso*, and an old William Higgins flick called *Sailor in the Wild*, which I had pilfered from Dan Savage's basement the previous winter. Both of them did the trick when I needed to rub one out. I was way too impatient with any kind of porn on the computer—loading up grainy thumbnails, having to wait two full minutes while the photo slowly revealed itself, by the centimeter. Sometimes, though, in a pinch, just the suspense was enough to get me off.

Mary and I talked at least a couple times a week. Neither of us could afford the long-distance bills, so we had to fill in the blanks by mailing each other collages of JonBenét Ramsey and Phyllis Diller cut from tabloids, or just plain old letters. I would receive envelopes from Outwater Plastics, the office she worked at, where she killed time at her desk by penning me acidic notes. Sometimes we would include pictures of ourselves with Post-its on them.

"I'm doing it," she said one evening on the phone.

"What, rejoining Amway?" I quipped. Once, a coworker had taken her out of town to try to get her into that scheme. After a lecture, she'd been somehow lured by motivational speakers/proselytizers onto an RV in a parking lot where she'd pretended to "find Christ." Mary would sometimes do something just for a good story.

"Seattle," she said. She was going next week to interview for jobs and find an apartment.

But she didn't know anyone up there. "Do you want me to come and look at places with you?"

"Nah, you've got school, and my mom is coming with me anyway. You can visit when I'm settled."

I was excited for her but felt a pang of anxiety. It was great she was getting out of Arizona, but would she be able to navigate a new city completely by herself? It could be a fresh start for her, and maybe she could find a way to get healthier. She was so bored in Arizona, and I knew she longed to be somewhere more sophisticated. At least she was taking the initiative to make a change. It was a good sign. I just hoped it was the right decision.

14

IT WAS HOT OUT NOW AND THE AIR WAS VISCOUS.
Smells wafted through the city like dead seaweed in a sour-cream
ocean, scents of hot nuts and melting butter. The heat seemed to expand sounds that had been absent in the freezing temperatures. Doors
of buses hissed louder, stray street chatter became piercing. Pipes blew
hot exhaust in my face as I jaywalked through traffic jams. Sometimes
I raced in front of cars. Other New Yorkers didn't seem to mind being
in a cab's crosshairs. A couple times I saw a bicyclist or pedestrian lying
on the ground, a driver nearby pacing and pulling at his hair, in tears, a
crowd gathered. A friend told me one day that a woman had just been
backed over and crunched by a garbage truck in Union Square.

The Cake Factory was no longer frozen like a meat locker. It had
become the opposite, a place for things to rot. I rigged an air condi-
tioner to hang out of my window, which was loud enough to block
out the sound of the rooster crowing in the morning. Some heavy
rains blew through the city and caught me by surprise.

One night I lay propped up reading *White Noise*. I could feel the
hard wall behind my head through the thin pillow. Above the top
of my book, I saw something glimmer. Water was sluicing down the
entire length of my blue wall. The steady trickle ended in a long, sad
puddle on the red synthetic carpet. My heart sank. It was like finding
out my room had herpes.

I grabbed my only two towels, moved the heavy furniture into the center of the room, and peeled the carpet back. The water just pooled outward. I tried to contain my tears and sponge up the mess with my bath towels: They were soaked in seconds.

I thought of my little studio apartment in Seattle and its homey, wooden smell. And now here I was, watching it rain in the middle of my room. I pulled myself together, dried my eyes, and walked into the front space to find my roommate Leonard. He was lying on his couch, watching a small TV, which was plugged in with an extension cord. *Anaconda* with Jennifer Lopez was on.

"It's raining in my room," I said.

He swiveled. "Oh shit, man. That's right."

" 'That's right'? You know about it?"

"Yeah, there's a little leak in there."

"It's kind of more than a little leak."

"Let me see." He pushed his burly body up off the chewed sofa, and I followed him to my room. "Ohhhh," he said, as if he'd discovered a lost hat he'd been looking for. "Yeah, it's definitely gotten worse. It's puddling down there." He laughed and poked my side. "It's like your own water feature, man."

I was out of towels. They were all wet. Leonard finger-motioned me to hang on and left the room, returning with a big pile of dirty drop cloths to line the wall with. "Hopefully they'll keep it from turning into a lake," he said.

I thought of the landlord. "Do you think Graham would come look at it?"

Leonard shook his head. "I heard a few months ago he was thinking about trying to patch up the roof with cement. Guess he didn't do it." He glanced at me from the side. "You can talk to him, but you'll probably just have to live with it."

Leonard walked out and I sat on my bed. The entire wall was leaking; it was like being under a bridge. Why the fuck couldn't I get a break? At the very least I needed a room to sleep in that was dry, that wasn't like some squat in an apocalypse. With the carpet peeled back, my plastic clothes bin of drawers and the low red velour couch looked like proper junk. My room was nothing more than a child's fort. I curled up under my thin top sheet and tried to keep reading.

My parents tried to put a hundred bucks or so in my bank account every week for the train and some food. They weren't going to allow me to starve, but they let it be known that it was necessary that I find a job. I did my best to think about what kinds of things I could do. Retail would be miserable: I was good with people, but folding clothes endlessly and pretending to know anything about fashion would have been a disaster. I wasn't brave or savvy enough to attempt to wait tables. A bookstore job would have been cool, but it seemed like everybody wanted one of those. I didn't feel ambitious enough to try.

I responded to a help-wanted ad on the bulletin board at my school. It was for the Association of American University Presses: They needed somebody in the mailroom. I arrived for the interview in a building at the corner of Twenty-Third Street and Sixth Avenue, and rang the bell of the nondescript office. In the waiting room was seated a perspiring young man in a sopping-wet plaid oxford. He nervously held a bike helmet in his lap.

I wore blue jeans and a small short-sleeved, red-gingham snap-button collared shirt. My short hair was combed over and pasted down with tiny bangs sticking up like sports fans in the middle of doing a "wave." I got the job.

It was pretty easy working in the mailroom, plus I got to take home all kinds of books after they were mailed back from their respective conferences. I was in for about three or four days every week, and there were only about eight people in the office. My boss was a handsome gay guy who seemed to like me. I wondered if at some point he would get flirty, but then I decided he was too professional for that. But not too professional to order two dirty vodka martinis when he took me to lunch. And besides, he went on and on about his boyfriend, some loaded guy he was in love with.

Around this time, Lucy's boyfriend, Linas, tipped me off to some kids who were creating a show in the Experimental Theatre Wing at NYU. They were writing it through improvisation and they needed one more person to join the ensemble. I was intimidated that I didn't know any of them, and didn't even go to NYU, but my curiosity was piqued.

When the day came to meet everybody, I chugged an obscene amount of coffee—I guess to ease my fears, but the caffeine just made me more nervous. By the time I arrived, my ears were ringing and my skin itched. The rehearsal space looked like an empty dance studio, a large mirror lining the length of the room. An attractive, baby-faced fellow named Ryan greeted me and we sat down cross-legged as a couple girls and another guy meandered in. They all seemed to know each other well and I felt shy as Ryan introduced me to each person. I was thinking, *What am I doing here? I'm not an actor.*

Ryan started by thanking the six of us for being there and said we were going to begin with a warm-up. I followed along with their strange yelps and whooping. After a round of making weird bird noises at each other, Ryan announced that we were going to take the next hour for free improvisation. "You can do whatever you want," he said. "Create characters, talk to each other, but listen and respond. Be specific with your body."

Everyone immediately began to hunch and stretch. A couple girls started moaning and writhing like evangelicals possessed by the spirit. I bent over and walked on all fours, sweating caffeine and needing to pee. Everyone just tripped out: It was as if we were in a locked padded room and someone had taken our straitjackets off. I lost track of time, thrilled to be pretending with no one looking at me funny.

Ryan called the end of the session. I was covered in sweat and everyone snapped out of their trance as if nothing had happened. "I love what I'm seeing, lots of energy. One thing. Please no retarded people, thanks. On Tuesday we're going to start playing with some characters and scenes." Everyone gathered their stuff, said goodbye, and left the studio. I didn't know if I'd see any of them again.

"Are you open to doing the show?" Ryan asked. "I know it probably feels weird, not knowing any of us. But I need one more guy. I think you'd be great."

As I gripped the sticky handrails on the L train, headed back to Williamsburg, I was elated. Despite the rain in my room and being perpetually broke, this was my first opportunity to perform in New York. It wasn't clear to me yet, but I was becoming more and more drawn to situations that made me uncomfortable, whether it was by jumping blindly into a show or even my strange living scenario. Being in over my head must have been an instinctual way to discover new parts of myself that I hadn't even known were there.

When I got home to the Cake Factory, most of the lights were out, and the loft was silent. I walked down the hallway and turned the corner, threw my jacket on the couch, and gasped: Someone was standing still in the middle of the main room. It was my roommate Donavan's dark silhouette backlit by a tiny lamp. I could see individual hairs that had come loose from his ponytail. He was upright, head resting on his chest, with a lit cigarette dangling from his mouth.

"Jesus, you scared me." I forced a laugh. He didn't move. "Donavan?" I took steps toward him and touched his shoulder. He raised his head up a couple inches, weaving, eyelids heavy. "You okay?" No recognition in his eyes. He said something unintelligible, lowered his head again, and the cigarette dropped to the concrete floor.

I stepped backward toward my room. "You should to go to bed, man. Let me know if you need anything. I'll see you in the morning." He was catatonic. I had never seen someone so fucked-up. In my doorway I looked at him for one more moment, perplexed by how someone could seem asleep but still be standing. I closed my door, turned my lock, and sat on the edge of my bed, scared. It felt like the Cake Factory was suddenly haunted. Who the hell were these people I was living with?

EAT ME was the name of the play we made. It was about a lesbian carpenter who lived next door to a manipulative, homophobic, grifting 7-Eleven checkout lady. My character, Joey, was her son, a gentle boy obsessed with turkey and Thanksgiving. The play ended with a big dance number led by Cher, and for some reason, I was dressed as a giant hot dog for the curtain call.

My Joey had stiff, slow, and specific movements of his arms and his neck. He had a bow-legged gait and talked in a low voice, sounding something like a sweet cartoon tortoise. I'd practice him at night when I walked home from the subway, running my lines over and over. Joey would come out on the train, or while I was eating a sandwich at the diner. I was doing the character so much, sometimes I would slip into him without even realizing it.

On opening night, our two leads burst into an uncontrollable laughing fit and ruined the whole performance. I was so angry. I couldn't understand; it seemed almost like they had done it on purpose. But that was the only incident in our six-show run. I loved my time working with those NYU kids, overcoming my initial fear and learning basic improvisation. Plus, I got to date the director, Ryan, for a month or so afterward.

It was a hot Sunday afternoon, and my roommate Donavan gave me a pill, saying it would give me some energy. We went to Vinyl in TriBeCa for Body and Soul, a beloved afternoon house-music party. It felt decadent being inside a dark club, knowing that it was a warm,

sunny day outside. The crowd was mixed and the dance floor comfortably snug. The smell of fresh sweat in the air wasn't unpleasant.

Donavan's eyes were wild as he let his hair free from its ponytail
and started dancing, all elbows and knees. "Dude, this shit is just like
Chicago in the eighties!" He was slack-jawed, as if he'd never set foot
in a club before. Whatever upper he had given me kicked in. I felt its
initial rush of effervescence, but I still felt like a stranger. It seemed
everyone was smiling only at each other, like they all knew something
that I didn't.

I took a break from dancing and wandered through one of the side
rooms. Ernesto, a gay guy I knew from Seattle, was leaned up against a
wall. We used to hang out and get dinner, had slept together on occasion. Now, his clothes were tighter, his body had grown since I'd seen
it last, his hair was shorter. I threw my arms open and gave him a hug,
so happy was I to see a familiar face. He was a little stiff.

"Oh my God! How cool to see you here!" I said.

Ernesto glanced around me, like there was someone else he was
expecting to see. "Who are you here with?" he asked.

"My roommate is in there somewhere, I think he's grabbing a
drink. I can't believe this. What are you doing in New York?"

"Working for Wilhelmina," he said, his voice flat.

"I don't know her. What kind of work?"

He looked as if he felt sorry for me. "It's a modeling agency,
babe. Good to see you." He turned and left me standing alone. I
felt sick to my stomach. He seemed embarrassed that he knew me.
As I watched him reenter his circle of friends, the atmosphere in
the room became distorted. People's faces looked waxy. Was it just
me, or had the music taken a dark turn? I became suddenly self-
conscious about my plain jeans and Hanes tank top. I found Donavan and we took the L train back to Williamsburg, staring at our own
reflections in the glass.

When we returned to the Cake Factory, Leonard was waiting for
us on his mangled sofa-island. "We're getting another roommate!" he

said. I didn't even know we were looking for one. She showed up later that night and I knew right away why we had a new addition to our rotting concrete palace: She was stunning.

Leonard had met her while she was shooting a music video with a crew at our place the week before. When he found out she was looking for somewhere to live, he offered to build her a room. She was a film student from Texas named Anne Marie and looked like a ravishing raven-haired villainess in a Disney movie. She was tall and floated through the room, her eyebrows arched, her smile disarming. I listened as she and Leonard discussed the dimensions of the bedroom he was building her. She walked around, looking up in the corners, arms folded, heels clicking on the dirty floor. Leonard said he would start construction the next day. And Donavan, between earnest mouthfuls of weed smoke, said he would love to give it a special paint job. I didn't quite know what to think, other than that it would be nice to have a woman around.

Leonard spent the following weeks nailing Anne Marie's room together in the front corner just beside the main entryway. His dedication on display was unparalleled with anything I'd seen him do, and I wondered if he thought he was building their love nest. Anne Marie dropped in to check on the work between shifts bartending at Black Betty down the street, giving directions on the job that Leonard was doing. She became a cool girlfriend and would visit me in my room to talk about guys, or different movie projects she was working on.

"Okay, we are mixing the colors, right now!" Donavan called out, a cigarette dangling precariously from his lips. Wearing a kimono, he was crouched over a big white bucket with Anne Marie towering at his side. "It's definitely going to be red!" Like a witch with her wand, he swizzled his mixing stick in a noxious brew of pigment and God knows what else he'd whipped together.

Anne Marie pulled me aside a few minutes later, concerned. "He said he 'blessed' my room? And he put a piece of coral from the Dead Sea into the wall and sealed it. Also, he just spat in the paint."

"It's cool," I reassured her. "I think he just takes this kind of thing very seriously." And *serious* was the only way to describe the finished job. When Donavan was done, the room looked like an explosion of gore and guts. The shades of red could have been called Afterbirth and Crimson Grit. Anne Marie seemed pleased enough, but I couldn't have even slept in that bloody box. She then convinced Leonard to build her a loft bed as well.

Anne Marie was friendliest with me. She knew I didn't want anything from her, like I'm sure a lot of men did. We'd stay up after she was done bartending and gossip about our weird roommates. When she was working at Black Betty and it wasn't too crowded, I'd sit and gab with her at the bar, eating chicken kebab. It was a scene loaded with artists and musicians, and some nights bands played.

Our dynamic as roommates was relaxed and cordial. Sometimes there would be extra characters hanging around, like Donavan's emaciated girlfriend. We'd smoke from a bong and the girlfriend would tell me stories of all-night parties with magical sunrises and DJ sets. She was obsessed with Kruder & Dorfmeister, and claimed that one of them had saved her during a time of emotional distress. ("It was like . . . he really understood me, you know?") As the night wore on, Donavan and his girlfriend would grow quieter. I'd take one last hit of weed and excuse myself to let them go about their business. I had deduced by this point that Donavan was shooting up again.

15

MY HEAD WAS ALWAYS FISHING. WHEREVER I WENT, I was casting an invisible net, trying to capture some idea that I could bring home with me. I yearned for a sensation that I couldn't quite name. But I believed if I just kept my eyes open, the true reason I was in New York was going to rear its head. I had an inkling now it was going to be performance-based, yet when I tried to visualize how I would do it, I drew a blank.

I got a ticket to see Beck on the *Midnite Vultures* tour at Radio City Music Hall. Not being able to afford two tickets, I went alone and ended up with a great seat, very close to the stage. Beck's performance was assured, and the absurd world he created around him was specific and fully formed. There were zombified backup dancers dressed as football players with spare limbs coming out of their crotches. He sang "Debra" writhing around on a bed with satin sheets, a midnight cowboy with blond ambition. It was ridiculous and free. For him, sex was something to poke fun at and celebrate. I kept turning around during the performance to look at all the people in Radio City, out of their seats. It was arguably the better view.

Kiki and Herb at the Fez was an act that everyone was talking about. They were a duo played by Justin Bond and Kenny Mellman— respectively, Kiki, an old, washed-up lounge singer; and Herb, her "gay, Jew, 'tard" piano player. Kiki belted out left-field covers and monologued about her long-departed good old days. She got progressively drunker and surlier, walking on tables, harassing the audience, throwing drinks around. As the show continued, the lines blurred, a magic trick where the character became very real. The darkness was unexpectedly moving. When the show ended, I was shell-shocked, never having seen a performance with so many layers. I turned to my friend, the playwright Tom Donaghy, and surprised myself by saying, "This is what I want to do."

"Then you have to just do it," he replied. That sentence I uttered was a pivotal moment. I realized I wanted to make people feel how I was feeling right then, at the end of a show. The simplicity of Tom's response was nothing but the truth.

I saw Fischerspooner play the Warm Up, a Saturday-afternoon outdoor party at the PS1 museum in Queens. The "band" was four singers and dancers wearing warped beige tunics, wrapped around them like tumors. They played no instruments; the music was automated and prerecorded, their lip-syncing skills immaculate. It was as if Kraftwerk had scored a Bob Fosse musical. Casey Spooner, the lead "singer," kept stopping the numbers midway because of wrong dance moves or "sound issues." His prima-donna act was convincing, leaving the crowd wondering if what they were seeing was for real.

It was at this performance that I met a handsome black man with muscles, short shorts, and a skimpy top, who proceeded to tell me I had a piece of corn stuck on my cheek, from a cob I'd just devoured. I wiped the remnants off and we both agreed we'd never seen anything like Fischerspooner. His full name was Seth Sharp and I was drawn to his cutting magnetism right away. He had a demented glee; everything he said came across like a private joke just between you and him.

The music stopped, the show was over, people clapped. The singer, Casey, brushed past us, sweaty and glowing. "I fucking loved that!" I called to him as he walked by. He politely thanked me and kept moving.

Seth asked me if I'd accompany him that night to see some DJs playing at Windows on the World. It was located at the top of the World Trade Center, and riding the elevator for the first time was like being catapulted into the sky or squirted out of a needle. It was swankier than the daytime shorts we were wearing, but no one stopped us from entering. I approached the huge windows and put my fingers on the glass. Other than being on an airplane, I had never been so high. We met a guy that night from Argentina who worked at a fur-coat shop on Houston Street. He and I made out and smoked some weed in the bathroom, and then he invited Seth and me to some party in Chinatown.

A night out in New York was like playing a board game. The goal was finding the quickest shortcut to the most fun. It was like Chutes and Ladders for grown-ups. One silly hour at a dive bar could lead you to a warehouse, then maybe a penthouse. On a good night, someone with actual cash was around to buy you enough cocktails to keep the night going. They were delectably sticky summer evenings, with no one to answer to, and no telling whose bed I'd end up in.

Seth and I went out constantly. I knew we'd have a big night ahead when he'd ring my heavy cell phone and say, "Let's go tippin', honey." We prowled the streets of the East Village, talked up any cuties we could find, made faces over unsuspecting people's shoulders, drank until our legs did the sidewalk jitterbug, and started tiny fights with each other about some assumed slight.

At Wonder Bar, it was pretty easy to get loose with Nashom's stiff drinks. They fueled Seth and me with the courage to chat any guys up we wanted. We made a good pair, both of us dressed in clothes meant to be taken off easily. My bar conversation improved. I'd learned the skill of keeping a ball in the air, and also knew how to hit it into the outfield, for the guy to take one look away, and I'd disappear. Some evenings led to shadowy corners, making out with strangers, or to the entryway of a freshly locked bar at closing time, getting a blow job from the bartender.

Seth and I were relieved when we realized we were into different kinds of guys. He liked them younger, small and skinny. That's probably why he had talked to me in the first place. My tastes ran older and rugged. I wanted somebody I could climb on. Some friends around my own age seemed repulsed that I could get into a guy in his thirties, but perhaps they were just butt-hurt that I wasn't eyeballing them.

One midweek night at Wonder Bar, Seth and I were in the mood to cruise, but it was quiet and neither of us saw any sexy offerings on the table. "Hey," Seth said, his eyes sparkling. "Let's go down the street."

"To that straight dive bar?"

"No, next to it. You haven't been?" He looked at me as if I were kidding. "Shit. Come on, trust me."

You'd never have known the place was there: It was a conspicuous storefront with a dark tint on the windows, good for blocking out the chaos within. Upon entry, it looked packed. And it was—but with only about fifteen people. That's all it could fit. A Hole song struggled out of mounted speakers as two almost-naked dancers gyrated on the splintery bar. Christmas and disco lights flashed on a muscled guy standing on a wood crate. He smirked at no one as he rubbed oil all over himself. The barman, shirtless and stoned-looking, was lobbing beers at patrons as fast as he could throw them. It was a like a raging party that was being held in someone's storage locker.

The bar, IC Guys, had no liquor license, only beer and wine. Apparently the name of the place was always changing because—rumor had it—the owner was trying to dodge taxes. The bartender, Dave, who came in from Jersey City every day, was the sole employee. He juggled bartending, DJing the music, and operating the intricate makeshift lighting rig, not to mention minding the dancers. With shaggy grace he swung like a spider monkey from the laptop, leaped onto boxes to adjust the lights, and hauled beer out of the closet. It was like manning a three-ring circus that only had one ring.

IC Guys had a kind of homespun atmosphere and was a party

boiled down to its essence. The close quarters provoked the awkward laughs. The wonky decor provided the mise-en-scene. The dancers brought the sex. I couldn't afford to tip them very much, but they seemed to know we were both in the same financial boat. They ran the gamut from scrawny, doe-eyed young guys to road-hard types that didn't smile or speak very much. Everyone wore some version of short shorts, Adidas or denim cutoffs. Athletic socks were pulled up to the knee, no shirt, headbands optional. The shorts were eventually pulled off to reveal either a pair of threadbare briefs or a G-string. Their facial expressions were an art form unto themselves, a projection of nonchalant stone-faced disassociation. They stared through the patrons with their X-ray vision. When the crowd was semi-ignored, it almost made it easier for them to part with their bills, in the hopes that they might finally be seen. Other dancers used engagement tactics, grinning eagerly or pursing their lips. They'd whisper in your ear, dangling the carrot. Usually it was a row of older men that sat at the bar. A beer in front of them next to a stack of bills, they brushed the dancers' legs with their fingertips, a signal that they were ready to feed the boys like a slot machine.

Seth and I spent our free afternoons on the beach; he liked the clothing-optional section. I've never been a total nudist; I needed some kind of swimsuit to feel comfortable. Seth had no problem strutting through the sand, his cock bouncing with each step. There were cruising trails that wrapped around the dunes behind us. We didn't use them but craned our necks to see the diverse plethora of men furtively strolling around the bushes to peddle their wares.

"I want to go to Europe," I said aloud one day as I was lying on my back.

"What's in Europe?"

"I don't know, I've never been." I had dreamed of backpacking by myself since high school. I wanted to ride trains and not care where I ended up. "I think it would be fun to just *go*. I'd need some money."

"You're certainly not gonna make enough packing boxes in a mailroom." He was leading to something. "Take out an ad, honey."

"Anne Marie and I already have one up in the back of the *Voice*," I said. "But she's scaring all our customers." We both howled and clapped our hands. I loved Anne Marie, but somehow she had become the abstract butt of every joke. All Seth had to do was say her name and we'd start laughing.

He shook his head. "Nah, you're too sensitive to be a hooker, hooker."

It wasn't as though the thought hadn't crossed my mind, in a sexy-fantasy sort of way. I could imagine myself answering calls on my phone, setting up dates, an independent professional. The friends of mine who were sex workers had their shit together like anybody else. But in reality I didn't want to risk changing my own relationship with sex. I'd managed in the past five years to rid myself of any hang-ups about sleeping with men, and I didn't want to jeopardize that.

"What about dancing? I'll bet you could get on at a night somewhere. You'd be good." He'd already thought about this.

"Oh Jesus . . ." I laughed, red-faced. "You think?"

"Well, you're definitely social. It ain't much, but you gotta body. You like to go out, meet guys. Bitch, if you started dancing, you could pay for you *and* me to go to Europe."

He was right: I loved going out at night and talking to people, was crazy about cutting a rug. The star filters in my head right then weren't just the sun playing tricks. I could see myself, standing above all those people's heads, my hands touching the ceiling, others' hands wanting to touch me. I started the following week.

16

BEFORE LEAVING THE CAKE FACTORY THAT FIRST night as a dancer, I laid my paltry options on my bed. There were some denim cutoff shorts and a pink string men's bikini that I had BeDazzled with silver studs around the waistband. There was a red and blue headband with matching cuffs. And a pair of sad, gray New Balance sneakers. I sighed, picking up and examining each item as I placed it in my backpack. It felt like I wasn't in my own body, like I was about to jump out of an airplane. So I actually yelped when I heard a crash hitting the other side of the wall of my bedroom.

I ran over to see what it was. Donavan was standing confused in his kimono, heavy eyes bloodshot and bleary, his room crumbling around him. Pieces of a broken vase lay underneath a dent on the wall where he had thrown it. "There was a demon in it," he said. "I had to let it out." I backed out of the room, got my things, and left. Something was gonna have to give, this place was getting seriously weird.

As I rode the subway, I thought of my mother's face. What would she think if she knew I was about to get on a bar and take my clothes off? Another subway pulled alongside and began racing with ours. Through the window I could see people reading, staring off into space. We were all headed in the same direction but oblivious of one another. Every time this happened, I'd wonder, *What if the love of your life was over there, in the wrong car? What if you caught a quick glimpse and never saw him again?*

IC Guys didn't look as festive as usual when I walked in. It seemed dirty, all the surfaces covered in a film. The room was mostly empty, with two guys standing around, none of the party lights on. The music was set at a soft volume. It occurred to me that I had never been there that early.

I nodded and said hello to Dave the barman, who showed me the "changing room," which was also the beer-storage closet. I wrestled the door closed behind me. Under the dim, bare bulb I began pulling my civilian clothes off, knocking my elbows and forehead into the shelves. My body had started to take on a more distinct shape, from working out. But I was still skinny, with a little pooch of a belly. I looked down at it. This was a terrible mistake. At least Seth was going to show up to offer moral support. I figured if there was someone I knew there, it wouldn't feel like I was doing something so seedy.

I walked out of the closet in a white tank top and denim cutoffs, my socks pulled up all the way to my knees. There were a couple more people in the bar now.

"Might be slow tonight," Dave said, his eyes sleepy but smiling. "I only put one other guy on, but you never know, might make a cool million. . . . Beer?"

I shook my head. It was going to be water from here on out. A drink would have calmed my nerves, but I didn't want to be fuzzy. I sat at the side of the bar, my mind racing. A few more middle-age guys with beards and shorts came in.

"Time to get up there." Dave slapped the counter. There were only a few customers. I was embarrassed. "What song you wanna start with?"

"You got 'Sexx Laws'? Beck?"

When the familiar horn riff started, Dave adjusted the volume, jumped up on a stool, and fiddled with some switches. All the lights shot on like a holiday feature in someone's front yard. I put one foot up and lifted myself onto the scarred wooden box, squinting my eyes at the spotlight. Dave was adjusting it to my height to focus on my torso. I was only about a foot and a half taller than the five people in the room. Lasers with no smoke skittered around like digital bedbugs on my skin.

I didn't know what else to do other than smile at whoever was looking and shuffle my feet. After Beck, Dave put on "Sexual" by Amber and I allowed myself a little more sway. The swing of my hips grew wider. When was I supposed to take off my shorts? I gave it at least ten minutes and pulled them down ungracefully. The elastic waistband got stuck on my sneakers and I almost fell over. My neon-pink G-string was awarded a couple glances from the guys. Finally one man who was there with his friend got off his barstool and tucked my first dollar bills into my waistband. It was official. He punctuated the gift with a pat on my ass and a smile, which I returned.

When a few more people came into the bar, I started to loosen up, my elbows raised, fists clenched, hands doing a jackhammer motion. As small as my audience was, it was still dizzying and mortifying at the same time. There were about ten people in there now, which in that place felt like a crowd.

Seth walked in, saw me, and started laughing and pointing, doubled over with his hands over his mouth. I flipped him the bird. For a split second, I felt conned. Had he suggested this just to see if I would do it? He wiped his eyes. "I'm sorry, I can't believe it. You're a natural." He stuffed a wad of cash under my belly button. "Honey, I'm afraid you've found your calling."

The other dancer showed up. He was around my age with a similar body, not the sharpest knife in the drawer. The two of us rotated stations. I watched him for cues, still having only half an idea of what I was doing. As the night stretched, I saw him get semi-hard. And he was letting guys touch it. I tried following suit but was too nervous to get anything near resembling a boner. But I still let some of the guys touch me.

By 2 a.m. the place had mostly cleared out, the music at a lower volume. I hopped down to have a drink at the bar with Seth, who had remained there with me to the end. I was relieved he'd stayed, because something in me felt awful.

"Well, you did it," he tittered. "What'd you make?" I had retreated to the broom closet only once to pull the bills out of my G-string. It wasn't much. Thirty bucks. "Ooh." He winced. "Yeah, it's a Tuesday. I wouldn't worry."

"No?" I looked at my sad stack of cash. "Do you think people will think I'm a hooker?"

He rolled his eyes. "And they'd be right, hooker. No one cares about that shit in New York." I felt like I had done something shameful and cheap. I had let guys feel me up for dollar bills.

"I'm not sure that was my idea of a great time," I said, folding the cash in half. That night I put the wad in an empty shoebox and slid it underneath my bed.

I did some serious thinking about whether I wanted to dance at IC Guys again. I loved the attention, entertaining a room, feeling desired. On a busy night, I could make enough money for it to be worth my while. But offering myself up like a goat in a petting zoo didn't sit well. So I made a decision: Every time I danced, I would pretend that my mom was in the room watching. Not that she'd be thrilled at my new vocation—I told her I had gotten a part-time job bar-backing— but I never wanted to do anything that I'd be ashamed of doing in front of my mother. From then on that was my rule.

The crowds got bigger and so did the cash flow. I preferred dancing on the bar, where I couldn't stand all the way up. But the ceiling gave me a place to put my hands. I could press upward and let my hips do all the work. There were a couple of exposed wires hanging above me. When I brushed up against them, I would feel a little electric zap. I tried to avoid them when I was dancing around in spilled beer.

The men sat at the bar, most of them alone and not saying much to each other. They just drank and stared straight ahead. Most of the time they wouldn't even be looking at me. But every few minutes they'd glance up, expressionless, and stick the bills in my shorts like I was a jukebox about to run out of songs.

I always had a squirt gun on hand. It was a fun way to flirt with people, and if someone became too frisky I'd squirt him in the face. Everyone got the point and no one seemed to mind. It didn't make me any less money, either.

I had a much better time if I didn't drink any booze. The tiny bar could turn into an oven, rendering me drenched with sweat. A quick shake of my head and it would fall like rainwater onto the heads of men below. To avoid getting dehydrated, I kept a jug of melon-flavored Gatorade at my feet, and every fifteen minutes or so I would tip it back and chug, letting the sugary liquid trickle down my chest. It gave me the energy for my piston hips, which were like a machine with multiple settings. I would leave the bar only for the broom closet, scooping the huge handfuls of gamey-smelling cash accumulated. Each night, my jockeys would fill up faster than the last. I'd have to take off my shoes and socks, where the money had been crammed in.

When I danced I'd feel the spirit of the room lift; people were more playful and exuberant. I began having fun, being an object of desire; people wanted to look at me, sleep with me, they were being entertained. But still, I was a boy—one without the body of those gods I saw every day at the gym.

Some guy named Tim approached me one night and asked if I would dance at a party called SqueezeBox at Don Hill's. It was a queer rock and roll night that had been going on for years already. I had been a couple times and it was fun, but everyone groused that it used to be better and that its days were numbered. Rock bands would play between Miss Guy's DJ sets. It was quite a change from IC Guys:

The ceilings were high enough for me to stand, and there were actual dressing rooms to change in. One of my heroes, Sandra Bernhard, was singing the night I danced.

During a break in between sets I went down to my dressing room and was organizing my bills in front of an old-style theater vanity, the kind with the light bulbs surrounding it, when the door flew open. An older, bleached-blond woman sauntered in with a couple of the go-go boys and they plopped down at the dressing table next to mine.

"You want some blow, doll?" she said, chopping up lines on the table next to mine.

"No, thanks. I'm okay for now," I replied.

"Good," she said. "Don't touch the shit."

Coke wasn't my favorite drug. I had dated a guy briefly who had a taste for it. I found it to be pleasurable for at least a half hour. My confidence doubled and my head felt like it was bolted on a little more straight, the eloquence of my words elevated. I would feel a tingle of possibility and optimism in my center. Then, as fast as it had come on, I would become uncomfortable. Sadly, the only thing that could make you feel better was having some more.

I glanced at the woman in the mirror as she cut her lines with determination.

"It's always wet, this stuff. Al. Ways. Wet. You'd think they'd have a microwave or something back here." Her lips smacked when she spoke. I knew that voice. I knew that face, had seen it many times years before on record sleeves, at my not-boyfriend Pete's apartment in Seattle.

"Are you Jayne County?" I couldn't believe it.

"What's it to you?" she replied, not looking up from her current project. Jayne County was formerly Wayne County, as in Wayne County and the Electric Chairs. My Pete had spent many an afternoon playing me the Wayne County records: loud, inspiring, grating stuff. And here I was, half-naked in a dressing room, watching her about to snort some lines. This is why I had fucking moved to New York.

"Oh my God, what are you doing here?"

"What the hell does it look like I'm doing? This isn't baking soda." She blew a rail and fluttered her eyes, tapping her nostril. "I saw you dancing up there," she said. "There's a good time written all over that ass."

"I just started. You think I'm all right?"

"You're all right, doll." She gave me a kind smile and laughed. "Keep it up and someday you might get a real job."

17

open window and stuck my face into the breeze. I needed air. The taxi smelled like an armpit—and not in a good way. The ride from the airport into Brooklyn was surreal. I had been gone only for about five weeks, but I could see right away that certain details of the city had switched, places had been renamed. Every new café awning or HSBC spotted was like being cheated on, proof that the world just went ahead without you. It was New York saying, *I think we've met. . . . What was your name again?*

My exhaustion was tinged with disappointment. I was like a kid who had opened his last Christmas present. After hitting Amsterdam, Berlin, Paris, and Barcelona, I'd found my last stop in London to be a let-down. When I'd arrived at my hostel I'd been finished with making new friends and had just needed a bed to pass out in. My camera had gone missing with a whole roll of film, pictures of people I wasn't sure if I would ever remember. My backpack was crammed with dirty T-shirts and crumpled brochures. I had managed to navigate my way around Europe with no plan, few clothes, not a lot of money, and a Bible-size *Spartacus International Gay Guide*, now warped and worn, marked with pens and stuffed with frantically scribbled phone numbers.

Already, the last month was a dreamlike blur of blisters, train rides, furtive glances. I'd slept in hostels or on the couches of strangers, dined with whoever was next to me. I'd dived like an Olympian into beds of boys who spoke no English, lost hours to my own daydreams, cruised bathhouses that were older than I was, spent afternoons with random people, playing walk-on roles in each other's lives. I'd cried on park benches in moments of sheer loneliness. Each new place felt impenetrable, and my aimless walking rarely revealed clues as to what it was I was supposed to be doing.

I wrote every day, high on hash and caffeine, and filled up notebooks with thoughts that could only come from social deprivation:

I feel like I have a constant need to perform for others. How often do I become detached from myself by playing to be someone who I think others want to see?

Why do I feel sometimes like I'm trying to imitate the boys who tortured me in high school? Maybe I loved their superhuman powers as much as I couldn't stand them. I want that ability to command. How easy it is to become a twisted version of yourself, stepping into roles inspired by people that we hated, turning into our own worst enemy.

With the detritus stripped away, the total anonymity, I had nothing else to offer but my own self. The only exception was when I was in Berlin, where my friend Andy was now living. It was the first time on the trip I had met up with someone who knew me well. We hadn't parted on the best terms when he left New York, so initially I was nervous about seeing him. But it turned out to be a reset button for our friendship. East Berlin had been just what he needed in his life. The city was popping off and Andy seemed truly happy for the first time.

I soaked up Berlin's blocky streets, the unkempt parks. People did as they pleased, without anyone looking over their shoulder. Andy and I spent our days going to gay beer gardens and DIY bars, some in people's actual apartments. The men were aggressively sexual, the music consistent and solid. Two DJs, Boris and ND, showed me around the city's techno underbelly. I ended up staying in Berlin the longest. But the guys, as hot as they were, could come across cold. I got my feelings hurt a few times. A guy whom I had a fling with told me at one point that he thought my friendliness was a put-on, like every other American's. That my warmth wasn't real. Nevertheless, I had a ball sleeping around and carrying on with Andy at all hours.

Back in Brooklyn, the cab pulled up to the front of the Cake Factory and I slowly shuffled up to the front door. As ratty as it still looked, it was home. The loft was quiet when I entered. There were a couple of lamps on, but it seemed like no one was there. As I approached my door, I saw a light coming from under the bottom of it. *That's strange.* I'd locked my room when I left. I twisted the knob and walked in. Leonard jumped up from the computer at my desk.

"What are you doing here?" he asked, his face flushed, trying to shove himself back in his jeans. On the computer screen was a JPEG of a naked woman with her legs spread.

"Leonard, why are you in here? My room was locked."

"I—I thought it would be okay if I got some . . . uh, work done on your computer."

"Yeah, looks like it." I threw my backpack on my bed. "You really shouldn't be in here, but whatever. I need food, I'm starving."

I shrugged off the fact that Leonard had broken into my room and was masturbating at my desk. I knew he meant no harm—he was just horny. I could relate. Desperate measures for desperate times. Leonard and I caught up over a burger and I forgot about the incident while I told him about my trip. It sounded like life had been uneventful around the Cake Factory. But that wasn't what Anne Marie said when she got home a couple hours later.

"Oh my God." She stepped into my room, wide-eyed and serious. She closed the door behind her as if there was a killer on the loose. "Jason, it's been really bizarre around here." I told her about the masturbatory spectacle I had just witnessed. She in turn revealed that Leonard wasn't the only person who'd been fucking with my stuff. Apparently, he had rented my room out to a couple from Brussels. They were in there for a month. "Total trash," she said. "And Donavan has been seriously out of it. I think he's a full-on junkie."

I could feel the blood pumping in my ears. They had rented out my room? People had been sleeping in my bed? I tore into Leonard's space and kicked his couch. "What the fuck? Renting my room? Are you kidding me?" He looked up at me, opening and closing his mouth, no sound coming out. I was boiling. "Fuck you guys. Your days are numbered here, you fucking prick."

My heart was still racing when I slipped into bed. I stared at my peeling ceiling. Strangers had been poking around my stuff, seeing my notes on the desk and flipping through my records. Those were my things, imbued with the meaning *that I had given them*. I imagined the couple from Brussels looking through my notebooks and laughing, making fun of my music. I was raging, but my thoughts soon puddled into my pillow. Sleep wasn't as hard to come by as I had thought.

After the room invasion incident, I refused to speak to Leonard and was only cordial to Donavan, who had really started to lose touch. One day I found him wandering around our floor wearing a nurse's face mask and wielding a machete. He drew a pentagram near the kitchen floor and placed two pears and an apple in it, told me he'd put his blood in the paint, and that it was a spell to capture Anne Marie's spirit. Neither Anne Marie nor I would touch the thing, and the fruit started to rot. Despite it being creepy, I thought the whole situation was kind of hilarious. I believed that Donavan wasn't capable of inflicting any real harm, and I still feel that way. Even when he was walking around with a machete it never seemed truly dangerous.

Anne Marie hatched a plan: We were both going to approach Graham, our landlord, and explain that Leonard had broken into my room and had pocketed money off of renting it out, and that Donavan was on a steady diet of heroin and wandering the place dressed like he was in *Mortal Kombat*. Graham's art studio was in the building. He was assembling some rusty-looking, boatlike structure. It was pretty ugly, but such things probably got him laid.

Anne Marie dressed the part, friendly and flirtatious. She was great at this. I marveled at her strategic body language, her subtle manipulation while I nervously wrung my hands. I had been wondering what was in this for her, but then realized that she simply wanted Donavan's bedroom, which was about three times the size of the dripping blood sac she'd been sleeping in for the past six months.

I felt guilty about all of it. I wasn't very good at ratting on people, so it was good to have someone as assertive as Anne Marie to help get the job done. I wanted Leonard out for sure, but I still felt bad for Donavan. Even though he was a junkie, I still thought he was a sweet guy. But then, on the other hand, he *was* painting pentagrams in the kitchen. Graham agreed that he didn't want those guys renting the floor and would start the proceedings to throw them out.

"Hey, by the way," he said as we were leaving. "If we get inspectors in the building we're going to need to move your beds out for a couple days." Oh, yeah, that's right, the whole thing was an illegal living space.

"Graham," I said, "is there any way you could take a look at the ceiling in my room? It's flooding every time it rains."

He paused for a second and looked at me, just like those mean boys in the hallway at school, like I still had teased hair and a skirt.

"You ever heard that song by Janet Jackson? What's it called? 'What Have You Done for Me Lately?' You've put enough on my plate. Don't forget to put your rent check in the freezer."

18

IT WAS FRIDAY AND THE COCK HAD SO MANY PEOPLE
crammed in it, you could practically swim through the crowd without
touching the floor. There had been the customary *New York Times*
article about how it was the new hot spot, so it looked like every
muscle queen in Chelsea had traveled down to inspect the plumbing.
The invasion was apparent just from the average circumference of
everyone's chests and the higher arch of their eyebrows.

The night was called Foxy, and the person responsible was Mario
Diaz, a swashbuckling party promoter from Seattle. He'd almost
single-handedly given the East Village its sleazy gay resurgence. The
party's slogan was "What would you do for a hundred bucks?" People
got up and displayed such talents as mixing cocktails in their rectum,
or attempting some drunken striptease. I heard a rumor that a girl I
knew had gotten up a few weeks before, taken her clothes off, and
ground the stage like a roadhouse stripper. When she bent over and
caressed her flanks, there was toilet paper hanging out of her butt. The
humiliation was part of the exercise, and to participate was to wake
up the next day and wonder where your life had gone wrong. But
each person was egged on in their act by the cheering crowd. At least
whoever achieved the most impressive display of depravity walked
away with a hundred dollars.

Justin Bond and Jackie Beat were hosting. I was amazed at

how fast those New York queens were: They made forked-tongued split-second decisions, brave enough to offend, their wit seeming progressively sharper the more drinks they consumed. Justin was gorgeous and imperturbable, looking like some '70s movie siren with her shoulder-length brown hair and smart backless dress. She had become almost mythical to me, ever since I had seen her Kiki and Herb show at the Fez. Jackie Beat, a brash drag queen, writer, and comedian, sat in a chair on the micro-stage, as standing for minutes might have proven too difficult. She was very large at the time, and I couldn't help but think of Mary when I watched her.

Behind where Jackie and Justin sparred with the crowd, you could see the "dark room" bottlenecking with people trying to get in. My writer friend Mattilda appeared at my side, wearing a glamorous polyester shirt with a butterfly collar, and a jump rope as a necklace. "There's a guy by the bathroom selling some coke," she said. "I'm just going to get some, do you want any?" I didn't do coke often, but I was already a little drunk, so I shrugged and said I'd split a bag with her. They were small, anyway. I could afford fifteen bucks' worth.

We elbowed our way into the back, where you could discreetly partake in the illicit activities of your choice. They were called "dark rooms" for a reason. Once you were beyond the entryway, only silhouettes could be seen, heads tilted back, spaced-out grunts pushing up from the inside, while teeth gnashed and lips parted. I blindly walked forward and tripped over someone crouched down, giving a blow job. Once we found some room, we dipped into the tiny bag, squinting our eyes to see if any powder had actually made it onto the key. Doing my best not to drop any of it on the floor, I inhaled deeply. My nose was suddenly on fire.

"OOWWWwww." I grabbed the side of my nostril. "Jesus Christ." My eyes watered. "That feels like fucking dishwashing detergent."

Mattilda frowned and decided to try some anyway, then held her face in pain. "Delicious! Unbelievably fresh," she said, laughing, her hands pinching her nose. "Only the finest coke at the Cock. Holy shit, that's bad. Laxative for sure. Probably going to be shitting for days. Guess I'd better do some K first." Mattilda started riffling around in her purse in the dark. "Found it! Talk about good luck," she said, and snorted some from her wrist.

"Let's get the hook," I said.

As we sidled our way out, some guy onstage was pulling out his half-hard dick and bouncing it around to "Magic" by Olivia Newton-John. I couldn't get a clear view of what exactly he was doing, but the crowd loved it. If it was a magic trick, there was no way it could beat Amanda Lepore pulling thirty feet of scarves out of her pussy.

Mattilda and I headed the six blocks to Wonder Bar, our conversation getting more abstract with each step; her K was kicking in. Wonder Bar was busy but not jammed. Mattilda excused herself to go to the bathroom and I found Seth, who was standing near the entrance, with some pale, sweaty guy who looked wasted. It was almost 2 a.m., time to go to my friend Matthew Delgado's penthouse.

Mattilda eventually came out of the bathroom and stared straight through me, upright but completely unresponsive. It looked like a pretty fierce K-hole. When she snapped out of it, she said, "Girl, you won't believe this. I had a hallucination that all the walls disappeared and everyone was watching me shit." I just grabbed her by the shoulders and steered her along with the group of about seven guys, including one stripper who had just finished for the night at IC Guys. We took the ten-minute walk to Matthew's place.

Matthew Delgado was a man who had tipped me fifty dollars in each one of my shoes one night at IC Guys. He was probably in his late forties. I made it clear that I wasn't a sex worker, but he didn't seem to care either way. Sexually, I wasn't attracted to him. But I liked his half-nurturing, half-sketchy demeanor: He was chatty, secretive, and charming. Most of his stories of sex and celebrities were horseshit, but I found his heart and love of a good time irresistible. Also, his two-story penthouse on the Bowery, with its terrace and hot tub, made it easier to forgive any minor shortcomings. It was fun to invade the place, pillaging his endless supply of alcohol and flopping around in the Jacuzzi like untrained dolphins.

Matthew's normally grouchy face couldn't hide his childlike glee as we blew in, everyone already casing the joint for plates and straws. He had already gotten some kind of party started, and there were a few hot guys there. I spotted a fledgling photographer whom Matthew let sleep in his windowless storage space in the basement. There was a ditzy and blitzed model, who already had his shirt off and was dancing to "One More Time" by Daft Punk. He was clearly celebrating his new Dolce & Gabbana ad campaign that was currently plastered all over the city. I pushed Matthew's two gigantic, unruly Rottweilers off of me and stepped into the kitchen to make drinks.

As I carried the cocktails up the spiral staircase to the second floor, I stepped around the piles of clothes already accumulated. Three guys were in the hot tub, a mess of barking queen soup. I stripped down to my underwear and joined them, gingerly sinking into the water, holding my drink so as not to spill it or slip and nail somebody with my elbow. The briny bath bubbled and popped around my shoulders. Oh, to be a little high, kind of drunk, floating over the Bowery. Arms and legs, boners and vodka tonics.

Matthew was going to let me house-sit for him the following week while he was out of town, in exchange for my feeding the dogs and watering the plants. That, plus going to visit my parents, would give me enough time to let my roommate business blow over. Anne Marie and I had managed to get Donavan and Leonard kicked out of the Cake Factory. I felt terrible, like I had betrayed Donavan. But he'd started acting stalky, showing up at Anne Marie's bartending job and staring at her from across the room, like a maniac. We'd had to file a police report.

The laughs and chatter came into focus around me. It was a conversation to be expected: Britney versus Madonna. Female pop star versus female pop star—the kind of thing many gay people talk about when they can't think of anything else to say. I let my eyes glaze over and lolled my head.

A man with a shaved noggin and tattoos was sitting next to me, not participating in the moldy dialogue. I made a face and shoved a gag finger down my throat. He flashed me a lovely, crinkled smile. His name was Steve. He was a bartender at the Hangar on Christopher Street, and the hottest thing I'd seen all night. We talked about music: Mouse on Mars and Pizzicato Five, which led us to extolling the virtues of Other Music, a record store on West Fourth Street and Lafayette that carried every record you've never heard of. I extracted myself from the man-bath to trot to the kitchen, dripping, to refill our drinks. Mattilda was doing runway in front of the stereo to the Grace Jones version of "Warm Leatherette" and had turned a blanket she'd found into a cape and a head wrap. She stopped and looked at me. "Girl, you want to try this on?"

I returned to the tub and sat in Steve's lap, his hairy chest on my back, his dick getting hard beneath me. Some other hot guy with a beard and short shorts emerged from the apartment, introduced himself, then got interrupted and caught up in another conversation.

"Who's he?" I asked.

"Ah, that's my boyfriend," Steve said.

That was a naive rookie move on my part. I'd let my guard down and gotten my hopes up at the same time. Excusing myself, I toweled off and dressed, making sure Steve got a good look at the ass he was missing as I hiked up my jeans. I threw my underwear in Matthew's dryer and passed the open door of his bedroom. There was a black leather sling hanging from bolts in the ceiling. *God help 'em*, I thought. They were going to have a long night. Without saying goodbye to anyone I slipped out and started the walk up to Fourteenth Street to catch the train.

19

IT WAS FEBRUARY OF 2001, AND I WAS WORKING at *Paper* magazine.

"So the Gucci sandals are priced at $399?" I asked with the phone pressed hard into my ear, cradled on my shoulder. I marked up my page with a red pen as fast as I could.

"That's correct," the man on the other end said. He was the head buyer at Barneys. I was halfway through fact-checking a small fashion piece that had to be turned in later that afternoon.

"Are the sandals from the summer collection?" I asked, moving down the list.

"Yes."

"Okay. Next, there's some kind of key chain thing from Hurmees that's priced at two hundred."

Silence on the other end of the line, then a laugh.

"What was that?" He paused. "What did you call it?"

"A key chain? Hurmees?"

He cackled. "Jesus Christ, did you just get here from Nebraska? It's pronounced 'air-may.' How can you not know that?"

"I'm sorry." I could feel my face flush. "I usually work on music articles."

"You might want to stick to that," he said.

I hung up the embarrassing phone call and turned to Gary Pini in the seat next to me. "How was I supposed to know it's not Hurmees? I can't afford to buy that kind of stuff."

"Not to be confused with herpes." He didn't take his eyes off his bulbous iMac. I sighed and realized I was crumpling the copy in my hands. I glanced around the office, worried that someone might have heard my gaffe.

Gary spun around in his seat, all sympathy. "Oh, those retail queens. Think they know it all. You got what you needed, just go turn it in." Gary was in his fifties, and the nicest guy in the office. He had formerly run a record label, and now Kim Hastreiter and David Hershkovits, the co–editors in chief, let him have his own space to work on various projects in his retirement. He always gave me tips on good parties that were happening downtown and seemed to know just about everything going on in the city at any given moment.

"You going to Click and Drag tonight?" he asked.

"Yeah, I'm dancing. You coming?"

"I'll make it eventually. I have to stop by Deitch Projects first. There's some dinner where these artists are apparently building a walkway over people while they're eating."

"Maybe that buyer from Barneys will be there and they'll drop a hammer on his head." I stood up and went to deliver the piece.

The office for *Paper* was a maze of desks and anxiety, deadlines and heads down, hushed conversations punctuated with loud exclamations, personality the most valuable currency. Mickey Boardman, the fashion editor, strolled up the aisles in his sequined cardigans. "I want cool kids doing fabulous things!" He clapped his hands, talking to no one and everyone at the same time. "That's what this magazine is about!" Copy was handed off as in a relay race, and any nonchalance was a ruse: With so much going on, everyone had to ignore each other to get any work done.

"Mark!" I grabbed at his sleeve as he shuffled past my desk. Mark Jacobs was one of the editors: a gangly, Roman-nosed party boy with a penchant for wearing '90s rave T-shirts. He was so ahead of the curve, he made things ironic while they were still in circulation. Mark stopped and looked down at me, expressionless. He didn't bother with a greeting.

"I'm dancing tonight, at Click and Drag. It's at FUN now . . . in Chinatown." I pulled out a flyer and placed it in his hand. He grimaced and walked away as if I had just handed him a religious pamphlet. "Debbie Harry's singing . . ." I called after him. He collapsed into his chair and put his head in his hands.

"Jason!" To my right, Erik Meers, my boss, materialized. "I've got four Beautiful People for you. I'll need them by the end of next week." He placed a small stack of xeroxed photos in front of me. "The contacts are on the back. Just take it from here, please." Erik was the managing editor, square and uptight, but gay with a pair of baby blues that were easy to get lost in.

I'd known I needed to find an internship somewhere, and working for a magazine sounded like the most fun. *Interview* was a long shot, and *Time Out New York* was utilitarian but not cool enough. I had been reading *Paper* since I had arrived in the city, and Peter Murdock, an interiors photographer I had met at the Cock one night, was a contributor and had taken me to a couple of their parties. They drew a pansexual mix of sophisticates without being too exclusive.

Paper's focus was on the creatives of the city. And through that office I saw a way in. I could eavesdrop and learn what people were up to, where they were going. To my interview, I had worn a maroon turtleneck and tight jeans, with a fake-fur-lined brown pleather snowbunny jacket. They called me to come in and work the next day.

It was my last semester at school and I had two writing workshops left, so I could be at the office most days. I was fact-checking and running samples to fashion shoots, and was eventually given small articles that no one else wanted to write. The first time I held an issue with two of my pieces in it, with my own byline, it was the closest thing I'd felt to fame.

Paper was started in 1984 by two friends, Kim and David, who were both imposing, intimidating figures. I marveled at the perspiring assistants with their thick skins as they frantically multitasked. When Kim or David walked by, I did my best to look busy, hoping both that they would and wouldn't notice me. I was ecstatic to contribute to the magazine, but understood that I didn't want to spend my life in an office. The best thing was the opportunity to interview people and get a glimpse of each person's creative process.

Whenever I was chastised for not getting an article turned in on time, I just stared up at the walls. They were lined with every *Paper* cover in order of the time they were published. It was a lineage of celebrated artists: Björk, Sandra Bernhard, the B-52's. I told myself that one day, my own face would be on one of those covers, up on that wall.

I took the xeroxed photos off the desk and slipped them into my backpack. It was five thirty, time to head to the gym. I stepped out onto lower Broadway, and the pedestrian traffic was a churning whirlpool. It took me a second to orient myself and find a walking rhythm before I accelerated, navigating my way past Canal Street, where the throng was the most dense. The sidewalks were full of Midwestern women with updos, walking in groups, on the lookout for bootleg bags. It was a strange ecosystem, these women doing deals in side alleys with people from all over the world, passing off cash for phony purses. Performing a kind of acceptable drug deal, they must have felt a simulacrum of danger as they stole away with their score to show off to their friends back home.

Crunch Fitness on Lafayette was packed by six. It was a warehouse of mirrors, all squatting, pushing, and heavy breathing. We gently flexed at ourselves when we thought no one else was looking, pulled up our tank tops for a quick peek at our abs. I stared at the older guys with their facial and chest hair, bubble butts popping as they climbed StairMasters to nowhere.

On the floor I did my best, learning form from watching others. I still thought I was too skinny, and never meant to be one of them.

After workouts, I'd look for any new signs of a body in the mirror and then scold myself for wanting what they had. I resented that I'd been trained to love such physiques.

At the machines I saw Benjamin, a bartender from Barracuda, pumping his legs. They looked like they could have their own address. He was a big French guy, out of my league, but always lovely to talk to. "Those hamstrings." I sat on the machine next to him and shook my head. "How the hell do you get those things?"

There were lots of characters around. Randy, the cowboy from the Village People, was always working out. Matt Damon was in the boxing ring occasionally. A few times even Britney Spears could be seen on the stretching mats. My favorite, though, was a guy who never left the treadmills. I called him Swamp Thing. He had an unhealthy green pallor and was always chugging two Venti Starbucks coffees while he ran for hours, his greasy hair hanging over his wet forehead. Super weird. I swooned over a hunky, rugged daddy type who'd had one of his ears torn off. Once, he honked the horn of his truck at me and waved as I was crossing the street on Lafayette. I felt like Sally Field winning her second Oscar.

In the locker room, it was hard to keep my eyes to myself. All the goods were on full display, muscles exposed, not having to strain against their stretchy gym clothes. V-shaped silhouettes soaped themselves up through thick banks of steam in the showers. Guys would keep the curtains only half-drawn. There were tiny holes ripped in them so some could peep. But it was creepy when you just saw eyeballs poking through the holes in the plastic. Eventually the gym put up more durable curtains, so people just had to leave them open, no more ripping.

Guys were more well behaved in the sauna. But it was still a morphing tableau of towels and glistening skin, a cramped box where everyone pretended not to look at each other. It was where I had met Iannis, with our towels barely draped over our dicks. He was a beefy Greek guy with a voice like Kermit the Frog, which drove me wild.

We exchanged small talk as we put our clothes back on at the lockers. I asked him if he had a boyfriend, which he confirmed. "But he'd love to meet you. What are you doing right now? Do you have time to come over? It's just up the street on St. Marks Place," he had said.

Their apartment was one long shabby rectangle; the bathtub sat in the kitchen, and the walls were lined with books. They had a pet tarantula in an aquarium. Iannis's boyfriend was an attractive poet in his thirties named Tom Breidenbach. He was quiet, with strange mouth tics and a steely reserve. Their apartment became my second home. Tom and I would get stoned on strong weed, listen to Patti Smith, and talk into the night, losing track of time. He'd flip through poetry books and read aloud. Some nights he would start his paranoid conspiracy-theory talk and a dark anger would bubble out of him. The three of us watched VHS Werner Herzog movies on their old TV, while I drifted to sleep on the couch, which was really just a twin bed. Sometimes we would have sex and then fall asleep until noon. I'd wake up first, wrap a blanket around myself, and sit by the window, maybe looking at a fresh coat of snow on the street.

They weren't the only ones I met at the Crunch locker room. I'd make small talk with half-dressed guys and get numbers to dial on weekends. A couple months before, I'd met a stunning boy named Ned Stresen-Reuter in a steam room at a Crunch in Midtown. I recognized him from the current Gap campaign. We hung out a few times, chastely, as if having sex would break whatever spell was pulling us together. Finally after a dinner at the Cowgirl Hall of Fame in the West Village, he came home with me. We made out for about five minutes in my bed, ravenous, gnawing each other's faces off, having held back for so long. I started barfing before we even took off our clothes. Must have been food poisoning from the dinner.

One of the hottest guys at the gym lived in an apartment above mine. He was a square-jawed superhero with preppy clothes, topaz eyes, and a Colgate smile. I couldn't understand why *he* of all people was flirting with me. Our location made things convenient: If we were both around I could jump up to his place, take care of business, and be out in an hour. Sometimes when we had sex I would go back downstairs, lie in my bed, and stare up at the ceiling, as if I could see through his floor. But the joy was fleeting. Sometimes we'd be covered in sweat, and I'd trace the lines of his form. He was literally in my hands, but still felt unattainable.

I had moved out of the Cake Factory in the fall. One night I was boiling water to make a pot of pasta, stepped out to pick up some laundry, and realized I had locked myself out. I didn't want to call the fire department. I thought they could break in our door and get us all busted for living in the space. So I decided to sprint as fast as I could to the L train, rode into the East Village, and ran all the way to Bowery Bar, where Anne Marie was bartending, me panicking that the loft was going up in flames. I arrived coughing and sweating. She gave me a set of keys and ten bucks for a cab ride back. By the time I made it back into the Cake Factory, the saucepan was burning and smoking the whole place up. I had been so close to setting the place on fire. I took it as a sign it was time to leave.

I moved into a spot on Bleecker Street, a block away from CBGB. It was a basement that used to be an old black-box theater. There were still pulleys and contraptions screwed into the wall where curtains had once been. I found the room from borrowing printouts that a friend had received from Rainbow Roommates, a service that helped queer people find fellow queer people to live with.

The apartment was basically one big room, with three makeshift "bedrooms" built inside. But the walls were only partitions, rising to about two feet beneath the ceiling. The entire place had no windows except for a tiny one in the kitchen. My roommates were two gay guys in their thirties named Matt and Tim. Matt had an office job and was obsessed with Broadway musicals. Tim was a DJ I had met one night at IC Guys; he had hired me to dance at SqueezeBox, where he sometimes controlled the lights. They were both odd and melancholy. I was their wild child, and the relationship was familial and caring, even though I interrupted their peace with my cacophonous comings and goings. Still, I think they liked having my energy around.

That night, Tim and Matt were perched in their usual spot on the couches watching *SpongeBob SquarePants*. "Hey, guys," I said as I rushed past them.

"Jason, that guy Steve stopped by to see if you were around," Tim called over my wall. "I told him you'd be back, but he just said to leave a message on his pager." Steve Kramer still refused to buy a cell phone. He was the guy I had met in Matthew Delgado's hot tub six months ago, when he'd been there with his boyfriend.

I had thought about him constantly since we'd met. So, one early evening on a whim, I had grabbed my copy of *A Home at the End of the World* by Michael Cunningham (whom I'd been stalking and begging for an interview) and taken it to the Hangar on Christopher Street, where Steve bartended. He had served me drinks while I read, and we'd talked in between customers. I was happy to find he was now single. We started dating. He was an easy crush: thirty-three, mellow and artistic, prone to making eclectic mix CDs and crafting light boxes using vintage porn and real butterfly wings. He could be guarded, withholding, and standoffish, a tactic that worked: I was obsessed.

In the new apartment, I had a strange, unfinished, tiny square of a bedroom, which I painted bright yellow to make it feel less like a tomb. But no matter how bright the walls were, it still felt cramped and claustrophobic. The discomfort was worth it: I was smack-dab in the middle of downtown now. I could walk just about anywhere I needed to go: the *Paper* offices, Crunch. At a brisk pace, it took me about twenty minutes to get to the Eugene Lang campus.

My evening's go-go wardrobe lay before me on my bed. The night was "biohazard-military themed" or something, so at the army surplus store I had bought a union suit, some combat boots, a gas mask, and a camouflage G-string that was two sizes too big. I tried it on one more time as if my dick might have magically grown in the last twenty-four hours. It was going to take a couple cock rings to even begin to fill it out. I had a camo bikini, an army-green trench coat, and a trashy long blond wig with a soldier's helmet for my girlfriend Jess, who was coming with me. She was going to look like Private Benjamin at the Spearmint Rhino.

I put an evening bag together and returned to the living room. My roommates were zoning out with a VHS tape of *Kiss Me, Kate* on Broadway.

"Debbie Harry hasn't performed in a while," Tim said glumly. "I'd like to see her tonight."

"Why don't you throw something on and come out?"

"Eh, I wouldn't be any fun. It's not been an especially good day." Tim had been sick for years; some days he was spritely, most days he was pretty slow. He almost never left the house.

"Well, call me if you change your mind." I finished zipping the bag and threw it over my shoulder. "All right, boys, time to make the donuts. Don't overdose on musicals."

"Don't overdose on adoration," Tim said.

Click + Drag was a technology fetish night that Rob Roth threw and had been going on for years, originally at Mother in the Meatpacking District; it had now moved to a new space in Chinatown called FUN. Rob only threw one every season these days, which made them all the more special. But the old one was before my time, so I didn't know the difference. The room could have fit an airplane, and had towering walls for video screens that stretched in all directions, causing a pleasing sense of vertigo on the dance floor. There was an upstairs lounge behind glass. You could look down at the crowd as if observing zoo animals under strobe lights.

Tonight, with Debbie Harry being the musical guest, the place was, as expected, rammed with people, packed and raucous. I danced behind strips of biohazard tape hanging from the ceiling like Mylar curtains. My gas mask became hot after a few songs, but I kept it on, loving how weird it looked with the G-string. You could see Debbie in the upper balcony, behind glass.

After her set, I took a cocktail up to the second floor and was introduced. She had an air of poise and detachment. "Thanks for letting me dance tonight," I said. "And for the great set."

"The gas mask was a nice touch."

"I almost fell off the platform a couple times. I couldn't see very well."

"Well, I hope it was worth it."

"I think my dick looked really small," I said, letting my mouth get ahead of me. "The thong was way too big and even with a couple of cock rings, I wasn't filling it out."

She looked amused, a tiny hint of a smile, and turned to greet someone else. God, I was such an idiot. And that was that: an entry-level lesson in the art of Nightclub Small Talk: Get in and get the fuck out before you say something really stupid.

The rest of the night was all tracers, drunk laughter, drinks spilling, and lips smacking. My girlfriend Jess and I walked home from the club. She wore the bikini and wig, her heels hanging on two fingers. We held each other up, limped through Chinatown, and basked in our party mission accomplished. My bed could have been made from peat moss: We wouldn't have known the difference. Mixing our limbs up in the sheets we slept, knowing that no matter how much water we drank, it was going to be a rough morning.

20

I NEVER CONSCIOUSLY INTENDED TO START WRITING real songs. I tell myself that it was an exuberant accident. But in truth, it's something I had dreamed of most of my life. But how could it ever become real? I could barely play an instrument, yet I sang all the time. I'd sing songs when I walked to the subway, when I made food. I'd make up melodies as I put myself to bed.

The dancing I was doing at parties and bars was getting a little rote. I would work on making my outfits more elaborate and outrageous, but would still feel a kind of dissatisfaction when I stepped off a platform, wondering what the endgame was.

Scott Hoffman and I had been hanging out the entire time I lived in New York. We had met through my college friend Lucy originally when I was visiting her one Christmas in Lexington, Kentucky. He was one of her longtime friends; they'd met in high school.

Scott and I had crossed paths again, when he was taking a road trip across the US and stayed with me for a few days in Seattle. The two of us had books, horror movies, and video games in common. We could talk for hours on end about the minutiae of David Lynch.

When I got to New York, Scott and I would meet occasionally for drinks or I'd go see his band performing up at Columbia, where he went to school. Sometimes he and some of his friends would come see me dance. He told me he'd been learning Logic one night when we were out, a music program. He said the two of us should make something together. "I want it to sound like Depeche Mode."

Scott's apartment in Park Slope was college-straight-boy undecorated, with a whiff of mildew. We popped open some beers and went into the makeshift studio. There was nothing on the walls, just a desk and some notebooks stacked around. He showed me Logic on the computer screen, an all-gray palette of boxes and horizontal lines. I had no idea what I was looking at.

"It's basically a sequencer. Like take this keyboard, for instance." He had a Roland Juno-60 from 1982. "This doesn't have any MIDI capabilities because it's so old, but we can lay down some notes and map them out on the screen, push them around if we play them wrong. Listen. . . ." He played me a fuzzy lead line.

We built our first beat, assembling the sounds and assigning each one to a different key on a MIDI keyboard. Scott would hit the record button and I would do my best to play while a metronome beeped in the background. Scott could go back in and quantize what I'd played out of time, move the misfired beats onto a grid. We cracked ourselves up making Satan voices into the microphone or pitching our voices down to make ourselves sound like giants. We twisted knobs on the Juno for hours, losing time and listening to sounds modulate. Finally Scott said, "Let's just put a song together."

The first thing we wrote was called "Talking to Databases." I couldn't think of any lyrics off the top of my head, so I just read out of a computer manual in a staccato, sinister voice. We had a chord progression that lifted up the dark feel, and I came up with a melody for the chorus.

"Hey, I sound like Cher!" I said, referring not to robo-Cher but to actual Cher. We laughed and hooted at each turn, and at the end of the night we had a little song, perhaps a stupid one, but it was still a marvel to listen to something we had created.

During the weeks after, I returned a few more times in the evening. We would lay down a beat first and come up with a simple bass line with what we thought to be an interesting synth sound. The lyrics came quickly. We wrote one called "Step Aside for the Man." By no means did we strive for perfection:

> 'Cause I'm a real nice guy and I'm free as hell
> To be a cornpone faggot dressing really, really well.
> In my big black boots and my denim Daisy Dukes
> I got my bleached-blond hair and my leather underwear.
> You know I'm fine, 'cause I work it all the time.

The words just came off the top of my head, and I wasn't really paying any attention to whether they were good or not. Mostly we just thought they were funny. I was getting a kick out of poking fun at myself and the city around us.

There were a couple more tunes. One was called "Backwoods Discotheque." Another called "How Many Times." But summer was approaching and major transitions were happening all around. I was about to graduate school and leave on another backpacking trip to Europe. I didn't think about making music again with Scott for months.

My relationship with Steve Kramer was painful at moments. He enjoyed my company and liked having me around, but I wanted to get swept away, my emotions taken care of and looked after. His apartment had been a wonderful respite from the dank basement dwelling I had been living in, but the reality was that he was still having to look out for himself. He was in what he called a "deep thaw," coming out of a period in his early thirties of significant partying. He would look at me in the backs of cabs and say, "You know I adore you." But I knew well enough by then that adoration wasn't love.

My demands put him off. I insisted on time spent together, more sex with energy he didn't have after working in the bar all week. I knew when he told me it was fine if I wanted to fool around with other guys that his absence of jealousy was a sign of his lack of attachment.

I graduated college at the end of May at Radio City Music Hall, and my parents came to attend the ceremony. My father wasn't too keen on being in New York, but my mom was taken with its glamour. I could tell they were both proud that I had lived there for two and a half years and had somehow stayed on my feet. While they were in town I took my mom to the East Village bars one night, to all my favorite haunts, including the Cock and IC Guys. I refrained from telling her that I had been dancing at these establishments, but she was just thrilled to be out with me and basked in the lovely attention she got from my gay friends. She rolled her eyes and shook her head at some of the raunchier dancers. Surprisingly, she had a sense of humor about it. I think I inherited my mom's lovely capacity for handling just about anything.

I'd always had a safety net. It was called "Mom and Dad." If anything bad happened, if I were to run out of food, get stranded, abducted, whatever, I knew my parents would get me out of it. Their love was a luxury that afforded me more than perhaps I deserved.

By the time I had finished high school, my parents had mostly accepted my gayness. But it wasn't until I graduated college that I began to feel my dad's full support. I was the first person in our family to finish school; I think he realized that, gay or not, I had my shit together. The trust and the freedom, the low-friction ride they provided might have been a by-product of their pity. Perhaps by me turning out homo, they thought I'd been handed a shit deal, or perhaps *The Joy of a Gifted Child* didn't include a chapter on the ways my gifts could be a joy. They must have been amazed that I hadn't blown it, given the prior difficulties with my siblings. Yes, I did drugs, had sex with men, and stayed out late. But I still showed up when I was supposed to, turned my papers in on time, stayed busy with my passions. I'd mostly steered clear of being a mess.

The night I graduated, I had dinner with my parents, then decided to go out to the Roxy. I sat at the bar sipping a cocktail and letting myself feel proud for a moment. I'd majored in creative writing, and college was finished. There had been no stunts pulled, no crappy grades. (If you didn't count the last F I'd received in a writing workshop for forgetting to turn in a novella I'd written. The college let me walk in the ceremony, but to this day, I've never actually seen a diploma. Whoops.) Unease, though, traced itself around the good feelings. As I looked out at the packed dance floor, here in this city I loved, I thought, *What now?* I had virtually no idea how the hell I was going to make a living. Dancing certainly wasn't going to pay all the bills. The thought of getting some office job made my skin crawl. I knew nightlife or bartending could be an okay Band-Aid, but that wasn't where I wanted to end up in the long run.

I glanced up to my left, and there was a man with silver hair wearing a black T-shirt who was looking at me and smirking. He was a fox. His gaze was straightforward and at the same time a little bashful. We approached each other. His name was Anderson.

"Oh, wait." I suddenly realized that I recognized him. "I used to watch you when I was in high school. You were on *Channel One News*." It had been a show that was broadcast daily into public schools. Each episode was about twenty minutes and kept students abreast of current events. In my ninth- and tenth-grade years, we watched it every day in class. "I used to see you dodging bullets in Bosnia." His adventures had always stuck with me. "That shit looked dangerous."

"Ah . . ." He waved it off. "Wasn't bad. I liked it."

I asked him if he was still doing it, and he told me that at the moment he was hosting a reality game show called *The Mole*. But was still doing some news anchoring. "It's very early in the morning," he said.

"Does that mean you're leaving here in thirty minutes to go sit behind a desk?"

"I have tomorrow off—thank God. I just wanted to come out tonight and have some fun."

We looked around at the club and nodded our heads, silent for a moment. It occurred to us at the same time that we were both out alone. He took my hand and we went to the dance floor. I made faces at most of the circuit music, I was never a big fan, but I was just happy to be out, dancing with a handsome man. We got some more drinks and found a couch on a secluded side of the dance floor. I leaned over and we shared a sweet kiss. The bass vibrating through us only seemed to amplify the connection.

Anderson and I went back to his little first-floor apartment in the West Village and stayed up the rest of the night talking and thumbing through his book collection, laughing and making out. I was impressed with all his first editions and with the pictures of him all over the world, waist-deep in water, dusty in deserts.

After a few hours' sleep we got up and decided to go to the Ziegfeld to see *Moulin Rouge!*, which had just opened the day before. While we watched the movie, I laid my head on his shoulder, exhausted. But afterward, we still had enough energy to take my parents out to dinner at some Moroccan restaurant on Houston.

Anderson was sweet with my family, talking to my father, who could be formidable, with ease. I'm sure my mom was wondering where Steve was, but he hadn't seemed too interested in me lately. I told her he was out of town visiting his family in Pennsylvania.

Anderson and I met again two nights later. We had dinner and spent the night together. I told him I was going to be traveling Europe again, and it turned out he would be in Italy shooting his TV show. We decided that we would meet up, and though I wouldn't have a cell phone, we would stay in touch by email. On my way out the door he said, "Wait a minute," and handed me a picture of him standing by himself in front of a sunset. "Maybe you can take this with you," he said.

Before leaving on the trip, I was back with Steve for my last night in New York. I spent the time after graduation packing my stuff from the

Bleecker Street apartment and putting it in storage. My roommates
Tim and Matt seemed sad to see me leave the nest, but I knew there
was another go-go boy lined up directly behind me to take my room. I
took care of all my final business and brought my backpack to Queens
to spend one last night with Steve. We were contemplating what to
get for dinner when he picked up my huge gay *Spartacus* guide to
Europe and thumbed through it.

"Who's this?" Steve said. He held the photograph of Anderson
up. I hadn't even thought about him finding it, having forgotten I'd
slipped it in the book.

"His name's Anderson."

"Is he your cousin or something?"

I paused for a moment, knowing I could lie. But then didn't see
the point. "No, we met the night I graduated. We've gone on a couple
dates."

Steve's face fell. He stood up from the sofa, pale, and retreated to
the kitchen to pour himself a glass of water. I sat wringing my hands,
confused as to whether I'd really fucked up.

"So you have another boyfriend." He came back into the living
room.

"No, we just met."

"Nice," he said, bitter. "Nice one."

We went outside for a walk. Steve stared at the ground, knowing
he'd just lost a relationship, albeit one he hadn't necessarily claimed to
want in the first place. I'd thought we could be boyfriends, in my naive
way. But he wouldn't give me the attention I needed. What I didn't
quite understand yet was that no single person would be ever be able
to give me the level of attention I needed.

Barcelona was my first stop. I started there to attend an electronic
music festival called Sónar that Gary Pini at *Paper* told me about.

I arrived as planned the day before and spent the rest of the week-end there. The daytime part of Sónar was held at the contemporary art museum; the nighttime portion was at the soccer stadium. Every day I sat out in the sun by myself and listened to different DJs I'd never heard, playing sets of glitchy, sometimes challenging electronic music. At night, bands and more commercial DJs would play. Sonic Youth did an experimental set back-to-back with Richie Hawtin, that sort of thing. I took notes, took pictures of revelers. The crowd was studied and there for the music, eager to get turned on to new things. There were other shows going on around town, most notably Fischer-spooner, who played a set at a club called Lolita.

By now, I had been to multiple shows of theirs in New York. Their performances had evolved a bit, with more distinct costumes and ad-ditional dancers. It was a bigger production, an electronic flapper fever dream. Before their set started, I was by myself and looking around for some ecstasy. After I asked around to no avail, people must have got-ten their hands on some, because it seemed like everywhere I turned, someone was popping a pill into my mouth. By the time the band was finished my eyes must have looked like they were swallowing my face, I was so high. A cute young man from Venezuela took me by the hand and led me into the square to have a beer. I swear to God I was fluent in Spanish that morning.

When the sun started to rise, the guy took me on a train to a vil-lage in the mountains. It seemed like the middle of nowhere. A light rain started to patter around the greenery as we entered his modest flat, fooled around, and fell asleep for a couple hours. And so my sum-mer journey proceeded in this manner.

But with the time alone, I was haunted by my sick heart. I had to face the reality that Steve and I were over. I had acted fairly casual about our breakup, but I realized once I was on this trip that I was grieving him. There were many long walks alone, or train rides with no one to talk to that allowed too much space in my head. I seethed with jealousy when I thought about Steve back at home sleeping with other guys. In tiny rooms with single windows and stiff beds, I wrote letters that would remain unsent. Though I knew my heart would be stitched up and healed, there would always be a little scar with his name on it. In retrospect, Steve had been pretty good to me. I had been the one to be a demanding, sullen little fucker.

There was plenty of quiet time, but there was also a plethora of distractions. It was like my first summer in Europe, but the sequel was on steroids. I was a wandering drifter, in search of amiable people and moments worth remembering. Some towns didn't strike my fancy, but there were boys everywhere.

I snuck a guy and his dog into my room in Montpellier, France. I shacked up with a Danish couple I met at a party in Amsterdam. Sometimes a tryst would turn into an adventure. One evening, I picked up a man from a restaurant in Marseilles—which I was very thankful for, because I had found little worms in my bed in my disgusting hostel. When he dropped me off at first light the next morning, a group of boys stole my camera, while asking me some question I didn't understand. I chased them down the streets hollering; we ran for blocks in the early-morning light. When I threw all my cash at them, one of the guys gave me my camera back. I returned to the filthy hostel, grabbed my backpack, and headed to the train station to get the fuck out of there.

I was always pleasantly tired and slept whenever and wherever I could, whether it was under a tree in a park or on some kind stranger's couch. Sometimes I paid for places to stay; often I didn't, preferring to meet people and share food and stories. I prowled the discos and had drinks on the barstools whether the place was alive or dead.

By the time I got to Italy, I was relieved to see Anderson's familiar face. He was shooting the show in Lucca, a tiny walled-in village about an hour from Rome. I was taken to his hotel room before he got off work. When he walked in I had my contacts out and a mud mask on. We talked and slept for a few hours before he had to return to taping his show, tired but happy to see me. "I've been around these people so long who are so obsessed with this game, I don't really know how to act," he said. But we were content just being ourselves. The next morning we read the news together, and I headed to Florence, then Rome, where I would meet up with him in a few days.

It was the first LGBTQ pride week in Rome, and it seemed like everyone was in the streets. The days were a sweet blur of boys and food. I connected with some friends from New York, and spent a day swimming at a literal castle. I watched in horror as some new Italian friends I'd met dined on raw horsemeat in their kitchen. I spotted one of my favorite Bel Ami porn stars with an older American businessman who had hired him for the week. After a couple dinners together, the older guy tried to get me to come have a three-way with him and the model. I was tempted but didn't do it.

I met up with Anderson there, and we stayed at a flat of a friend of his, its balcony overlooking a beautiful piazza. We shopped and lounged, wandered the Colosseum, napped and fooled around, ate giant plates of pasta. It was just for two days, but we had a rhythm with each other, and established a friendship that is alive and well to this day. He remains one of the loveliest people I know.

My last night in Mykonos was heavy. I went out by myself and was picked up by a group of guys: two Germans, one Swiss guy, and two New Yorkers. One of them was a Broadway dancer who seemed to take himself the least seriously. We all went back to a hotel room and fooled around. By the time I shuffled back to my little rented room, I felt gross. The sun was coming up and the stores were opening. I had spent too much of myself.

The light was just starting to appear in the alleyway outside my room when I heard the first screams. They came from the window right across from my own. It was a man and woman in an argument. I couldn't understand what they were saying, because it was in Greek. Their voices escalated and I heard a huge slap and the woman shrieking. His big deep voice thundered into my room—it was like he was right there, sounding like a demon. Huge crashes, like he was throwing her into a wall. I ran into the main area of the house where I was staying, and the little old landlady who could speak no English was standing in the kitchen, listening as well. She had been sweet and taken good care of me, but when I walked out she put a finger to her lips and shook her head.

"But it sounds like she's being killed." I was frantic. Somebody had to help this woman.

The old lady said something in Greek and, with her hand motions, it said to me, "Be very quiet. This is very sad, but we don't say anything or talk about it."

I realized that it was probably a regular occurrence. I ran back to my room and amidst their screams I threw all of my clothes and books and my journal into my backpack and brushed my teeth. I was getting out of there, getting the fuck off this island. Obviously, I had overstayed my welcome. I gave a curt goodbye to the landlady and fled to the docks, where a ferry was just about to leave. I bought a ticket to the island of Andros and sailed.

The sea stretched before me and I grasped the rails of the ferry. It was going to be a hot day—I could already feel the sun burning on my skin. It was July 24, 2001, 8 a.m., and I hadn't slept. My large backpack rested at my feet as I watched the foamy wake of the boat as it sliced through the still waters. Mykonos was growing smaller in my sights, shrinking into a speck. I needed it to shrink. Everything had gotten too big in the last twenty-four hours. I felt empty. Something had shifted. I was rudderless.

The shining white of Mykonos was burned into my retinas. I had allowed myself to get sucked in, a wholly pleasurable experience, but now I was totally alone. I'd heard Andros was a quiet spot. I didn't need any more stimulation. But nothing would have prepared me for the earsplitting silence I would find when I arrived.

I had now been away from the States for a month, floating and roaming. I thought I was getting the hang of being on my own. But my heart was a tangle of romance and late nights. I had allowed it to open too wide, had let down my guard with everybody. My carelessness had left me feeling like shit.

Now it was just this boat on the blue water. I sat on a bench and rubbed my eyes, feeling the stinging tears well up, my throat closing. Andros was a big dirt rock in the distance coming closer and revealing itself as nothing but a dock. I disembarked from the ferry and walked toward the only building I saw, my backpack feeling as heavy as the cloud in my mind. The stumpy building just sat like a gravestone on the empty street. I turned and looked back as the ferry pulled away. There was no one here.

The lobby was dark and hot. All the windows were open and there were two fans above, their rotations lazy. The long-haired man at the desk gave me a room for forty dollars.

It was scuffed and simple, with a small window looking out at the sea. I set my backpack on my bed with unease. The only noise was the soft whir of the fan. I had just made yet another miscalculation. I had managed to place myself in a purgatory. I laid my face in my hands and cried.

That room was like an arid tomb. I missed Anderson and Steve. But perhaps I was just addicted to the feeling of possibility. I flipped through my CD book and pulled out the Tangerine Dream score to *Thief*, popped it into my Discman, and headed outside to find somebody renting scooters.

I rode to a beach and wandered down from a huge rocky hillside. Once I made it to the shore, there wasn't a single person there. I walked, pulling all my clothes off, the sea lapping at my toes. Like most times when I had nothing to do or nowhere to go, I decided to jerk off out in the sun. Around me it was as if the world had emptied out. It was like being in a blinding waiting room to the rest of my life. My sadness and boredom surged into momentary bliss.

After I came, I turned around and realized I hadn't been alone. A large white goat was standing on a rock, staring. "How'd I do?" I said. The goat looked unimpressed.

On my walk back, as I started up the side of the mountain, my footsteps became heavier, my breathing labored. It occurred to me that I hadn't brought any water as my vision began to swim. I was ravenously thirsty and tried to focus on the climbing, my general sadness taking a backseat to fear. I wasn't sure if I was going to make it back without passing out. There was no shade or escape from the sun. When I finally reached my bike and returned to the hotel, it was on burnt and weaving legs. I stuck my head under a cold faucet and gulped huge mouthfuls of water.

August 9, 2001

Last night I was in Berlin. Andy played me "Nutbush City Limits" while I lounged on his bed. Can't believe I've never heard it, holy shit it's good. I was so tired, but wanted to go out anyway, I didn't know if I could do it, so this guy Lester gave me

*a tiny speed bump to swallow that was wrapped in a little bit
of paper. We then headed to Ostgut. A massive wild club, must
have been an old factory. We danced and talked and finally at 4
a.m. we left. Some friends walked me to the ATM because I had
no money on me. But none came out. So I didn't think I could go
to Budapest. Someone gave me five marks for the train, and an
ATM in another neighborhood let me take some money out.*

At 6 a.m. I packed my bags and called Mary from a pay phone at
the train station, using a calling card number my mom had given me
for emergencies.

"Have you checked the children?" I asked in my gravelly devil voice.

"Where the hell are you?" she said. "You sound like you're underwater."

"I'm calling from a toilet bowl," I replied. "It's the best new club
in Berlin."

"What time is it there? Please tell me you've slept."

"With just about everybody. I'm headed to Budapest. Got a
twelve-hour train ride or some shit. I'm exhausted."

"I literally just read your horoscope in *The Stranger*. You wanna
know what it says?" I heard her rattle a paper. "'Okay, the fun is over
and it's time to get to work.' Baby needs to come home."

"I know," I replied. "I'm trying not to think about it."

"What is your plan exactly?" Her words hung in the air. I glanced
around warily at all the purposeful, fresh-faced Germans starting their
day. It was a question I'd been avoiding asking myself. I'd been winging
it for years, and now the protection that college had provided was
over. Reality was starting to encroach from the periphery: I had no
fucking clue what my plan was.

PART 3

SCISSOR
SISTERS

21

I WAS SLEEPING AT MY PAL GREG'S THE MORNING THE towers fell. There were four of us piled in the bed after a lovely drunken home-cooked feast the night before. The crash woke us up. We looked at each other bleary-eyed and confused, thinking that there had been a car accident down on the street. My friend Julie must have gotten up to go look out the window, because I had fallen asleep again when she ran into the room screaming about a plane.

We walked up a couple of flights to the roof, squinting our eyes at the bright blue sky. Still in my underwear, I had a blanket wrapped around me like a cloak. Greg's place was on Grand Street in SoHo: We were so close. The buildings loomed above us, one with a jagged mouth on the side, red flames lightly licking its perimeter. A plane had gone in, people were saying. No one really knew what kind it had been. Was it just a little prop plane that had lost control?

We didn't see the second plane, because it came from the south side toward us. There was just a huge explosion, a fireball shooting out of the tower. Everyone jumped and screamed, suddenly chittering like animals. Was it a missile, a bomb? Were there other missiles coming? "We should get inside," we said. Greg didn't have a TV, but we found a radio. Up and down the stairs I went. Trying to hear, trying to see. All the bits sparkling, falling from the building. What looked like confetti was people. When the buildings crumbled, I told myself they were just on a giant elevator, being lowered into the ground.

Greg and I ventured out into the street with no destination in mind. The sidewalks were jammed. I kept listening to bits of conversation, trying to piece together what others were saying. Thoughts were scattered, people talked about other things, in shock. We went to Matthew Delgado's penthouse for a few minutes and had some coffee and then walked to my friend Mark Tusk's, where we smoked some weed and listened to soul records. We finished off with some tuna sandwiches at Veselka. The transactions were grim-faced but kind, a sick understanding unsaid. Word was that we were going to have to get out of downtown. Everyone under Fourteenth Street was being evacuated.

I found a working subway to Michael Warner and Sean Belman's, two friends I had recently made in Brooklyn and was staying with. I'd had an apartment I was about to sublet on Twelfth Street and Avenue A. But now, after the evacuation, I wasn't going to be able to move in for a while. Who knew when they were going to let people back downtown?

Michael was on his way back from his teaching job at Rutgers. Sean and I gazed out their window at the sunset, looking at the neutered skyline. We turned to each other and kissed, had sex on the floor, trying to forget what we'd seen.

We convince ourselves we have some kind of control over our fate. And to a degree, I guess we actually do. But so much of life is a reaction to our surroundings and circumstances, on small and grand scales. Decisions are so often made for us; tragedy can define your direction. Starting a band was all I could think of to do. Maybe it was just that now I had an excuse. Maybe it was a brief window of time when no one was going to grab my arm and stop me and say, "Hey, what do you think you're doing?"

On September 21, Scott Hoffman and I were at the Slipper Room. The stage we stood on was dark, the curtain closed. I was nervous, and looked over at Scott, who didn't seem too bothered. The hostess of the night, Ana Matronic, was in front of the crowd, announcing us. "Ladies and gentlemen, I'm going to introduce to you a new band. All the way from Finland . . . Just kidding. But they are a new band, and I wish I'd come up with the name myself: Scissor Sisters!"

The curtains parted. The room in front of us was full. Faces stared back, expecting something. Scott pressed play on the minidisc player and gave me a nod, and our staccato synth started. I must have been inspired by my psychotic former roommate: I was wearing a kimono. I took the microphone in my hand and began to sing.

> *I see you dancing*
> *Damn, you look good*
> *I wish I could dance like you*
> *But I ain't got no legs*
> *I see you having sex*
> *Damn, you look good*
> *I wish I could have sex too*
> *but I ain't got no sexual organs*

People were laughing. My voice was shaking, rattled from my racing heart. But the number was landing.

> *I rode the bicycle of the devil*
> *Riding straight to hell.*

This wasn't my first time onstage at the Slipper Room. I had performed there the previous spring for a night called Knock Off. One of the hosts was Ana, whom I'd met at a party at this guy Joe Corcoran's house. He was a mutual friend who made music under the name Hungry Wives. He would throw parties in his loft under the Williamsburg Bridge.

The first time I saw Ana, she was wearing a green velvet dress and a red wig. We were both very drunk. She told me she threw a performance party called Knock Off that had different themes every week and handed me a flyer. The next one coming up was an aerobics theme. I internally rolled my eyes. Aerobics? I'd already thrown an aerobics party two years before. I could be such a snob.

But I did have an act I wanted to try out. For Halloween I had dressed up as a back-alley late-term abortion and my friend Lucy was the RU-486 morning-after pill. My costume had been vivid: a bald cap, umbilical cord, and coat hangers bursting through my chest, dripping with blood and gore, shit hanging off my face. It was hideous. I decided to try the outfit again and go as "Jason, the Dancing Back-Alley Late-Term Abortion." Hey, I never claimed I had any taste.

When I did the abortion routine at Knock Off, a drag queen in mom jeans named Mangela Lansbury, also performing that night, dragged me out to the stage inside a black garbage bag. I burst out, reborn in a glam New York nightclub, and did a dance routine to "Goddess," the main theme from *Showgirls*. Thank goodness the number came toward the end of the proceedings. The other performers probably wouldn't have appreciated the leftover blood on the stage.

That third week of September, with the smoke still hanging in the air, no one seemed to know what to do with themselves. I was supposed to be looking for a job, but hiring would be scarce. So I hung around Scott's apartment like some deadbeat while we started messing around with recording again. He would man the computer while I banged away on a keyboard. It was a lot of stopping and starting, but we were learning some new tricks as we worked. There was novelty in making sounds and hearing them come back out of the monitors. The time Scott and I spent together, laughing and coming up with rudimentary songs, was at least a way for us to get our minds off the chaos just outside our doors.

At his apartment, about a week after the tragedy, I went to get a glass of water in the kitchen and came back with an idea. "Let's take this song and go sing it somewhere," I said. People were sad. They needed to be entertained. We could go do it at that Knock Off party at the Slipper Room. There was one on Wednesday.

I had recently been walking down Fifth Avenue and had a vision of a stationary bike, with a fan blowing on me, wearing a kimono. The song would be called "Bicycle of the Devil." Scott and I thought it was stupid and hilarious.

Within minutes Scott had mocked up a logo of a pair of scissors wearing high heels. And there we were, three days later, singing lyrics maybe even more juvenile than my high school days, in front of a crowd with their mouths agape:

> I see you defecating
> Damn, you look good
> I wish I could take a shit too
> But I ain't got no anus.

Someone turned on a strobe light and my kimono went flying, revealing a leather G-string, combat boots, and a harness. The flashing lights reflected off Scott's round goggles while I finished the number, gyrating and grinding. It was all I really knew how to do at the time. When the number ended, people clapped and hooted. I felt like my heart was going to explode out of my body.

That was the beginning of Scissor Sisters.

22

NEW YORK WAS AN EMOTIONAL WASTELAND. PEOPLE were trying to find normalcy, going about their routines, but underneath it was an awful fear. You could see it in every stranger's eyes, in the reams of MISSING signs still on every lamppost and on the sides of bodegas. It was like an uncanny parallel world we'd been thrust into.

I finally moved into my East Village apartment on Twelfth Street and started putting together résumés for assistant positions at various magazines. But it was a charade: There were no jobs to be had. For extra money, I was writing articles for the local gay rags. But for the rest of 2001, interviewing Crystal Waters or Amber about their new singles seemed pointless. When I was talking to artists about their work, it was as if they'd run out of things to say. The walls of my new apartment were small and imposing, but I was comforted by their swaddle—it was a new kind of privacy. There was no one watching me: I was finally in a place on my own. The sex noises I now heard came not from roommates, but from pigeons hanging out on the window ledge.

The woman I was subletting from was uptight, but I had a feeling that she wasn't coming back. If I played my cards right, I could take over the lease, which was rent-controlled, to boot. As cheap as it was, I still had to come up with the dough. Magazine articles were a cushion, but they didn't pay particularly well.

A cloud of uncertainty lingered. I still didn't know what I was supposed to be doing. I loved the city, but I longed for more freedom inside of it. Having a boss in an office didn't feel free to me. I looked at friends of mine, college graduates who had been working for the new barrage of start-ups. Every subway or TV ad you saw was for some kind of dot-com. It seemed like all my friends had been hired. I watched them, actors, writers, and musicians chained to their hours and complaining that they didn't have time or energy to pursue the things that mattered to them.

The weeks through September and October were strange in that they became a lot of fun. Much of the city was at a standstill, but clubs and bars were packed at night, smelling of musky hedonism. My friends were getting drunker than usual, finishing the nights with tricks in tow. There was a sense of abandon, a communal shoulder shrug about the future. We'd go to a firefighter's funeral by ourselves, somewhere specific to cry. And at night our dark humor prevailed. *"What buildings, hunny?"* we'd say in our best bimbo voices, and cackle. Small talk was sweeter than usual, the kisses more lusty. I was living now almost right above the Cock, so it was easily accessible from my apartment. At any given moment I could walk downstairs and get drunk or laid.

A bar in Williamsburg opened up called Luxx and became a trendy place to go on the weekends. It was a medium-size joint with a long bar on one side and a sticky carpeted stage on the end. Next to the DJ booth was a go-go cage. The place was bursting with so many cool kids, their fabulousness almost canceling each other's out. On Saturday night was a party called Berliniamsburg that DJs Larry Tee and Spencer Product had started. The music was electro, abrasive and homemade, the kinds of tracks that people had started making in their own apartments. It was all flat kick drums and bored-sounding girls, lamenting the death of clubs, of fame.

"I mean—they don't want us dancing in the city, so we had to take it all the way out to Brooklyn," Larry said one night, flapping his hands as we talked outside the boys' room. He was good at sound bites, a master of spin: You could hear him saying it in the exact same way to three hundred other people. "The police'll just shut the parties down. At least here we have a spot where were not going to be bothered."

Berliniamsburg was tongue-in-chic, stylish to the extreme: Looks were layered on top of looks. Amanda Lepore (self-named "the most famous transsexual in the world") and Sophia Lamar (maybe not so much) were ever-present, presiding over their respective crews of young guys willing to do their bidding. They were like misfit gender-fucked sororities, the members worshipping their chosen club star, wearing lifted designer gear, or T-shirts they'd screen-printed themselves that read SOPHIA'S BOYS.

The party was so successful that Larry and Spencer started throwing more nights. Mutants was on Fridays. At one point I think they had four nights a week going on at the same club. There were performances, most of them electro acts that didn't need too much setting up. No one was playing any live instruments, but we still referred to them as bands.

Everybody had their own theme songs, regional micro-hits that only we knew. Larry had protégés, a pack of vampy girls called W.I.T., which stood for Whatever It Takes, with a fistful of catchy songs that Larry had written and produced for them. They were all feathered hair, Studio 54 dresses, a bemused affect. Melissa Burns, the obvious leader of the three, had perfected an air of stoned dislocation, a charming remove. The tunes were pure bedroom bubblegum and since they were Larry's band, he had them performing almost every week, insistent that the songs would catch on.

Spencer Product had his own act, Prance. He was petite guy, mustachioed, blowing onto the stage in dramatic purple outfits. He made his own grimy covers of Prince songs but altered the lyrics slightly. "Contra Pussy" was one of my personal favorites. Avenue D, two easygoing girls from the East Village in lots of gold jewelry, rapped filthy over electro beats. Their big song was "Do I Look Like a Slut?" Larry produced that one too. Everyone wanted to get up on that stage.

My friend and momentary boyfriend Joe Corcoran had his band, Hungry Wives. There were four members. Three of them played synths and one person sang, rotating positions throughout the set. They even had their own clothes designer: Andy Salzer, who ran a label called Yoko Devereaux. Sometimes they dressed in white with inverted collars, almost like dentists. Grainy projections of Gothic imagery behind them were synced to the music. It was fitting: The music was creepy, but had a sense of humor. "It's Over" was their big song. A lament on the death of New York club life:

> *The Palladium is now a dorm, sweetie*
> *The scene is dead, honey, Twilo was sold on eBay.*

Joe was the mastermind of the group, and I fell for his strong nose and crinkly eyes. He wrote reviews for dot-com sites that needed content, and minded a stuffy antique furniture shop on Lafayette. Music was his real passion, however, and you could hear the gloom and sarcasm from his personality in the songs. Hungry Wives was his baby, and anytime he wasn't doing his day job, he could be found on the simple music rig in his bedroom, a Nord synth in front of a Mac. One of the best Hungry Wives songs was called "I Can't Find My Friends" and was based on some (apparently) true story about the bouncers at Twilo throwing overdosing club patrons into a broom closet, leaving them to die. It was hilarious.

These were all the local small-timers, inspired by the electro stars that were making it big—well, at least it seemed that way to us: Peaches, Le Tigre, Chicks on Speed, Fischerspooner. We would go see their shows in mammoth rooms with real crowds. Their CDs were for sale in Other Music or at the Virgin Megastore. When it came to the bands coming out of Luxx, everyone was just passing around their own bootlegs. A lot of times, your stereo couldn't even read them.

The place wasn't primarily queer; it was just weird, rowdy pansexual fun. There were no red ropes, and I never knew of anyone who was turned away. This wasn't an exclusive fantasy. If you had the wherewithal, you could record your own songs on just about any device and elbow your way onto the stage. And if you played your song a few times, people might actually start remembering it. Maybe they'd request it at the DJ booth.

At the beginning of October, someone asked me if they could link me up with some BBC crew from the UK. They were in New York shooting what life was like in the immediate aftermath of the towers falling. I called Larry and asked him if it was okay and, open to any kind of exposure, he said yes. So this film crew came into Luxx one Saturday and started filming us, interviewing people. It was strange suddenly for this moment to be on display in front of camera lights. But no one seemed opposed to being filmed. People didn't give a shit—the world felt like it was crumbling. There was now a crack in the earth that we all had witnessed with our own eyes. Niceties, modesty, and morality had stopped mattering. It felt odd, though, while I watched one of the queens do a spin on the stripper pole while the crew filmed. I wondered if we were just pretending to be having more fun in that moment than we actually were. Whether or not our exuberance was a performance, an outward denial of our sadness, there was no doubt that our surroundings and circumstances were prompting us to be creative. Every song made was inspiring somebody else to make one more. I guess that's how a scene happens.

23

SPENCER PRODUCT ASKED ME IF I WOULD DO A GO-GO number before he performed one night at Spa, a large club off Union Square that was hopping on Thursday nights. The night was called Ultra and was hosted by Eric Conrad, a sunglasses-clad fabulist that had started the gay staple Beige party at B Bar. Eric loved telling tall tales about various celebrities, pretending Liza or Madonna or Britney were on their way, just stuck in traffic. You'd laugh and forget about it, and then one of them would actually show up.

Many from the Luxx crowd would come and boogie on the souped-up dance floor or get drunk in a futuristic lounge room with banquettes. Any given week there'd be garish combinations of people drinking rivers of champagne: Jocelyn Wildenstein, Boy George, Richie Rich.

The thought of just taking my clothes off and dancing on a box wasn't as exciting anymore. I'd still been doing it for some spare cash, but I felt like my act had become stale, to myself at least. Grinding my ass for tips had run its course. When I brainstormed, the best thing I could come up with was maybe I could be a singing go-go dancer. It hadn't dawned on me yet that I might turn Scissor Sisters into a real project. The Slipper Room had just been a one-off. Besides, I couldn't imagine Scott getting up onstage with me at a club like Spa. He was a computer nerd, not a flashy ham.

Spencer told me that the theme for his performance and for the night was "Electro Yoga." I had no idea what that meant, but I nodded and said it sounded fascinating. I was just flattered that Spencer wanted me to perform with him. It was an opportunity, at least, so I asked Scott if he'd help me with an original song for whatever number I was going to do.

I was strolling in the West Village days later and a melody popped into my head. New ideas were often coming to me in my daydreams. Electro yoga . . . electro aerobics . . . Perhaps, Electrobix? It made zero sense, but something about it sounded good. I called my home phone number and left the tune and some lyrics on my voice-mail.

The next day Scott and I wrote "Electrobix." We still hadn't figured out how to make anything that sounded remotely fleshed-out, so I would bring in some CDs I'd been listening to, and we would sample a few bars from a song, lay additional beats on it, and write melodies on top. That day, we sampled the beat of Bryan Ferry's "The Chosen One" off the *Boys and Girls* album and overlaid some basic synths on top.

Not that any of it made much sense with the title. But the imagery from the song described how I felt about my body growing up. Some of lyrics were sloppy, but the chorus worked:

> *You gotta pump your body*
> *If you wanna be a hottie*
> *You better like to party*
> *If you gonna pump that body.*

Sometimes I have a difficult time speaking about things that I really care about without getting choked up, especially if it's to more than one person. I'm a total crier. Even when I'm simply excited my eyes can well up with tears. This is often really embarrassing, and why I have a mild fear of public speaking. If I'm writing something that has a deep meaning to me, when I listen back and get a lump in my throat, that's how I know I've made something real. As silly as "Electrobix" was, it was still about my lingering insecurities.

The "Electrobix" performance at Spa felt off. The crowd was supportive, but when I exited the stage, the number left a bad taste in my
mouth. My look was terrible. I had worn an off-the-shoulder black
blouse and some leggings. But the worst of it was the plain, short
bobbed wig I had decided on. I guess I felt like I needed an asymmetrical haircut like everybody else was wearing, so I placed it on my head
sideways. Hell if *I* knew what I was trying to do. Self-styling has never
been one of my talents.

I didn't enjoy singing by myself, either. Even though Scott was in
the crowd watching, I felt too vulnerable up there alone, singing along
to nothing but a prerecorded track. Afterward, he gave me one of his
half hugs, patted me on the back, and told me it was fine, but I knew
that whatever I was doing up there, I didn't want to do it by myself.

So I convinced Scott we should start playing together wherever
we could: at the Slipper Room, on the bar at the Cock, even at friends'
birthday parties. We were writing about a song a week, and once we
got a keeper, I would find us someplace to perform it. We were a long
way from being able to get up onstage at Luxx, but every weekend, I
was there, watching the shows and knowing I could do something just
as good if not better.

My friend Mark Tusk was around a lot during this time. A disheveled
stoner in his late thirties, he lived on Seventh Street in the East Village.
A few years back he had been a producer on the *Hedwig and the Angry
Inch* movie for New Line, but at this point he was mostly taking photos
of nightlife and just hanging out in his apartment, where he'd play me
soul records from the '60s and '70s. He always had a camera in hand and
would show up, even when Scott and I were singing "Step Aside for the
Man" to a mostly empty room at one in the morning at the Cock.

I had asked him what he thought we should do next one night.
"Bringing in some female energy would be great," he told me. "It'll
broaden the vibe of your performance. You've got to figure out how
to pull an audience in."

I was high at a birthday party for Joe Corcoran, and Scott and I volunteered to perform "Electrobix." Around midnight, when the party got full, we dimmed the lights and loaded the cavernous room with fog. Scott and I took off our shirts and sang the song into a cheap microphone, over a house stereo. I can't remember how I convinced him to do it, but my shirt usually came off onstage because I didn't have anything particularly cool to wear.

I'd dropped a hit of ecstasy earlier and felt giddy. High from the pill and performance, I felt the room begin to spin, a blur of friends' faces, cute guys wearing black, European girls in denim dresses and mullet hairdos. I remember it seemed that though most people had a day job, everyone around us had their fingers in something creative, whether it was clothing design or making music. It wasn't just a bunch of dilettantes, either—everyone lived there for a reason. We all wanted to impress our ideas on one another.

"Scott." I put my arm around his neck. Not one for physical affection or engaging in lascivious activities, he gave me a suspicious sideways glance. I'm sure he knew exactly what I was up to from the size of my pupils. But he still put up with me when I got wild. "I think we should ask that Ana Matronic to join Scissor Sisters," I said.

"Like, right now?" he said.

"Why not? She's right over there!"

"Well, because your eyes are both going different directions."

"Your eyes always go in different directions." It was true, Scott was a little wall-eyed. It was cute.

"Go ask her," he said.

She was dancing when I approached. We'd been hanging around each other more recently: She was hilarious, outgoing, but I didn't know her very well. Her delivery onstage was cutting, and she was innovative with her numbers. They were mostly drag and could have a conceptual bent that reminded me of a combination of Beverly D'Angelo and Ann Magnuson. But my favorite thing about her was that Ana seemed like she already had a history and was an actual grown-up.

It was late and we were trashed, but she screamed and threw her arms around my neck. "Oh my God, fuck yes!" We danced together in circles. Scissor Sisters was now a threesome. No one else remembers it this way, and I could be wrong. But that's how I remember it. That night, as we spun around to the cranked electro, fucked-up and happy, we had no idea what we were in for.

24

MY PARENTS SOLD THE PLACE ON SAN JUAN ISLAND and moved to a modest farm in Bristol, Virginia, so my mom could be closer to my ailing grandmother. The farm had horse stables, fields, and a strange Suburban Gothic house on a picturesque hillside. Mom could now visit my mamaw in her new convalescent center a few times a week. And my father, who had recently gained a fascination for race horses, loved having a new shop to tinker and learn saddlemaking in.

On my first visit down there I was charmed by the farm's beauty but horrified by the surroundings. It felt like nothing but freeway off-ramps leading to the Golden Corrals, TGI Fridays, and Olive Gardens littering the landscape. There wasn't a bookstore for at least thirty miles, and compared to the island, I found the area to be unspectacular in every way.

When I went down to visit my folks, the boredom came in handy. A lack of stimulation can make it easier to pluck ideas out of the air without distraction. Sometimes I sang not even knowing I was doing it. At Christmas in 2001, I was in my parents' horse barn, kicking hay and just wandering around daydreaming. But in one moment I realized I was singing "Comfortably Numb" by Pink Floyd in my falsetto. It occurred to me that some kind of an electro disco cover of the song could be interesting to try.

When Scott and I laid "Comfortably Numb" down in the studio, we sampled a beat from some random sound library, and put a bass line down on the keys. The first versions of the song were wonky. When I recorded my vocals in our makeshift sound booth, which was just some plywood nailed up as a separator covered in egg-crate foam, we didn't know how to listen at the same time to the other vocal tracks that we had recorded. So I had to harmonize with my own imagination. I laid it down and then we'd go back and listen to all the vocals together, surprised how the harmonies overlapped. Later I realized that the song always sounded like it was speeding up or slowing down because the drum loop was imperfect. The whole song is a tiny bit out of time, but nobody has ever noticed.

Dan Savage and his partner Terry Miller were visiting from Seattle and staying with me in my East Village apartment when I played Terry the first few demos that I had. He listened to a couple songs and looked at me with all seriousness. "Jason, you've got to get a new vocalist. You sound awful."

Anderson expressed a similar sentiment. He was a great supporter, but one night as he was walking me home, probably listening to me spin my music wheels, he said, "You realize you're going to have to get a real job, right?"

I lied to the manager of Leshko's when he asked me if I had ever waited tables before. It seemed easy enough. The schedule gave me time to work on any articles I was writing or go over to Scott's and make music. Leshko's was a diner on the corner of Seventh Street and Avenue A, right beside Tompkins Square Park. Next door there was an old ragtag shop with this ancient, toothless man who made pistachio frozen yogurt with rainbow sprinkles on top. The yogurt was an electric green color and tasted like chemicals, but fuck me if it wasn't delicious.

There were a lot of junkies around, and we weren't supposed to let them in to use the restroom. I was really bad at this, always telling some strung-out chick: "Okay, just this one time." But then on one of the night shifts, the waitstaff ended up with a stiff in the john.

I would forget to put people's orders in, distracted by the action. But then Martin Pousson, the tattooed bartender, would make strong cocktails that I'd slip any unhappy customers for free. Usually if I messed up it wasn't that big of a deal. But once, some guy during a busy weekend shift took his pork chop on the end of his fork, shook it in front of my face, and said: "You can go tell the chef to go stick this under his shoe and step on it and it would taste better than this shit."

The Strokes' studio was down the street, so I would always wait on Nick Valensi and his girlfriend. When famous people were around, it was uncanny that they were there in front of you but also everywhere else. I wanted to have that omnipresence, too, be able to occupy multiple spaces at once.

I had just broken up with a grad student I'd met in the fall named Dominick, and I was lovesick. Dominick looked like the statue of David and was a hell of a lot smarter than I was, but he'd bait every conversation with his pointed socialist discourse. I grew tired of his didacticism, but the sex more than made up for it. We'd only been dating for three months but I was prone to falling in love as accidentally as one might step in some Tompkins Square Park dog shit.

I had become close with the queer theorist Michael Warner and his partner, Sean Belman, who ran *Bound and Gagged* magazine at the time, and was headed upstate to their place for the weekend. I assumed that Dominick would be coming with me. But he materialized at my apartment the night before to tell me we were over. I cried after he left with *The Wall* cranked up at full volume. Those tears were justified, it had been some damn good dick.

I still decided to go to Michael and Sean's place in Poughkeepsie. They called it Camp Climax, a little hippie haven where everyone could laze about or get lost in their own creative projects. The other guests that weekend were a radical faerie named Granite, performer Justin Bond of Kiki and Herb fame, and fiction writer Stacey D'Erasmo and her anthropologist girlfriend, Beth.

Justin Bond was my neighbor on Twelfth Street now. I idolized her: a true downtown performer able to sustain herself off of her raw talent and imagination. This was the first time I had spent with her in a private setting, which for me was like hanging with a celebrity, just like my nights with Ms. Brown in the second grade. I wanted so badly for Justin to notice and like me, but I could tell that she still thought of me as a kid.

That night after dinner, I lay on the floor in the living room as Justin improvised a long, sorrowful song on the piano, her hair hanging in her face. Granite sat on the couch, making a giant collage out of vintage porn magazines, delicately gluing cutout dicks and spooge. Stacey and Beth quietly read. Not able to stop thinking about Dominick, I wanted to walk out in the snow and not come back.

After falling asleep on the floor, I woke up the next morning feeling horrible. But this wasn't just my heart hurting—my whole body ached. I tried to stretch and yawn it out to no avail. A flu was coming on. A bad one. I decided to wait a couple hours and see how I felt. We had a Scissor Sisters show at Marion's that night on the Bowery.

"I'm so sick, Scott," I said later, my teeth chattering from the chills. I wasn't able to stand up all the way. I was crouched down in the hallway, clutching my phone. He knew I wasn't faking, I wouldn't miss a performance for anything.

"So what do we do about Marion's?" he said.

"I guess see what Ana thinks," I said. "You guys just might have to go with my vocals on track."

"Oh God. This'll be classic."

It was going to be our third gig with Ana. The last two had been successes, though they'd been sparsely attended. For one of them, we'd played three songs on the restaurant side of B Bar, for some kind of variety performance night. I'd worn a leather harness and cutoff denim shorts. Scott's look was an ill-fitting union suit with the sleeves off. Ana wore a dark-red wig and square black sunglasses. We were doing our best, but there was no budget for clothes.

We each had our own microphone now, and Scott still pretended to play keyboards as usual, running the backing track on a minidisc player. Our rehearsals were in Scott's kitchen, where we came up with a little dance for "Electrobix." It was clunky but worth it to see Scott try and keep up with the moves. The two of us didn't excel at choreography.

Scott and Ana played the show without me that night. It had been snowing in the city and there weren't very many people there anyway. Ana apparently told the audience that I was "off fucking Liberace's ghost." I wish I had been: I felt like death. The fever finally broke, leaving me drenched in a pool of my own sweat. I felt useless. It would take a couple weeks to feel better, emotionally and physically, and get over missing Dominick, or at least him giving me the what for.

When we played a makeup gig at Marion's a few weeks later, this time with all of us present, I was disappointed not to see Amy Sedaris waiting tables. I'd heard she took shifts sometimes just because she liked the place and had done it for years. The restaurant was full, but it felt a little like a dinner theater: Everyone was sitting at a table. Ana used this to her advantage, however. She was brazen with the crowd, fearless with her jokes: If one didn't land, the next one would. We were working without a net and having unbridled fun with each other onstage.

Somebody liked our set enough to steal the backup CD from the sound booth; we kept it there in case the minidisc player didn't work. Two guys from a record label had watched the show. They left us a hundred-dollar tip, along with a note that said they wanted to put one of our songs out. It turned out the label was called A Touch of Class and was run by two Swiss producers named Oliver

Strumm and Dominique Clausen, who worked out of a loft turned music studio in SoHo. I was familiar with one of their previous songs on the label, a twelve-inch single from my friend Nashom's band the Ones. It was called "Flawless" and had been a big club hit. ATOC did all their own artwork and each twelve-inch had its own special look.

Our first meeting with them was congenial. Scott and I were impressed with their office's all-white interior and studio rig, which was legit. When they talked about our songs, they acted energized and mentioned they would like to release a single of "Electrobix" with "Comfortably Numb" as the B side. They said they loved how "honest" our music was.

Scott and I left that meeting buzzing. "They've got their shit together," I said. We walked at a brisk pace, our eyes straight ahead, both processing whatever this could mean.

"Someone's gotta look at the contract," Scott said. "It's not like we have any idea what this stuff means." We walked in silence for a block. In my head we'd already signed everything and were moving forward. Scott was more careful and pragmatic to the extent that sometimes I felt like he savored dousing my fantasies.

"Any ideas?" I said. "Do we know any lawyers? And where would we even find the money for one?"

"My uncle? Not sure if he knows anything about entertainment law, but we can try him. This kind of stuff is hard without a manager."

We ended up signing away some important points on that first contract, which we'd painfully find out later. But at the time, I was intoxicated with the thought that anyone wanted to release our songs. We didn't realize it yet, but every decision we made from here on out was a possible pitfall. The more songs we wrote, and the more time we put into our little shows, the more we had to lose. Young kids with talent and no money can be perfect targets to be taken advantage of. The initial paychecks can seem worth it at the time, making it easy to sign away what should remain yours.

I was going to Luxx in Williamsburg almost every weekend at this point. Friday night was Mutants, which wasn't as big as Berliniamsburg on Saturday, but there was still a decent amount of people showing up, and Larry Tee was in need of more acts to perform. So I gave him our demos and got Scissors a gig.

We needed a look, so I had Scott and Ana bring in some black clothes, which I laid out on Scott's living room floor and splattered with a toxic-green paint. It didn't look great by any means, but I figured it would at least give us some kind of visual unity.

The night of our first Luxx show, it was freezing outside. I had been posting flyers everywhere downtown that just had the Scissors logo, our name, the date, venue, and two lines from "Electrobix": YOU GOTTA PUMP YOUR BODY, IF YOU WANNA BE A HOTTIE. Just seeing the flyers on bulletin boards or taped up on a lamppost filled me with pride. We were real. I had also been ironing the logo onto some of my clothes, denim jackets and T-shirts. When I wore them in public, even though I was the only one who had them, I knew people could see it and might wonder what it was.

The show was no later than 9 p.m. that night for some reason I can't remember. And the room seemed bigger than I'd ever noticed. We decided to actually plug in Scott's keyboard for a change, as well as a bass guitar that could be played live over the minidisc playback. Just rehearsing with the microphones before people came in I realized that even though the stage wasn't very far off the ground, at least we weren't using a wooden box or standing on the floor anymore.

The dressing room barely fit the three of us, with a cracked mirror and a curved black pleather seat that fit two. Scott had his feet up on the dressing counter. "Ana just called, she just missed the train, but she's on her way."

"Are the flaggers here yet?"

"I stuck them in the men's room. What are they doing exactly?" For each show now we tried to think of some kind of feature or gag. We thought it would be ridiculous to have gay flag dancers behind us for our last number. Flag dancing was a holdover from gay parties of yore. Though it was easy to poke fun, the dancers themselves notoriously felt a spiritual connection to the style. And if you really watched it, it was quite beautiful. The only thing was, we were paying these two flag dancers every cent we were making off the gig. Which wasn't very much, probably just over a hundred bucks.

"They're just doing what they do, I guess. I told them to come onstage for the last number."

"Does that include ketamine?" he said. "They were just snorting some in the bathroom."

Before we went on, I felt like my insides were getting squeezed. No matter how many times I went, I still needed to pee. It was hard to speak. I was so distracted and nervous that when we got onstage, my energy was overwrought. In front of an audience, I didn't know yet what to do with myself or the crowd. It was as if I could look past and around them, but not at them. Ana's presence made up for this, however. She worked the drag banter angle she'd learned on the San Francisco stages and smoothed over any obvious nervousness I brought to the table. My friend Mark Tusk had been right: She loosened up the room, whereas I was projecting a pent-up, manic energy.

We had about fifty people at the show, most of them friends and charitable former lovers. Our set lasted twenty minutes and the dancers added flair, though their flags kept scraping the low ceiling.

Larry Tee in his thick glasses approached me afterward, clapping. "That was great. There's so much new stuff!" He said he couldn't wait to play it in his sets. His sentiment was sweet, but I knew that a lot of our music was a little too quirky and not quite electro enough to be DJed at his and Spencer's parties. It didn't bother me, though. I was just happy to be embraced by the club in a live capacity.

The most exciting time for a successful band isn't necessarily at its peak, playing huge sold-out shows, or (back in the day) selling a ton of records. It's at the cusp, the split-second hairline fracture that precedes a break. It's a beautiful limbo when people are discovering the music, when every day is full of inquiries from surprising sources, the achievement of small goals that start adding up into something significant. It's a time that feels so special in retrospect because it can never be returned to. Once a band truly breaks, it can't be replicated. The magic trick is impossible to pull twice.

If there was any time in my life I wish I could freeze, live inside perpetually, it would be in this spot. Making my work, I was an unspoiled bonehead, innocent and happy. The joy of creation was coming from the purest place it possibly could. It would take me many years to truly be able to tap into that same unfiltered reservoir again.

I wanted to write about my world—both internal and external—to multiply the fun I was having by just being myself, maybe inspire other people to do the same. Bit by bit, we were creating a vessel for what I was envisioning. But if I had stopped myself, been realistic about the real chances of success, if I had actually paid attention to having to get a "real job," the momentum would have sputtered. I was living in my own boy-crazy music-fantasy world, scribbling incantations in notebooks, improvising with a pencil. I would force myself to write even when there was nothing coming out but nonsense. I had a magic and manic ability to conjure my own excitement, half dancing, half shuffling down sidewalks, talking and singing to myself. It was an extended trancelike state that kept me productive, but the freewheeling discipline would eventually harden and escape my control.

25

I WAS DRESSED LIKE A MIME, SITTING ON THE BEACH, high. The sun was barely peeking over the horizon, turning the sky into delicious streaks of pink and orange. Peals of laughter bubbled up nearby from small groups on the beach, the sound traveling across the mostly flat silence. They were all straggling revelers not yet ready to call it a night. My jaw was clenching; with my right hand I rubbed the side of my face, massaging my mandibles. My other hand, after pulling my cap off, stroked the hair on my head. MDMA made me happy most of the time, but this was something else. The night had been an epic neon spectacle. I wasn't sure how I was going to get back to the hostel, but at this point I didn't care. I just wanted to stay in this moment, right now, alone.

Something had clicked inside me with the high: I'd held a hunch that I'd been on the right path, and now I knew for sure. The previous months spun in my mind's eye: the work, the hustling, the shows and lyrical epiphanies. On this dusty beach in Barcelona, I was so far from New York, across a whole ocean. But it still felt so close. The world was smaller than I thought.

Only two weeks before, Scott and I had gone to the Touch of Class office and seen the vinyl in person. We held it in our hands, impressed with the artwork of grotesque muscle, collaged to form our name. It was the real thing, not just some iron-on I had put on an old denim jacket. It wasn't a black-and-white flyer that I had tacked up on the bulletin board at the gym. People could buy this, in actual stores!

The Touch of Class guys seemed proud to put it out, but I still wasn't sure what their role was supposed to be. No one had explained to Scott and me what we should expect from an indie label. I had been reading some music business books, but it still felt confusing. Did they put money into promoting our stuff? They did give us a stack of records. I took them downtown to all the record stores: Rebel Rebel, Other Music, and some other place on Avenue A that I shopped at sometimes. Other Music and Rebel were happy to take and feature the record. But the guy on Avenue A wasn't interested. He just shook his head with his arms folded. "Yeah, man, I heard it already. Not my thing." I asked if I could just leave one there. He shook his head again. I walked out thinking what a jerk the guy was. He could have taken one just to be polite.

I was burning copies of our demos faster than I could give them away. People weren't sending digital files around much yet, so I always had a stack of homemade Scissor Sisters EPs that I would pass off to anyone that seemed interested. They went over the front of every DJ booth I encountered. When I saw Björk at a party, I discreetly tapped her on the shoulder, slipped it into her hand, smiled, and made a quick retreat.

A few weeks before, my pal Peter Murdock had taken me as his date to the B-52's twenty-fifth-anniversary show at Irving Plaza. No one would be more thrilled than me. They were my lifetime heroes. Yoko Ono came out and guested on "Rock Lobster." Riding Peter's shoulders, singing along to every word, I thought of my twelve-year-old self, dreaming about a moment like this.

When the show finished, I met Fred Schneider at the after-party. I wasn't shy. I gushed. I couldn't believe I was actually meeting him. I told him I was in a band and that maybe he could help us produce some songs. He was nonplussed and didn't seem interested. "That's not something I really do," he said. I was a little disappointed at his response but didn't take it personally. It was people like him who had the juice. Fred was a human talisman. I felt that by just shaking his hand, magic would rub off on me as if it were covered in glitter.

On a weekday afternoon I was still waiting tables at Leshko's and two men with British accents sat down in my section. One of them looked familiar, and I realized that it was Phil Howells, the head of the City Rockers record label in London, a subsidiary of Ministry of Sound. I knew an opportunity when I saw it. The single had been pressed, and the record was sitting on the counter in my apartment. I couldn't let this pass. I tapped a fellow waiter on the shoulder and pulled him back to the bussing station.

"Just one favor—please can you watch my tables for six minutes. I have to run home and get something."

"What?" He was confused but game.

I told him to look after my tables and pretend that I hadn't gone anywhere. If anyone asked, I was in the bathroom. I stepped out the door of Leshko's and broke into a sprint for six blocks, not looking back. I flung the building door open, took the stairs three at a time, unlocked my apartment, and grabbed the record. It was ten minutes by the time I got back to Leshko's, dripping in sweat.

"Sir," I said, approaching Phil Howells's table, in between gasps for air, "I know you don't know me but I have this band. . . ." I handed him the record and one of my homemade EP CDs. "I just want to give you this. I think you might like it." He seemed genuinely surprised and shook my hand, said he'd give it a listen and that in fact he'd recently heard something about us. In six months, that same guy would fly back from London to offer us a record deal.

I decided to return to the Sónar festival in Barcelona, this time with our record in tow. Scott and I would take stacks of the vinyl and give one to every DJ we met. Our flight was late, so we missed our first connection and had to repurchase our tickets from Paris to Barcelona, but we finally arrived and stayed at my favorite spot, the Hostal Que Tal, where I had stayed in previous summers. Carlos, the sweet manager, welcomed us in his Spanish style, making us coffees and clucking about the local gossip.

Gary Pini, my friend from *Paper* magazine, was in town for the festival, and said he had a pal named Neil Harris that he'd like us to meet, a former A and R guy from London Records. "He's smart and could be a good manager for what you do." At one of the Sónar afternoons that they held at the contemporary art museum, Gary introduced us to him. But before he did, he said to me, "Just be cool and don't bug him about anything."

Neil Harris was a tall, husky, pale-skinned man with a stern face and a fast, staccato delivery. When you spoke to him, he leaned in and squinted his eyes, but when he laughed, his whole face opened from this dour expression to a lit-up smile. That afternoon we rapped about music and watched a bunch of DJs—after which Scott and I went to the gay beach, to catch some rays before sunset.

Carlos, the hotel manager, was there, with one of the editors of *InStyle* magazine, who was also staying at Que Tal, along with a photographer and artist named Tim Hailand. We lay on beach towels and yammered. Tim talked a ton about Pete Burns and Vivienne Westwood; apparently they were all friends. The guy from *InStyle* kept saying things like: "New York is so over, it's just dead. There's nothing going on there."

His comments made my blood boil. I snapped at him: "Maybe it's time for you to leave then. If you think there's nothing going on in New York, it's your own fault. It just means that you're not doing anything worth talking about." The guy looked at me like I had just peed in the punch bowl. I couldn't help but take that statement personally. *Don't sit here and tell me that nothing's going on in New York City.*

That night Scott and I went to Metro, a cavernous gay discotheque that I dubbed the "Spin Cycle." It was so labyrinthine and strobed that you lost all sense of direction, especially if you were fucked-up. The bathroom smelled like someone's rotted insides, but was packed with guys around urinals, porn playing on screens above each one. I never could figure out what everyone was doing in there. Probably drugs. Right outside the bathroom door was an entrance to a big dark room where you couldn't see your hands in front of your face.

Scott and I spied two really sexy men. One was short, spark plug–shaped, and beefy. He was with a hunky blond guy who was in a wheelchair. "What do you think?" I said to Scott. "Are they boyfriends?"

"I'm guessing so. Let's talk to them anyway."

We approached and chatted them up. It turned out they were both military and, yes, they were boyfriends on vacation. The blond guy in the wheelchair had been hit by a car a year ago and was still recovering from the accident. I got everybody drinks and then went to the back room with the two of them. The blond guy gave me a great blow job.

Right then, the club announced last call and I looked at my watch. It was almost six in the morning. I said goodbye to the two guys and hoofed it up the stairs into the bright, hot summer morning air. In the taxi I laid my head back, so excited for a bed. Out the window, I spied Scott, having found the two of them on his way out, pushing the blond guy's wheelchair down the street toward their hotel. That was the first and only time we ever hooked up with the same people.

Back at Sónar that afternoon I started hearing from multiple people that they were hearing Scissor Sisters being played in various sets. Apparently, many DJs were playing "Electrobix" as well as "Comfortably Numb," which was on the B side.

That night Scott and I went to a label showcase for Kitty-Yo at Nitsa club, where a hot Spanish boy in the bathroom asked me if I wanted any "white diamonds," whatever those were. He said they were four euros apiece. Cheap drugs are usually a red flag, but I was empty-handed and willing to try out the local goods. The boy smirked as I handed him the cash, and I realized he was giving my outfit a once-over. I was wearing a white flat cap with a black-and-white-striped tank top, white suspenders, white pants, and white gloves. I hadn't heard that mimes were a thing that season, but I thought I looked striking and it was pretty cheap to put together.

Afterward, we attended the main party at Montjuïc stadium, where Tiga was DJing an outdoor stage for what seemed like ten thousand people. The "white diamonds" I'd bought in the bathroom started to surge, and within no time, I was completely off my face. Scott was eyeing me with his usual skepticism. He wasn't used to parties this big and he had tripped down some stairs earlier, spraining his ankle as I pointed and cackled. We were an odd couple: I looked like a madman dancing, all huge eyes and jazz hands, while Scott limped around in pain. I was feeling none.

Suddenly, I heard a familiar bass line. "Oh, I know this song. I love it!" I clapped my hands. And then I realized it was our own. Tiga was playing "Electrobix." I screamed, my eyes bugging out of my head. With the song being played on such a massive system, I could hear every flaw. It was like being naked in front of everyone, but I was still ecstatic. Galloping toward the stage, where Tiga was playing, I screamed and jumped, waving my white-gloved hands. "This is our song!" I turned to the people around me. "Oh my God, this is our song!" We hollered and hugged, strangers happy to share the moment.

After Tiga's set, I ran down to the side of the stage, embraced him, and introduced myself. "Dude, are you a mime?" he asked, amidst my babbling of thank-yous. "I love 'Electrobix.' I just got my hands on it last week." Tiga and I would end up recording some big songs together: "You Gonna Want Me" and a cover of "Hot in Herrre" were the first. So began a collaborative friendship with him that lasts to this day.

Scott and I took the bus back into Barcelona as the sun was about to rise. I was still very high, so I disembarked, said good night, and strolled to the beach. People from the night before were strewn about like debris, flopping around in the sand, some in their sunglasses, some still in their evening clothes. Some had stripped down to their underwear. I walked to the shore, sat my butt down in the sand, and just gazed out at the water.

Something was happening. It was like there was a wire loose inside me, flapping around, spraying sparks. There were so many voices in my head speaking at once. "I'm gonna be in for it," I said aloud. This was going to be my life. I took off my clothes and got in the crisp ocean wearing only my underwear. It was like being dunked in the river out in the desert when I was fifteen, but instead of surrendering to Jesus, I committed myself to a life in music. I was capable of making whatever I wanted. As long as I could dream it, I could make it happen.

There were three Brits sitting near me on a beach towel, two guys and a girl in their twenties. They had a bottle of champagne and asked me if I wanted a glass. I obliged and told them that I'd just had one of the most exciting nights of my life. "Ah, then this is a special toast," one of them said. We tapped our plastic cups together, half covered in sand grit, and I tilted my head back and took a strong swallow.

My dad, Archibald Borders Sellards, at age twenty-four, 1952, in Safford, Arizona.

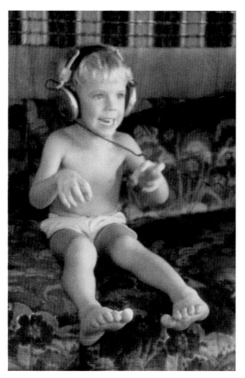

Age three, most likely listening to Barbara Mandrell.

Chillin' with my sweet pops. Was probably about five.

Doing my best nine-year-old impression of Henry Fonda in *On Golden Pond*.

Me and my second-grade teacher, Ms. Brown. The first of many teachers I would force to be my friend.

My sixth-grade teacher, Ms. Dyer, and me on my front porch. We had quite the rapport.

Jennifer Lebert and me during my eighth-grade year. We'd become such good friends we decided to take a school picture together.

Which one of these things is not like the other? My family sometime around 1996.

Mary and me in my dorm room at Occidental in 1996.

The night of the blackout. At the Slide. Looks like someone is tipping me for old times' sake.

Having a dinner date with Anderson in Rome. Summer 2001.

This was at a loft party at Joe Corcoran's loft. Scott and I are singing Electrobix, and if I'm not mistaken, this is the night we asked Ana to join the band.

January 2003, playing a gig in SF, when we were a threesome.

Me, John Cameron Mitchell, and Mark Tusk at some house party. John and I would go on to make the "Filthy/Gorgeous" music video.

Scott and me, having just finished the tracking for LP1 at the Shed in New York. On the mixing desk, you can see we had a little shrine to some heroes that included Dolly Parton, the Bee Gees, and Gizmo.

In our fineries, shooting the "Take Your Mama" video.

Scott and me in the studio with Bryan Ferry in Scott's apartment. We recorded "Heartache by Numbers," which ended up going on his album *Olympia*.

In England, holding our first Gold Records.

The first night I met Elton and George, in February 2004.

Scott, me, and Elton writing on the Colosseum stage at Caesars Palace. Spring 2005.

Me and Scott with the Heatherette crew. They made a lot of stuff for me for stage at the time and really embodied the spirit of NYC in 2004. From left clockwise: Traver Rains, Richie Rich, Aimee Phillips, Scott Hoffman, Amanda Lepore, Macky Dugan, and me.

In the studio for the first time with Kylie Minogue, making "I Believe in You" in 2004.

The night we fell in love. Glastonbury, 2004.

Our drummer Paddy Boom out on the street with Johnny Blue Eyes while shooting the "Filthy/Gorgeous" video, 2005.

Our first time in Russia, 2005. From left to right: Paddy Boom (Patrick Seacor), Ana Matronic, me, Babydaddy (Scott Hoffman), Del Marquis (Derek Gruen), and our keyboard player, J. J. Garden.

Ana and I during our first Barcelona show, when we were all deathly sick. My lack of food that week was probably good for the abs.

Not sure what show, or where, but I'm probably spotting a hot guy in the balcony.

26

I WAS BUYING A CAMERA IN B&H PHOTO VIDEO WHEN the power went out. The inside of the store was like the inner workings of a huge clock. If Willy Wonka had an electronics shop run by Hasidic men and robots, it would look like B&H. The whirring conveyor belts overhead transporting baskets of goods came to an abrupt halt. I was standing at the counter, only daylight now illuminating the racks of gadgets. All was quiet except for the sounds of huffing voices and the shuffling of feet. The man at the counter who had been ringing me up shook his head and said I'd have to come back later.

I walked out into the streets of Chelsea, one hand holding the straps of my Rollerblades and the other shielding my eyes from the blazing sun. People were streaming out into the street, curious and confused. It was a blackout, at least through the whole neighborhood.

I perched on the ledge of a store window, pulled off my shoes, and stuffed them into my backpack, then swung my Rollerblades around and clinched them to my feet in a practiced matter of seconds. They were my fruit boots. Every time I put them on I thought of that old joke:

What's the hardest thing about Rollerblading?

Coming out to your parents.

My Rollerblades were indispensable for getting around the city, like cyborg legs strapped to my feet. I wore them so much, when I took them off, the act of walking felt as if I were wading through molasses. I was careful not to fall, zipping through people and weaving between cars. Somehow I hadn't had an accident. The back brake was worn from excessive use. A few days before, I had gone into a Union Square sports shop to replace them and gotten into a verbal shouting match with the guy in the department. He was rude for no reason. The more years I spent in New York, the easier it had become to tell someone to go fuck themselves to their face.

I skated to the newly constructed Christopher Street Pier, where I knew plenty of gays would be gathering, having left their dark workplaces, happy to be pulling their shirts off and getting some sun, enjoying a surprise half day off. The boys were already sprawled in the grass, all bacon and eggs, doing their best to get burnt. As I skated, I could feel their eyes following me. I had become more recognized around town. Sometimes they'd call after me, using my new name.

I saw an olive-skinned, dark-haired guy with a questionably applied Superman tattoo on his shoulder. I'd seen him at the gym, and he'd flashed his junk at me once in the locker room. I floated over and we made small talk about the outage. Apparently it was covering the whole city. There were murmurings about another terrorist attack. But he'd heard that wasn't the case. Instead, the grid was overloaded. Superman Tattoo didn't have much to say, but he was stacked, so I asked him if he wanted to hike back across the city to my apartment, and we could throw down.

Our walk across the island was odd, the city draped in a placid chaos. People and cars meandered, seemingly aimless, waiting for electricity. By the time we got to my apartment, it was like a stuffy terrarium. So it made plenty of sense to just take off our clothes. After we fooled around, Superman Tattoo left. I never saw him again.

Sprawling around the swampy apartment, I racked my brain as to what the hell I was going to do. The post-sex sweat permeating the room smelled like I was cooking a pelican in rancid milk. I picked up my cell phone and tried to call Scott, to no avail. It was dead. I refused to rot in my place, especially when the city's current strangeness beckoned.

It had cooled off outside on Twelfth Street. Locals were sitting on stoops, talking to one another, drinking Cokes. My super and his drug-dealer cousin were outside my door. The super seemed wary of me, though I'd never asked him for anything. His cousin eyed me for other reasons. Usually when I was on my way home from the Cock, as I unlocked the front door, I would hear him chanting under his breath, into the quiet night, "Coke. Coke. Coke. Coke."

I headed to this guy Andrew's, a handsome young man I'd met at the gym. He was sweet and slender, could have been a model if he wanted, possibly a little too delicate for me, and he didn't know much about music. I had taken him to a Roxy Music gig at Radio City, but he had never heard of them. We ran into Fischerspooner's Casey Spooner and his boyfriend Adam Dugas at the gig and afterward we all had dinner at Sardi's. Casey pulled me aside that night and said, "Jason, that guy is a babe, but doesn't say much." I couldn't tell if he was just a guy of few words, or if he just wasn't very smart, but no matter, he was a good lay, so I rang his doorbell.

Andrew answered, and we went up to his equally baking place and fucked. His body didn't have much hair on it and got slick as a mole when he sweated. When it was wet, you could see every single ropy muscle. He shuddered and sighed, smiled down at me. Sopping in our secretions, we slid around on each other, kissing whatever skin happened to be in front of our mouths.

I lay in his arms and asked him what he was going to do that night if the electricity didn't come back on. "I'm supposed to work first thing in the morning," he said. "So I'm probably just going to go to bed." BORING! That was my cue. I wiped myself down with some dirty T-shirts and threw on my shorts, leaving my underwear to find its own way in the world. I kissed Andrew and walked to Tompkins Square Park, where people seemed to be gathering. The sky was turning. It was dusk. Reality was setting in.

There were no streetlights, no phones, there was *no electricity*. The streets were getting dark. I saw Sammy Jo, my DJ pal who lived next to me with his partner, who happened to be Justin Bond. "I'm gonna grab a boom box," he said. "We need batteries. What say we light some candles and throw a party at the Slide?" This was a bar that party promoter Daniel Nardicio had purchased that was right next to Marion's on the Bowery. The Slide was a sloppy, happy watering hole that was known for its encouragement of lewd behavior. As Sammy and I spoke, his features were in shadow. Not only was everything getting dark, in five minutes you wouldn't be able to see where one foot was landing in front of the next. The oncoming lights from the few cars out were blinding, as if alien ships were touching down.

A couple hours later, I felt my way down Avenue A as if I were blackout drunk. The East Village was in full-swing mayhem, total anarchy, disorienting. There were whoops and hollers, flashlight beams cutting erratically through the darkness, constant bumps of shoulders and lots of cheerful "Excuse mes." The view from the sidewalk by Tompkins Square Park was downright apocalyptic with bonfires, all surrounded by drum circles. The wild things had emerged, circling the flames and relishing the chaos. I caught glimpses of people completely naked, like cats darting between trash cans, reveling in an unspoken lift of clothing restrictions. The Slide had transformed as well. I arrived into a semi-Gothic dream, lit entirely by candles.

The air was filled with cackling laughter and Donna Summer's *Greatest Hits* CD on the battery-powered boom box. The drinks were being poured aplenty. (For free? Awesome.) After a few strong cocktails, inspired by Sammy Jo's choice of "Baby I'm a Star," I decided to pull most of my clothes off and surf the bar for old times' sake. Gripping the ceiling, twisting my hips, underwear pulled down just enough to cover my dick, I felt a tingly thrill over the tangle of skin and unfettered grins beneath me. At some point Sammy Jo and I started humping and riding each other (which was absurd—we were sisters, for crying out loud!). Justin Bond held court at the bar, sometimes hollering upward and slapping my bare ass. Almost everyone had their shirts off.

A guy I was dating named Mark strolled in by himself. Dark-skinned with a beak-like nose, confident, and always good-smelling, he made me insatiably horny. I knew in that moment with whom I would spend the duration of this strange night.

Mark and I had met a couple months before at one of Daniel Nardicio's late-night parties in a barren industrial aquarium, with stacks of glowing fish tanks lining the walls. Mark, who was go-go dancing in a tiny Speedo, climbed into a nine-foot-tall tank with a small shark swimming around below. I dropped a hit of ecstasy and decided to strip off my clothes and join him. We chatted and swam around, our heads peeking just above the water; we brushed limbs and kissed each other under the fluorescent light, hanging about eight inches overhead. If we had accidentally knocked the light down, we would have been electrocuted. It was time to get out of the water when our sliding fingers became prunes and the shark bit Mark's foot. He accompanied me home that night, and after a few dates I had developed quite a crush.

Back at the Slide, Justin Bond wrapped her arm around me and shot me a dreamy smile. "I'm so proud of you," she said. The place was a sight, all of these East Village friends and queers together in one room, dancing with abandon. Even the freaky glow-stick guy was lurking in the corner, wide-eyed and staring, covered in neon tubes and flashing lights. I never saw him speak and he wasn't conventionally attractive by any means. But I always liked seeing him out, decked in his finery. Even he had carved out his own place in New York nightlife.

We stayed at the Slide until four in the morning and closed the bar, sweaty and drunk. Mark and I ambled a couple blocks to the home of some friends who lived on the top floor of a walk-up. I stepped out on their fire escape by myself and gazed at the pitch-black city. I felt a new sense of independence now. It was the giddy, propulsive freedom that I'd been striving for. Grinning at the inky blots of buildings, I knew it was a silent, special vision that I would probably never see again. For a moment it seemed like I was the only person alive.

27

THE MEMBERS OF SOME OF MY FAVORITE BANDS, LIKE the Cramps and My Life with the Thrill Kill Kult, all had monikers, like Lux Interior and Groovy Man. I reasoned we should all have pseudonyms to help give us our special powers. Ana Matronic already had a cool name. Scott was nicknamed Babydaddy by some friends. I had decided on Jake (short for Jason), and Shears, being a play on *scissors*. Years afterward I realized a strange connection: Billy Shears, a fictional character from "Sgt. Pepper's Lonely Hearts Club Band," and Rhonda Shear, a busty blond late-night trash movie presenter from the '80s on USA's *Up All Night*. I always like to think that if Rhonda and Billy had had a baby, it would have been me.

After I tried the name on awhile, I thought it sounded too much like a porn star's. So before we played a gig at the Knitting Factory in the fall, opening up for Kiki and Herb, I decided that I wasn't going to be Jake Shears after all. Maybe changing my name was a stupid idea. But Neil Harris, our new manager, whom we had met in Barcelona, thought otherwise. "Too bad," he said. "It's too late, dude. You're stuck with it."

Every day there was some more news or opportunities, mainly having to do with this scene we found ourselves in the middle of. "Electro-clash" was what they were calling it, and Luxx was the self-proclaimed epicenter, with Larry Tee as the ringmaster. There was so much hype. Fischerspooner, only recently still playing elaborate underground shows, had just signed a reported million-dollar record deal with Ministry of Sound. When the media found out, the pressure was on: With everyone knowing how much the album had been bought for, they were now waiting to see what was going to happen with this flagship band on the cusp of this craze. Casey Spooner wasn't particularly helping the situation by saying outrageous things in interviews like "This is going to be bigger than *Star Wars*." Whatever the perceived movement was, Fischerspooner were the acting ambassadors. With such high expectations, the whole thing had the potential to fizzle rather quickly.

I ended up in a photo shoot that summed it all up. It was a fashion editorial in *Out* called "This Is Electroclash." I arrived on the day without much to wear. Some cool people showed up: the girls from W.I.T., My Robot Friend, some of the Hungry Wives, and Avenue D. Those people made sense, we were all musicians. But I didn't understand what the extra models were doing there. They were attractive and had asymmetrical haircuts, but when the piece was published, all the artists were standing around in these shots peppered with models. Something was awry.

When Scott and I got a call from London's *The Face* magazine ("Hey, this is Cookie, but playse coll me Cook. I'm cawling from *The Fay-ce* magazine? It's *The Fay-ce* off Lohndon and wey're doing a HUGE payce on electro-closh. You MUST absolutelay be there, wey loff you . . ."), we sat in the studio, alarmed, listening to this absurd woman yammer on our speakerphone. We told her we'd get right back to her, but it was an easy decision for us to skip the shoot. Our instinct was to sit back and wait, let the media pass over us for now. We knew we had the potential to outlast a genre trend that might be over tomorrow. For now, we could fully take advantage of the stage that the scene was providing us, but we would politely distance ourselves from the bandwagon.

That proved not difficult to do. Suddenly, our whole next wave of songs were piano- and guitar-based, not straight dance tracks anymore, and had more complex chord progressions and arrangements. Our shows at Luxx were getting bigger, and seemed to delight and confound the crowds we were drawing. "Comfortably Numb" was starting to get played out in clubs frequently, but the new stuff sounded different. We were performing rock-structured songs in an electro club; it didn't make sense, but people were paying attention. Every time we played, we would experiment with new looks and props. For some reason I don't recall, we did a show dressed as pirates. I pulled rubber snakes out of a basket wearing a peasant blouse and Ana wore an eye patch. It was a queer Pentecostal revival on the high seas.

Still, as successful as the shows were, I could feel an invisible wall between me and the crowd. It was as if I resented any expectation the audience had, and my rancor just bounced off of them and reflected back on me. It was like I was reenacting my days of being fifteen years old again at Mountain View High, allowing a roomful of people to watch and observe me, making a spectacle of myself. I was subjecting myself to their judgment and it made me feel like I was wearing a dog's shock collar that was twisted up to ten. Every joint and muscle in my body seized and twitched, my head swinging all over the place. It must have been exhausting to watch. My friend Tom Donaghy would tell me all the time with a straight face, "You've got a lot of rage. If you don't get famous, you're going to kill somebody."

Scott and I were in the studio now every day. We aimed for at least one new song for every show we played. It kept the performances exciting and unexpected. We never knew how the new material would read. Sometimes when we started playing a new song, we could feel it work right away, or it would sit there like a dud, and we'd never touch it again.

One of my secret weapons was my friend Martin Pousson, the bartender at Leshko's. He attended every single show, and had strong critiques and opinions. He adored the music and the band, but I could count on him to dissect the performances. Sometimes it was disheartening. But whether I agreed with Martin's feedback or not, it was always helpful. He would talk to me about band dynamics onstage, the archetypes we were projecting, body movements, and queer theory. Martin viewed the band through an academic lens that I didn't feel we were entirely worthy of. Every week, he bought me albums I needed to hear: *Make It Big* by Wham!, or *Dare* by the Human League. He fed me a steady diet of brilliant pop, a stream of inspiration.

Lyrics were coming to me loud and clear. I had recently written the chorus of a song called "Take Your Mama" at my parents' farm. I'd been listening to Steely Dan's "Can't Buy a Thrill" on repeat all morning when I decided to rinse off in the shower. With the water beating down on my head, the words and melody came out of my mouth while I was just standing there, spaced out. I ran naked and wet across my bedroom and recorded it into the voice-mail on my phone. I was doing this now when I had a new idea. If I didn't record the melody right away, I knew I'd forget it.

The same was true of notebooks, I always had one in my backpack. If I heard something while eavesdropping at a party or a restaurant, I would immediately grab a pen and scribble it down. The previous summer on Fire Island, I'd been drinking a cocktail when I heard some queen I knew behind me talking about Britney Spears: "Well, you can't see tits on the radio," he said. There was a song.

In the back of a cab, staring out the window, I thought of one of my favorite movies as a kid: *Return to OZ*. The story was so bleak: When Dorothy returned to the Emerald City, it was a decaying shadow of what it had once been. I began to sing a soft melody:

> *Is this the return the return to Oz?*
> *The grass is dead*
> *The gold is brown*
> *And the sky has claws.*

What if Oz were a metaphor for some tweakers I'd known on the West Coast? Seattle was the Emerald City. My writing and ideas came out of daydreams, those moments when my eyes glazed and my thoughts wandered. The shower remains one of my favorite places to write. It's the lack of stimulation, the beating of the water. And besides, everybody sounds better singing in the shower.

When we performed "Take Your Mama" for the first time, at a Knitting Factory show co-headlining with Hungry Wives, the band reached the chorus and something jelled. In real time, we leveled up. You could feel it in the room, a reveal of where we were going, and the potential for what we could achieve.

After that night, Ana was pissed off at me for days. "You ignored me onstage," she said. "You acted like I wasn't even there." I was defensive, but when I really considered it, she was right. It wasn't a conscious thing—I'd just been so amped up and nervous to keep the show moving, lost in my stage hang-ups, that I'd had a hard time bantering or singing together with her. Figuring out how to do it all at once was like rubbing your head and patting your belly. I was learning how to juggle, but sometimes dropping my balls all over the place.

Ana and I had a certain chemistry onstage—our personalities complemented each other's. But offstage I got tired of what I perceived to be flakiness. If she was late, it was always the subway's fault. There were a lot of excuses and finger-pointing.

The tension would increase when she'd come into the studio and learn that Scott and I had made new stuff. The first time she heard "Take Your Mama," she grimaced and said: "We can't do this. It sounds like 'Loaded' by Primal Scream. It's been done." Or she would listen to a new song and flip through a magazine, feigning being bored. I can see now that she felt left out of the writing process, but I was truly doing my best.

Solid collaborative relationships are tough to find. It can be just like a marriage, flowering into trust and stability, or it can wilt with a hardheaded approach. Scott and I have always made a wonderful pair, as cohorts as well as friends. There have been both fruitful and dry patches, triumphs and horrific fights. Our differences are the key. We're almost opposites. He's the ground that tethers my floating; I'm the whimsy that decorates his technique.

The dynamic among Scott, Ana, and me vacillated between ease and tension. Ana was hilarious and vicious; in one sentence she could render us crying and out of breath. She was great at improvising, and there was no telling what could come out of her mouth. Her singing voice was limited, but when she got on the microphone, magic was made. There was usually gold in her first takes. Our output was best when we allowed ourselves to be stupid and absurd, concerned only with the joy of writing and having fun.

The good times inspired the songs. Two words Ana used all the time to describe something were *filthy* (which was a compliment) and *gorgeous*. My first idea was to make a record with a song called "Filthy" as the A side and a song called "Gorgeous" as the B side. But when we started playing with the idea in the studio, it turned out to be just one big song. The lyrics were a psychedelic-sex-work-acid fantasy, the most detailed thing we'd written so far. Once we had the finished demo, we knew it was something special. The story and world we were concocting had just gotten bigger. Not only that, we had a few songs now that were pretty damn good, and they made sense next to each other.

I thought our productivity had been going great, but Ana came in the studio one afternoon solemn-faced and said, "I need to be a part of making these songs. I'm not just window dressing, you know." Of course Scott and I didn't want that, either. She was already far from window dressing, even if she hadn't been writing many of the songs so far. The flamboyance and energy she was bringing to the shows—and even the studio—were vital. But in that moment, I suddenly felt both guilty and defensive. Scott and I were already a songwriting team by the time we decided to bring more people in. I was happy to collaborate, but I'd made no promises that we'd write everything together. There was some unspoken jealousy there. If Scott and I wrote a song on our own, it could be uncomfortable playing it back for her. I sometimes felt punished for writing good stuff. It was my view that just because a new person had joined the project, it didn't mean they were entitled to the songwriting.

Her dissatisfaction was the spore for a subtle, sour dynamic that grew between us. I cultivated a defensive air and refused to hold myself accountable for anyone else's creativity. I thought resting her creative output on my shoulders was a cop-out. As much as I tried to include her, it wasn't my sole responsibility.

But whether we knew it or not, each of us was bringing something invaluable to the table. If you took away any of the elements we were bringing individually, it wouldn't have been working to the extent that it was. As high as tensions could be sometimes, generally we were close friends, confided in one another, and cared for one another's well-being.

Tony Moxham, a friend of Ana's, was one of the editors at *Interview* and got us a full page in the magazine. At the shoot there was a stylist for us, and we played dress-up for the first time in designer clothes. The final shot they used looked strange. You can see a band still trying to figure out who we were. I wore a sparkly sequined top and Scott was in a *Battlestar Galactica*–style square-shouldered vest. Ana looked extreme in huge platforms and vertical-striped tights. A big black wig was perched on her head and thick black makeup was slathered over her eyes: She'd become skilled at applying it after all those years in the drag clubs. I was happy to have the piece in *Interview*, but I didn't think it really looked like us yet.

I hadn't had a boyfriend since Dominick, and though I hooked up frequently, I didn't feel a strong pull to have one. I had everything I needed in my own neighborhood. The proximity of my apartment to the Cock made it easy to meet somebody and then dip back to mine. I was there often, and it was a convenient spot to do impromptu Scissor gigs when Mistress Formika was hosting. If I was drunk enough, I would just hop on the bar and sing one of our songs.

Though we'd achieved local notoriety, there was no money yet coming in from Scissors. In fact, Neil Harris was fronting us money, with faith that we would eventually make enough to pay him back. So I got an extra job bartending a block away at a tiny movie theater called Cinema Classics, which would show Fassbinder movies and things like *The Wizard of Oz* with *Dark Side of the Moon* as the soundtrack, a personal favorite. One night, we played a gig in front of the movie screen there. The crowd were just people from the neighborhood, I wore an orange sarong I'd bought in Greece and a tie-dyed Pink Floyd *Division Bell* tank top. Afterward we packed up our equipment, walked down the street to change clothes at my apartment, and then went and played a four-song set on a row of boxes at the Cock.

Our future guitar player, Derek Gruen, was there that night. "I was like, 'Ugh, I hate this stuff,'" he told me later, tuning his guitar in Scott's apartment studio. He was a handsome, steely-eyed cutie with good blue-collar style and drove around a shoddy van that he kept in Brooklyn. We'd found him through this guy I had been dating off and on named David Russell.

When I was still dancing, David was the only guy I ever picked up and took home from the job. He was a huge music fan, obsessed with Belinda Carlisle and Kylie Minogue, and was on the management team for Robbie Williams. We started hanging out regularly, often just strolling and talking music. "My best friend plays guitar," he told me one night. That's how we met Derek.

It turned out that the moment I ran home to get our record when I was waiting tables at Leshko's had paid off. The label head from City Rockers liked our stuff and flew back to New York to listen to our songs in the studio. "Comfortably Numb" had well taken off at this point, especially after its first radio play on Pete Tong's BBC One radio show. He introduced the song saying we were "cross-dressers from Japan." This would be the start of the insidious phobia that permeated much of our media coverage.

Once we acquired Neil Harris as a manager, he started steering the ship with purpose, and the fallout with A Touch of Class records was immense. Scott and I hadn't been trusting ATOC for a while. They sat us down and wanted us to sign the full-length album over to them. The conversation was peppered with calculated nuggets, them saying they wanted to take us "to the next level." But the contract they offered was laughable, attempting to take a huge slice of our publishing basically for nothing. Neil had been consulting for A Touch of Class on some other business. But he saw more potential in us than they did, so we both gave them the finger and split ways.

Now, City Rockers wanted us in London, and had offered to fly us there to play a couple shows, spend a week in the city, and let them convince us to sign a deal with them. London was a go, but we needed one more person. We needed an extra guitar. So when David introduced us to Derek, it seemed serendipitous.

Derek was a slightly nervous person, but I thought he was cute and had a fairly controlled crush on him. He had never been in a band but had been shredding in front of his bedroom mirror for years. A huge fan of the Cure and the Cult, he had a playing style at that time that was big and brash; he'd never really played rhythm guitar. Sonically he wasn't a perfect fit for the music we were making, but I didn't really care: He had a thing, and was handsome and odd. He confessed that he didn't initially like Scissor Sisters that much, but he seemed enthusiastic and available to go to London, so we brought him on and continued rehearsing in Scott's apartment.

That London schedule was bursting: We had three gigs lined up around town, and there was no downtime, but I was just stoked anybody cared enough to fly us out. We stayed at a hotel called the Columbia right on Hyde Park that was legendary for its cheap rooms and was where all the bands stayed. On any given night, you would go down to the bar and hang out with Franz Ferdinand, the Rapture, or whoever else was in town. The Columbia would become one of our second homes for the next couple of years. Scott and Ana split one room while Derek and I shared another.

The first gig we had was at a party called the Cock (unrelated to the bar in NYC), which was at Ghetto, behind the Astoria Theatre, the same space in which they were throwing Nag Nag Nag, an oven-like gay electro party that everyone was in a flutter about. A kind, burly guy named Jim Stanton, who would go on to cofound Horsemeat Disco, set it up and had a tiny stage prepared for us. I had a bad cold, probably brought on from anxiety over the shows, and wasn't feeling well. The place was teeming with surly drag queens, gays in ripped tops, and coked-up club freaks. It was a memorable first show; we received an extremely warm welcome and, from that night on, felt London embrace us as its own.

The second show we played was at DJ Erol Alkan's party Trash. It was a mad, eclectic free-for-all where Erol was touting his own movement, a mix of New York electro-rock, '80s classics, and left-field deep cuts. The Trash gig turned out to be in the lobby of the club and not in the main room itself, and Scott forgot our minidisc player back at our hotel, so it almost didn't happen. While we performed, people half paid attention, but it wasn't at all terrible. From the combination of my cold and the late night at the Cock, I lost my voice and could barely talk. But Neil assured me that my adrenaline would kick in, and I was able to pull off the show.

The third gig we intended to do was for the City Rockers label, but it never got off the ground. Probably a hint of things to come with the label itself. We set up and did a sound check, but come time to play the set, the PA wasn't working and the sound guy never got it running. So finally we gave up. I just took a hit of ecstasy and milled about, disappointed that the main gig we had flown there for had never even happened.

That night, Derek and I returned to our dilapidated hotel room. I was still fucked-up, but it was late and we had nowhere to go. "I don't even know what the fuck this is or what I'm doing," he said.

"Do you need to know?" I didn't see the point of worrying about it.

"It's like—I can just strap on a guitar right now and play along with these songs, but what is this anyway?" There was an old hurt in his voice. "I feel like we're gonna end up back in New York, and this will all just be some bullshit thing I did."

"But for now, this is great, no?"

"If I can just pretend to be what you want, it is."

We needed some press pictures and a shot for a sidebar in *Mixmag*, but were so unprepared, still having no solid idea of what the hell we were supposed to look like. I was by no means a clotheshorse; style was last on the list of stuff that I gave a shit about. I ended up in a sleeveless Jimi Hendrix shirt and 501s, as well as my janky white Skechers. We looked so ramshackle. But for the moment, fashion was the least of our worries. We needed a record deal.

The office meeting with City Rockers was on a rainy day and felt like a formality. I don't know if they were hungover, but the enthusiasm in the room was clouded. We agreed on the deal with a handshake. Then: "Guys, here's the thing," Phil Howells said. "I don't hear any other singles. Well, nothing as strong as 'Comfortably Numb.'"

I frowned. "You don't hear any more singles? There's about five of them." I was dumbfounded. "'Take Your Mama'? 'Laura'? 'Filthy/Gorgeous'?"

He patted me lightly on the shoulder, as if he were telling me a distant friend of ours had just passed away. He said, "There's a lot more writing to do."

He was wrong. I walked out of the meeting seething. The record wasn't finished yet, but there were a slew of possible radio songs. What, he was signing us on the back of this Pink Floyd cover but didn't hear the potential in the rest of the music? Why were they even signing us? I had a vision that was forming, and it set my alarm bells off that the label we were about to get in bed with didn't see it. I knew he wanted more of the electro that everyone else was making, but I didn't want to sound like everyone else. I got in the van with Ana and Scott and stewed.

A man named Michael Morley was hanging around us a lot; he worked for Zomba and wanted to sign us to a publishing deal. Which meant, in exchange for an advance, Zomba would always keep a portion of our songwriting royalties. God knows we needed the money. Scott and I spent many weeks mulling over whether we'd sign it or not. We were close. It was a hundred-thousand-dollar advance, but the deal was for fifteen years. We were almost going to sign it out of desperation for cash, but we decided against it, thank God.

There were so many of these land mines we managed to dodge. Scott and I kept betting on ourselves. If we hadn't, our careers and lives would have turned out very differently. It's a philosophy I still try to practice, not to give up the goods before they're ready and not to sell myself short. Complete faith has to be maintained while you figure out how to get your work out to the world.

I've never believed in bad luck. I mean, yes, awful things happen, a lot of times for no reason at all. But that's not luck. It's so easy to blame things on other people, situations, weather, whatever. Life is just the story that you tell yourself about what's going on around you. You can believe that your fantasies will become real, but you also have to hold yourself, and not the extraneous, accountable for when they don't.

The week we got back to New York, we heard that City Rockers was having financial problems. "Well, we got a trip and three shows out of it," Neil said. "Quite a few people saw you play. That's going to count for a lot." It was scary that a record deal wasn't happening now, but at least we hadn't officially signed. If we had, and the label ended up going under, who knows if we'd ever have gotten out from under that contract.

"Um, I haven't heard from you for weeks." Mary sounded far away, as if she was speaking away from the phone. I was in my apartment, my landline's black receiver cradled on my shoulder. She was the only person who had the number. Every time the phone rang, I knew it could only be her.

"Oh my God, I haven't gotten my head above water since we got back from London, it's been full-on. There was an *Interview* dinner last night for Miuccia Prada, you would have died. I sat next to this rapper lady named Medina. I actually asked her if she was funky and cold. Oh, shit—Cyndi Lauper was there, she was so nice. We were at some truffle restaurant. I didn't have anything to wear, so Prada let me go in the store and pick out a shirt and some pants. The shirt is so cute, it's like a navy blue button-up with all these stars all over—"

"It was my birthday on Monday," she said. "It was my birthday and you've forgotten it again. Just like last year and the year before that."

My breath caught in my throat. "Oh, fuck. Mary, I'm so sorry—"

"No. Not this time." She was crying. "Clearly you have your own life now. And that's fine, you can keep trying to pretend we're still best friends. But you have other things that are obviously more important. It's just different now, you can't go on and act like nothing is changing."

"Nothing has changed, Mary."

"Yeah you're right, you manage to forget my fucking birthday every year. I don't even know why you bother talking to me anymore. I've had it with you." She hung up.

That conversation with Mary stung. Partially because I knew she was right. I hadn't been as good a friend as I could have been. I wasn't good at remembering anyone's birthday. But I should have made a point of remembering hers. I could just envision her that night, sitting by herself in her Seattle apartment, watching TV, not having the will to go outside, where she'd be scrutinized. Mary liked living in Seattle, but I don't think she had made many friends. I suspected she was skipping workdays and not leaving the house.

Mary felt like she was losing me. During these conversations I would try to reassure her that I was still totally there for her, but to no avail. She refused to accept that I still loved her. One night I was out really late and got drunk. The next morning I realized I had a studio session with Scott. It was a weekday and we had laid down a haunting chord progression the day before. I was so hungover standing on the train platform thinking about how Mary must have felt on her birthday. In my head I sang the melody. "Mary, you shouldn't let 'em make you mad, you hold the best you can."

In the studio, even though I could barely open my eyes without a stabbing pain shooting between them, I sang the melody over the chords we'd laid down. As I wrote the verses sitting back on the couch, I thought of the friendship I'd had with her that had lasted almost ten years, and I just wrote the song for her. Multiple times that day, I was feeling so raw I teared up as we wrote.

I burned the rough version on a CD and mailed it to her with no note, wanting the song to be the last word in this conversation. The point, which I hope she got, was: "Don't you ever say again that I'm not your best friend, because I will always be, and I refuse to have this argument ever again."

28

AS OUR OPERATION GREW, OUR SHORTCOMINGS WERE becoming more visible, at least to me. All I wanted was for us to be a real band, but we still felt like an "act." Having Derek on guitar made a big difference, but how would people take us seriously when we were still using a minidisc player as a backing track? However, any small growth spurts changed the landscape of the venues we were able to play. It was a lot more difficult now to get the four of us performing on the top of a bar.

Formika was a drag queen staple of downtown. She used to host SqueezeBox and knew how to sell debauchery. The year before, she had roped me into hosting some weekly night in a Midtown theater. I made my own little flyers, thinking I'd give promoting a shot. Maybe it was one of the other mean hosts who turned me off, or the full bottle of poppers I spilled on myself and the dance floor, but I decided I was never really meant to be a party promoter, so after only a couple weeks, I gave up. But Formika was still friendly with me and booked the band multiple times at her party Area 10007. However, since we'd added Derek, it was going to prove a tight fit.

"I don't think we're going to be able to play the party anymore," I said on the phone, apologetic when she tried to get us back. "Our setup has gotten a little more complicated with the guitars and all. We have a manager now, too, who's handling all this stuff."

"Who is this manager person?" she huffed. "You're telling me you can't play my party?"

"Not unless there's a proper stage with more inputs, unfortunately."

I heard later that Formika proceeded to talk shit about the band around town. Apparently she was saying that she'd booked us to play and we didn't show up. This remains secondhand information, and who knew if it was true, but it still hurt my feelings. I thought Formika and I were friends, but I guess that's nightlife.

A drag queen I really loved was Sweetie. She was a very large broad, with towering hair and a foul mouth. Sweetie threw a party called Cheez Whiz at the Parkside Lounge on Houston Street, and the small room with its mini-stage was the perfect size for the four of us. But every Sunday night, it was Sweetie who was the real star. No one could nail a dramatic lip sync like her, a vision with her massive, sparkling frame. Her performance of "Light of a Clear Blue Morning" by Dolly Parton would raise the hairs on the back of your neck. To this day, she's one of the best performers I've ever seen.

A lot of weirdos and notorious downtowners would come to hear Sammy Jo DJ. Flawless Sabrina would show up every week, a living legend, working looks since the fucking '60s. The wig might have been as old as she was, but hell if she wasn't the loveliest soul. Rose, who served cocktails and dressed like an art deco lampshade, was kind, slipping us some free drinks when she could. Jayne County would amicably stand on the side of the stage sometimes, smiling with an occasional twitch.

At one of the gigs we did there, I tried playing an electric guitar for "Tits on the Radio." Neil pulled me aside later and said, "Please never do that again. You're a terrible guitar player. And by the way, you looked like a waiter in a bad restaurant in Tuscaloosa." I guess you could at least count on Neil for some gritty honesty.

I was soon hit with my first moment of songwriting depression. I came into the studio one day, and Scott and I started writing something that wasn't going anywhere. I thought about all the great songs we'd written so far, and I felt a curious, creeping dread that we'd be unable to write anything of that caliber again. All of a sudden our work seemed overwhelming and impossible. The first time this happened, it only lasted a day, but the feeling would eventually overtake my whole life.

Some friend of Neil's from Italy had been coming to our shows at Luxx, and he booked us to play this mega-club outside Florence. The trip was going to be very quick, just two nights, then back to New York. It was the farthest distance we'd traveled as a band. But we'd be doing it without Derek on guitar.

There was something wrong with Derek's leg. Doctors had found holes in his bones that were being filled by foreign matter. They weren't quite sure what was happening: No one was saying the word *cancer*, but it sure was bouncing around our heads. Derek was stoic and didn't let on that he was worried about anything. But he was saddled with appointments and had to stay behind.

The ride from the airport in Florence was all rolling hills and windy roads, so picturesque. It took forever to get to where we were going, which was a ways out of the city, but Scott, Ana, and I were happy to be on such a glamorous-feeling trip. The hotel was above standard, and our host took us out to dinner. Those hours before the show, often the promoter takes the band out to a nice meal. It's always a sweet gesture, but I've always found those dinners can be difficult. During the three hours before stage time, I can become both nervous and bored: Time can feel like it's dragging by in the dirt. I get too preoccupied to be able to carry on conversations. It can take too much energy before a show to be "on."

After dinner we were backstage waiting to perform, simmering in our excitement. This was the biggest club we'd played so far. I had a great feeling we were going to set the room on fire.

We were introduced, and hit the stage in front of the swarming, noisy club. I knew right away this was not going to be our kind of crowd. The women were in very high heels, short dresses, lips plumped, hair blown big. The men were all in suits. We began playing "Electrobix." The sound just kind of drifted out into the air, barely penetrating the noise of patrons, milling around and talking. They couldn't have cared less that we were onstage. A shot of panic hit me. How the hell were we going to get through all five songs like this? It was nightmarish, like we were singing underwater. People were actually pretending not to see.

During "Filthy/Gorgeous," Ana strode down the catwalk and asked a man and woman who were at the front of the stage but faced away from us, "Are you aware there's a band playing right now, sir, madam?" Ana bent over and aggressively stuck her face between theirs and started singing. The whole thing was getting borderline hostile. I signaled to Scott that we should break into "Comfortably Numb" next, because at least they might be familiar with the song, and we could win a few people over. When it started, my fear escalated. There was no recognition in the room. We cut a song and ended our set early. The gig was a flop.

Back in the hotel room Babydaddy and I were sharing, we fell apart. He was sick with some kind of strep throat. "Obviously we're doing something wrong." His head was in his hands. "How did that just happen?"

"They were a bad crowd," I said. "It's gonna be inevitable sometimes."

"Our style is totally off. We look ragtag. In fact, we don't even have a look. And people think this is just more electroclash bullshit."

"We need a fucking drummer." I was getting wound up. "We can't be just playing these dance club gigs. These kind of people don't want to see a band. They're out clubbing."

"We cannot be Fischerspooner! We'll look like we're following some kind of trend." We were now yelling.

"Of course we can't be Fischerspooner!" I screamed, and pointed at myself. "They wear fucking pantyhose on their heads!" The morning sun was already lighting up the room, and we had about three hours to sleep before we had to get up for the plane home. We were tired and hurt that we'd traveled all this way for the show to be so horrible.

When we met back up in the lobby the next morning, Scott looked like he'd just slept in a ditch. He was really sick. As we checked out, he asked me to get him some orange juice. "That's gonna hurt your throat," I said. "Scott, it's so acidic."

"What, are you my fucking mother?" He stormed away to get it himself and I felt like a total asshole. The ride to the airport was leaden. I just stared out the window feeling resigned. Something in me thought whatever just happened might be irreparable, the end of the band. We'd put in all this work to come out here for nothing.

Whatever bad vibes Scott and I had were quickly slept off and our next trip as a band was to Germany. I had spent so much time hanging at the Berlin mega-club Ostgut during my previous travels, it felt like an honor to play its last days, before it was to be demolished to make way for an O_2 arena. Two DJs named Boris and ND, whom I had befriended, asked if we would come out and play the last weekend at Ostgut, home of the infamous original Panorama Bar. We were to perform at Panorama well after midnight, and Peaches would do the main room at 9 a.m. This was all happening on New Year's Eve.

The club was in a desolate part of the warehouse district in East Berlin, seeming like the middle of nowhere, with dirt roads. It didn't even feel like you were in a city. The club was huge and unadorned, sharp and dangerous around its edges. Many of its industrial features were left untouched among the mixed crowd, queer and straight. The main floor played harder techno, and Panorama Bar was more eclectic. The smaller space was so named because it was flanked by two massive walls with windows that overlooked Berlin's city skyline: When the night brightened into morning, the sunrise and all its colors washed the room in a gentle glow. Within minutes, blackout blinds would be drawn closed. Then it could be any hour of the day and it didn't matter.

Derek came on the trip but was limping around, post-operation. He was on crutches and his foot was in a cast. Doctors had checked his bones, and now he was waiting to hear some kind of diagnosis. We stayed at the art'otel in Mitte and it was so cold, it felt like your body was shrieking when you walked outside. The night before the gig, we had all gone out to some bars, and Ana had barfed on the front of the hotel upon our return. We joked that she provided her own, special temporal art.

Jet-lagged, I slept through the entire day and got up in the early evening, knowing we would be up all night. The band ventured out of the hotel to find food in the freezing cold, but walked forever, not finding anything open. We screamed as firecrackers were thrown off balconies at us from all directions. Apparently that's what they did in Berlin on New Year's Eve.

I remember tromping through an iced-over grassy field. "Oh, we're in Mitte?" Ana said between firecrackers. "More like the Mitte of nowhere." We finally found a grotty sandwich shop that sold us some panini. As we clutched ourselves to keep warm, slowly plodding back to the hotel, poor Derek kept screaming every time he was startled by the firecrackers. He's always been sensitive to loud noises, and being on crutches seemed to make it all the sadder. By the time we all made it back to our hotel to be transported to the gig, we were traumatized, and Ana was in a bad mood over having forgotten her wig.

Our set was at four in the morning. The warm Panorama Bar was full of friendly faces, and the crowd was welcoming and excited. But the stage monitor scenario was a mess. Monitors are what make you able to hear what you're playing or singing onstage. We were having to use the room speakers to hear ourselves, which can cause weird sonic delays. But no one in the audience cared as we played the show; everyone in the room was just happy we were there.

Ostgut was set to be open for at least the next twenty-four hours, and I wasn't supposed to fly out until that night, so I immediately dropped an E and half a hit of acid. We were sharing a dressing room with Peaches and I was starstruck. It hadn't been that long ago that her performance at the Knitting Factory had picked at me like a loose thread on a shirt. Every artist I'd seen and loved had all pulled on that thread, making a hole that only I could sew up again myself with my own stitch witchery. Peaches was very kind, although everyone seemed to be calling her Merrill. *I guess a lot of us music folks have two names*, I thought.

At one point, I sat down next to Derek. He had his cast-covered foot set up on a chair and looked morose, kind of staring at the floor. "You okay?" I asked him.

"I just can't get my mind off this." He gestured to his foot and shook his head. "I want to be able to have fun with everybody, but I'm too distracted. I don't know what's happening."

"What was the last thing they said?"

He still didn't know anything yet. "I'm really scared." His face crumpled and he started to sob. I sat next to him and put an arm on his back while he cried into his hands. The bass pumped and throbbed, making the mirrors on the walls shake.

"Look, I think it's going to be all right," I said. With the drugs kicking in, I thought my voice sounded hollow. "Just try to be positive." There was a dull, sick feeling in my stomach. He wiped his face. "It's been a long night," I said. "We should get you to a car back to the hotel."

I spent the rest of the morning in Panorama Bar, pleasantly high, loving the music by DJ Boris, rubbing up on a stocky Turkish guy named Yusi. We danced together, flirted, and made out. Eventually he took me back to his place, on top of a high-rise overlooking all of East Berlin. We drew a bath and put on *Chill Out* by the KLF. As he held me in the bathtub, the sounds of trains, sheep bleating, and Elvis trickled around us. Before we went to sleep I put on my tacky velour purple sweatpants from Old Navy.

"These are my Liz Taylors," I told Yusi.

"So what are those, then?" He pointed to my tangerine glasses. "Your Melanie Griffiths?"

When I woke up at about 8 p.m., it was like the sun had never risen. I'd been living in the dark for days. I flew out of the old Tempelhof Airport that has since been closed down. It was beautiful and eerie, like being in some other time. I boarded the plane in a dreamlike state, remnants of the drugs still coursing through my system. Sticking my forehead to the frosty window, I wondered if this was what life was going to be now: just floating. We took off into yet another night.

***

"Jason," Mary said. "I'm sorry."

"For what? There's nothing to be sorry about." It was a Thursday night, and I was home, playing *Grand Theft Auto 3*. When the game got intense, I would forget to blink and my contacts would go dry.

"No, I'm a total bitch. Always whining, getting upset over nothing." She paused and I could hear her readjust herself wherever she was sitting. "I got your song you wrote for me and I've listened to it about two hundred times. Jason, it's beautiful."

I put my controller for the game down and sat up on my bed. "Babe, I'm so glad you like it. I wrote it just for you."

"Oh my God," she said. "What if I fucking hated it? Was like—this is terrible."

"And you were like playing it to people in Seattle and making fun of it."

"Even if it wasn't about me I'd love it. It's such a good song."

"Well, it's yours."

That night we made a deal. If her song for any reason turned out to be a hit and made money, we would use that money to get her a gastric-bypass operation, something she'd been wanting and fantasizing about for years. But it seemed like such a far-off prospect, there would never be enough money just lying around for such a thing. I knew she saw it as one of her only ways out. There was the possibility that she could live her life like a regular person, leave her house whenever she felt like it to go on a stroll, not be stared at when she got on the bus every day.

It was hard to imagine a healthier, happier Mary, but I knew anything was possible. It would be a huge life change, but above all else, I just wanted for her to feel like she belonged in the world, with me.

29

IT WAS TIME TO FIND A DRUMMER. SCOTT AND I PUT AN ad in the *Village Voice* and held auditions in a grim rehearsal studio in Midtown. The band and Neil were present and we had narrowed it down to two people. One was a really cute girl with shaggy hair and a massive smile. She played hard and straight and bounced along with the kick. Her energy was contagious, but it wasn't the right fit. The other drummer we were considering was a guy named Patrick Seacor. He was Lower East Side New York personified, like he had walked straight out of Scorsese's *After Hours*. Cute and blond, somewhere in his thirties, he wore a colorful scarf and a beret. His drumming was loose and cool, his face pouty and unbothered. We asked him to join the band.

Hearing our songs with live drums made a huge difference, black-and-white into color, mono into stereo. We were now a bona fide rock and roll band. My fears of being pigeonholed dissipated for the time being. Even though we would carry the electro label for a couple of years, people would now see for themselves something more than just a track act.

Patrick had his own low-ceilinged rehearsal space, directly under the Pink Pony in the Lower East Side. It was subterranean and dark, full of abalone shells, tacky ashtrays, and broken Christmas lights. But it was cozy, the perfect spot for us to rehearse a few times a week. The tangled cords and stacked, hissing speakers kept it makeshift. The place, as well as our playing, was a lovable mess, but we were fortunate to have it, as well as each other. None of us were spectacular musicians, but as long as we kept hacking away at it, I knew we could get good.

We were still trying to sort out our looks. Derek let me borrow one of his Paul Smith suits. My mom, in town to see one of the shows, took me shopping one day at Century 21 and bought me a purple leather vest by Marc Jacobs. The price had been slashed. My mime outfit always got me by in a pinch, when I didn't have any spare money.

The last time I had been down on the farm with my parents, I'd raced through a copy of *Everything You Need to Know About the Music Business* I'd bought at a Barnes & Noble. The different facets seemed complicated and I was overwhelmed by the commissions, the agents, managers, and lawyers. There were so many ways for a band to get in trouble. One bad move or faulty cog in the wheel could fuck everything up.

There was now interest from a couple more record labels in London. A man named Seb Chew from Polydor had been showing up in town to see us play gigs at the Knitting Factory and Joe's Pub. He told me my one dance move was getting old really fast. It was kind of a mix between the Charleston and the Mashed Potato. But he was right, I needed to expand my boogie. Overall I didn't mind when I got critiques of the show. This was entertainment and I wanted it to be as effective as possible. It was tough to give notes on the performance of other band members. But that didn't really stop me.

The other guy who was interested in signing the album was a notorious character named "Simon," who had an indie label in London. He'd released some albums that I had been a huge fan of. "Simon" was excitable and kind, but he'd show up at our studio to hear tracks, reeking of booze, immediately asking if there were any drinks in the house. I'd take him to the kitchen and watch him pour two straight shots of vodka over ice with shaky hands.

He was very enthusiastic about the songs, spouting ideas about marketing and how we could roll it out. On a car ride back into Manhattan from the studio, he told me about someone he knew, Fee, who was a clothing designer. "She did the Kylie look from the 'Can't Get You Out of My Head' video, you know. You should work with her." She was also at that moment outfitting the Darkness, who were blowing up in the UK.

There were a few other labels that were only half interested, some guy from Sony with whom we had sushi. He was on the fence. "I told him he needs to pay attention," Neil told me the next day. "I was like, 'Dude, the songs are exploding out of these guys. When Jason got up to use the little boys' room, he wrote a chorus to a new song.'" Neil was right. We were in the middle of our meal and suddenly a song called "Oooh" appeared in my head. I excused myself to the restroom and sang it into my voice-mail. We recorded it in the studio the next day.

Scott and I didn't know who to sign with. Our main two options were British—no label in America was interested. We had to decide between Seb Chew at Polydor or "Simon," between a major label under Universal or an indie. Scott and I gave both options serious thought. Or was I just pretending to? Was an independent label the more commendable and artistic route? Or was stepping into the majors an act of betting on ourselves and having a much larger infrastructure supporting us? There were many trips to London, a lot of meetings.

"Simon" from the indie had us play a show at Fabric for an anniversary party for his label. Our new drummer, Patrick, who had started going by the name Paddy Boom, came with us. I walked out on the Fabric stage in a Disneyland Star Tours–looking sweat suit that my friend Todd Thomas had designed. It felt luxurious on my skin, being the first thing anyone had designed for me. We tore it up: Having a drummer changed everything. I could strut bigger, throw my arms around, swatting flies that weren't there. The music's sturdier foundation bolstered my confidence.

After the gig, "Simon" walked up to me dressed like some sort of Amish priest, wild-eyed and frothing at the mouth. He grabbed my shoulders and, through his grinding teeth, all I could understand were the words *techno music* and *selling records*. He was mad out of it, off his fucking face. I walked from the dance floor and knew we weren't signing with him.

So that meant signing to Polydor. A woman named Orla Lee would be doing our marketing. She'd had a major hand in helping launch the careers of Daft Punk and Air. Our first meetings there were encouraging—everyone truly seemed to have an affinity for the music. We signed the deal. You always hear awful stories about bands and their record labels. That wasn't the case with Polydor. We got lucky with a group of passionate music fans who truly wanted people to hear the band.

My folks had agreed to help support me until we finished the album, but the band itself was still broke. There were so many costs that ran well beyond paying for silly flag dancers. When I looked at the actual numbers, they seemed really large and scary. This was real money. It was nerve-racking to know we were indebted to Neil.

Scott and I were in charge of finishing the album. We spent every day in his apartment starting at 11 a.m., poring over the tracks into the night, prepping them for the live tracking. We would have five days in a proper studio to get all the live instrumentation that we needed.

We recorded at a place in Murray Hill called the Shed, and right away we began learning new things about recording and about ourselves as a band. Derek was a frantic guitar player and was great at soloing, Scott was better at rhythm and acoustic, so we had to figure out who was playing what. The drums were a problem. Paddy was great live, but his style was too free to match the click track on the songs that were more dance-oriented and quantized. Scott and I had a lot of intricate work to do, piecing everything together.

The entire time in the control room I had some CDs propped up as a sonic shrine for what I wanted us to achieve. One of them was the *Annie* original motion picture soundtrack. Ever since my mom had taken me to see it when I was five, I'd been a sucker for its warm and flat production, the clanky pianos, the sound of tape.

Scott and I took all the bits back to his kitchen studio to weave them into the album. Some of the drums were usable, but a lot of them we had to program meticulously to sound like real drums and fills. It was tedious work. But the string arrangements that the New York singer and musician Joan as Police Woman had laid down lifted the songs in a way I hadn't expected. Composer Paul Leschen helped us out with piano on "Take Your Mama." The horn arrangements by Crispin Cioe and the Uptown Horns were revelatory, and I was in awe watching them work. They had played on songs like "Love Shack" and "Living in America" and were people we'd collaborate with for the next ten years.

But there was no money left for mixing the record. Both Neil and Polydor thought that Scott and I should mix it ourselves inside the Logic program. So that's what we did: We mixed the whole album in the kitchen.

30

January 4, 2004

The new year is here, and I've been very lazy today. It feels so nice sitting on my bed, ripping CDs and playing Zelda. This is all after a very busy, strange day yesterday, which was very Night in the Life of Jimmy Reardon *or something. It consisted of me waking up with this bartender I've been seeing, Jacob, hanging out, Nintendo, went to the gym, worked out, horny, watched guys jack off in the showers, went to band practice with Joan as Police Woman who's doing keys for the next show, went to Matthew Delgado's where I made a bowl of mac and cheese and then went to the Slide. Boyfriends Pinto and Paul were there and it was good to see them, but I still feel kind of dopey for having slept with Paul last summer. Met this kid named Jared who I've seen around for a long time. We went back to his place and smoked weed and made out and then I went home. Just as I was turning the light off I got a call from that old flame Mark, the go-go dancer I met in the shark tank. It was about 4:30 a.m. He came over, drunk, which I wasn't thrilled about.*

I made him just go to sleep. We woke up at noon and messed around, and I've spent the rest of the day hanging out on my own.

New Year's turned out to be really fun. Spent it with Tom Donaghy. We went to a friend's on St. Marks and took some ecstasy. Derek has been thrilled to find out that his leg is okay, and is almost back to normal. He got stood up, so he came out with us. At about 3 a.m. we went to visit Sammy Jo, who was DJing at the Hole. It had a real dark energy, but I'd like to think we brightened it up a bit. I took off my clothes and danced on a box. Then we grabbed some cute boys and went back to Matthew Delgado's penthouse for a hot-tub sunrise.

I think 2004 will be the year of the Scissor Sister. My main concern is to write an amazing follow-up.

January 7, 2004

Lying here in a bathrobe. It's freezing outside, listening to Station to Station. Had a slight cold for a couple days. Was in Fred Schneider's apartment last night. I couldn't believe it. My dream as a kid was just to have lunch with the B-52's and there I was, sitting on his couch while he played me demos they've been recording. He's singing with us onstage in a few days. It's beyond the call of duty on his part. He seems a bit nervous about it. Tomorrow is our last rehearsal for the Bowery show. It's going to be a blast, a little scary, a lot of press will be there, but whatever, no need to speculate.

The album got a five-star review in Uncut magazine. It's kind of a trip. I am (we are) going to write another album and it will be better than this one. The astrology column I read by Rob Brezsny this week used death as a metaphor for killing off beliefs and habits that are outworn burdens. This week he tells me to "seek up-close, experimental immersion, not conceptual understanding from a distance."

31

THE FIRST TIME I SLIPPED INTO THE WATER IT WAS JUST a few degrees under body temperature and was tolerable at first, but after hours of being filmed in the tank, we emerged cold and clammy, our bodies, scrotums, and hands shriveled from the dampness. The band had arrived in frigid, rainy Devon in January to shoot the video for "Comfortably Numb." It took two days in a gigantic, gloomy water tank that must have been fifty feet deep. The video was to be of us floating and swimming around in the water, with CGI creatures to be added in postproduction.

A kind of wet still permeated when I dried off for the last time. As we packed up for London, I wasn't feeling very well. Our driver was taking the scenic route and going about ten miles under the speed limit, pointing out landmarks. It was interminable—the car was crawling like my skin, like whatever virus was taking over and multiplying in my body.

By the time I got to my hotel room at the Columbia, I was gripped by a deep fever. The chills were so intense I couldn't get out of bed. I just lay there, moaning back to whatever hotel ghosts could hear me.

The next day we had the main photo shoot for the album. I had been unabashedly inspired by the Roxy Music gatefold of *For Your Pleasure*, the band shot against a stark white background, with Brian Eno on one side in a collar of feathers, which I jacked for my own look. Our shoot lasted all day and I spent most of it curled up on the couch in a fetal position, just standing up and lurching to the set at the latest possible moment. It was maybe the sickest I've ever felt. You can see my bleariness in the photo, my eyes hazy.

Days later we were in Barcelona playing a very late show at Nitsa, the same place where I'd bought those legendary "white diamond" pills a year and a half ago. I was by no means recovered yet, but whatever flu I had was now being passed around the band. It was brutal. Derek was in terrible shape, just as I had been, shivering and eyes watering. The whole night was bleak. At the hotel before the gig, Ana had a kind of sad fear attack. Scott and I met up with her in her bedroom.

"I can't keep doing this." She was sobbing. "I can't just ride around in a van, eating fried foods at gas stations!"

"Ana." Somehow Scott always kept his cool. "If we're still riding around in a van in four months' time, that means this whole thing is not working and we'll be done with it."

I went back to my room, with a horrible guilt. It was all my fault. Everybody around me was miserable and stressed-out, all because of some rock and roll fantasy I'd had since I was a little kid. That's one of the hardest things about leading a band: When things aren't going great, it's on your shoulders. I can't stand it when people around me are unhappy.

That night, the show at Nitsa was serviceable, but Waldorf, the band that had gone on before us (they were on A Touch of Class), had played a pretentious and sonically aggressive set with outlandish costumes and props. It not only fell flat, they had cleared out the club. By the time we went onstage, Derek was practically catatonic with the flu.

When I went to bed that night, I had a coughing attack with a tissue and there was a big smudge of blood on the Kleenex. I threw it away and pretended not to see.

32

WE'D DRAWN A COUPLE HUNDRED PEOPLE TO A VIRGIN Megastore in Central London. Not a line out the door, but a good turnout. After playing a five-song set on a tiny stage set up between CD racks, we signed records at a long table. The album was finally released that day in the UK—February 4, 2004. Not in North America yet: It was still a time when they staggered releases from country to country.

To see the album lying out on the table was surreal. An array of different people passed in front of us, clutching the CD to their chests, passing them toward us, nervously telling us their names. They turned from us grinning, walking away with a little piece of us in their hands.

If there was a panning shot down the table, from left to right, you would have seen the band in our elevated looks, our glam drag. I found myself now to be dressing up for all occasions. There was no such thing as casual anymore. Johnny Blue Eyes, our wardrobe guy, would hold an item of clothing in front of him, close one eye as if framing it on us. "Darling, you must understand," he'd say, his voice honey-laden, "you are now giving people a glimmer of fantasy every time they see you. Just a dollop of fabulousness, eh?" He'd tilt his head. "You now have the responsibility to brighten people's day. How magical is that?"

I think I was wearing a leather shrug, without a shirt no less, and a dead pink ferret or some such thing sewn on my shoulder, like half a boa, with black leather pants and a huge elaborate belt buckle, topped off by a fedora, and pointy black boots with a Cuban heel. I now felt like some heightened version of myself in these public scenarios. We had hooked up with a designer named Fee Jones; she'd started making clothes and styling for us and was letting loose on the whole band. We dressed like fun elderly people who had collided with a taxidermy shop.

"I just fucking love you." An unadorned teenage girl with plain, straight hair held forth a CD for me to sign. "My mum and I have been waiting for it to come out. Feels like forever."

"What's your name?"

"Evelyn," she said. "Linda," the next one. "Joe, and this is my friend Elsie, we drove from Nottingham." And so it went.

I looked into their eyes and wondered what they were seeing. I smiled at every person and shook their hand, tried to take a picture with them if possible, told them thank you for buying the record and for coming to see us. Scott, Patrick, and Derek were quieter. But Ana had a special way of making the fans feel like we were all just friends, normal people—albeit ones who dressed like bedraggled, world-weary pensioners turned club kids twenty-four hours a day.

The switch to this other life was drastic. Polydor placed the whole band in a fancy three-bedroom house in the posh Marylebone area. We were literally living together now in the heart of London. It must have cost the label a ton of money, but it was convenient for them to have us in one spot when they needed us to do promo, video, and photo shoots, which were happening now all day, every day. Our mood was jovial: Everyone was getting along, still enjoying the exotic pleasures of our new life. I was sharing a room with Derek, but managed to have enough privacy to jerk off at least every other day. All I had was just a centerfold of a shirtless tattooed porn star named Johnny Hazzard.

There was a scene happening around us—or maybe *we were* the scene. Two nights before, we had thrown a party in the flat. Our front door opened and in had poured a herd of eccentrics that rivaled any flashy night out in New York. Erol Alkan from Trash, Lady Bunny, Princess Julia, Tasty Tim, Pete Burns of Dead or Alive—each person a master of their own image and personality. With arms draped over one another, party cups tipped back, everyone seemed pleased to be in the moment itself. We'd made it this far, at least.

The weeks had been relentless: I had lost a lot of weight from all the work, being shuttled around to every corner of London. My face looked cracked from the makeup that was applied so my skin wouldn't shine in front of cameras. I was becoming all eyes: They seemed to get wider the smaller I got.

I was learning how to stare into the lens. Cameras were going off all day, and at every click, I imagined I was hypnotizing people. *Buy our records*, I chanted in my head. At first it didn't seem like it was working. Our debut UK single, "Laura," ended up charting at No. 56, a pretty dismal showing. But Polydor was undeterred and gave no external sign that we should worry, knowing it was in their best interests for the band to feel optimistic and confident.

I turned on the charm everywhere, going out of my way to be friendly with each writer, interviewer, and radio personality we encountered. For the most part the write-ups had been fantastic, though some old battle-ax named Kitty Empire said that our sound was as if someone had been thumbing through an old record box and just discovered Supertramp. When we finally showed up in a piece in *The Face*, they just gave us a corner of a page, with the headline "Karaoke Nation." But in general, their snark was obviously not on point (they'd be out of business in another two months). It stung, however, sitting at the Marylebone flat, scanning any lukewarm articles.

The band was getting pretty hammy in interviews. We were very pleasant to talk to, but it became apparent that we could get a lot of attention talking shit about other people. Ana told one publication that Britney Spears was "dumber than a box of hair." And I said that "she should be working at McDonald's." These would go into print, and then immediately every other interviewer would want to talk about these quotes, which would actually make headlines in the more sensational papers. This was treacherous territory. It wasn't a good look for any of us, and I got fed up with having to revisit something nasty I had said a week earlier. Scott and I tried to institute a band guideline not to say negative things about other artists to the press. With Ana, unfortunately, that was impossible. If you tried to tell her to do something she would just do the opposite, so there were a lot of moments of sucking it up and hoping no one noticed.

There were also bits of homophobia injected into even the praising articles. They were like backhanded slaps in between the lines, little reminders for us not to get too comfortable. When *NME* called us "camper than a row of tents," I seethed a little bit on the inside, knowing they believed they were putting us in our place. Some pieces were full of flat-out lies. Some would feature these weird paraphrases, injecting words and sentences we never would have said. At no point in her entire life can I imagine Ana saying: "Oh, only if it's Versace, darling!" I wanted people of all kinds to understand that the experience of being gay wasn't something separate from them. I wanted to tap into a truth broader and more universal, draw a line from my happiness and suffering to theirs, show that it's all the same. I've never made music just for gay people.

We let certain writers into our personal lives, only to be written about as self-absorbed egomaniacs. I was occasionally painted as an unaware and ambitious sociopath who loved talking about myself. *What the fuck else am I supposed to talk about?* I thought. The anger could color my outlook for days. Probably because I knew they were onto something.

I remember a quiet night in the Marylebone flat, when I lay on my bed and prayed aloud, "If anyone is out there listening, please, please, please make this work. I will put everything I have on the line, but just make this work."

A clear voice, inside my head, one that wasn't my own, answered: *If you get what you really want, it's gonna come with a price, you know.* "I'll pay it," I replied. "Whatever it is, I'll pay it."

One night, Derek and I went to Nag Nag Nag. The place was rammed. Justin Bond was there with this hunky guy named Christoph, all big muscles and a mustache, who looked like he'd chop the firewood and stick you for a spit roast. Christoph would later be responsible for introducing me to my future partner. On the side of the dance floor, some guy from New York named Ricardo shoved a bottle of poppers under my and Derek's noses. My head felt like a balloon.

Derek turned to me. "I suddenly feel like some trashy bottom about to get—" It was probably the poppers, but I didn't let him finish. I was seized with a sudden rage.

I shoved my finger in his chest. "Just because you're still not over getting picked on in high school doesn't mean you're any better than me, just 'cause I'm open about getting fucked." I could feel my forehead vein popping out. Derek took my pointing finger and bent it backward, and we shoved each other. The high of the poppers washed over me and I stood there in the bar, embarrassed and shocked at what had just come out of my mouth. We didn't exchange any more words; we just retrieved our jackets at the coat check and left.

Sheepish, I apologized on the walk home, interrupting the long silences. But something ugly had just happened. A jealous animosity had spewed out of me that I had been shoving under the rug. I felt threatened by Derek's fascination with representations of masculinity: the utility van he drove around, the butch-worship. I thought that because I was a freewheeling fag, it somehow made me less-than. I allowed myself to wear sequins and prance around the stage, performing queenery. But I told myself it was twice removed, an act. I still carried shame about who I was.

Also, it was an undeniable fact that I had a crush on Del, but the closest we ever got to anything sexual was taking Ambien, running down the hallway of the K West hotel in London naked, jerking off onto biscuits we found in the minibar, and then eating them. The next morning we looked at each other with amused confusion, having no proper explanation for what we'd done.

Having three gay guys in a band was tough for a few different reasons. We were probably measuring ourselves against each other constantly—the men we slept with, the groups we ran in. Fortunately, I think we all had our own, very individual sex appeal that attracted different kinds of men. There was, however, a hierarchy of masculinity between us that remained, and was constantly getting switched out as we attempted to one up each other, testing my insecurities. When Derek and Scott and I would check out a giant, muscular straight man, rather than enjoying objectifying him, I suddenly felt like I did when I was in high school. Like I would never measure up to the standards of what it meant to be a real man.

To prove that I was unafraid of myself, I wore outrageous looks, with tassels and sparkles, buckles and sequins. When I put them on, the shine was my resistance and rebellion to feeling inferior, just as it had always been. I knew I made ugly, sweaty faces onstage—I'd started seeing my distorted scream in the papers—but I didn't care about that, either. I didn't want to look handsome, I just wanted it to look like I was in control, and exorcise the hurt that remained under my skin.

33

THE HORSEMEAT DISCO GUYS WANTED TO PUT TOGETHER a club show at Crash in London on a holiday weekend. When we showed up at the big space in Vauxhall to do sound check, there was barely a half-broken drum kit waiting for us on the stage, which caused momentary drama. We thought we were going to have to call Pete Burns, who was performing with us that night, and cancel the show. Eventually a proper drum kit showed up and we were able to proceed.

I had been introduced to Pete by Tim Hailand, one of the guys I'd met on the Barcelona beach a couple summers before. Pete Burns was dialed up to fifteen, with his droll Manchester accent and constant desire to be wearing the most insane fashion at any given moment. He had a heavily augmented face—some people would say disfigured. I had no judgments about what Pete did; I saw an otherworldly beauty about him. I liked hanging around him just to see what he was going to wear or say. One night before our show, I watched him try on a closetful of stage clothes and listened to his running commentary regarding his own runway.

"Oh, here she is." Pete displayed a shapeless tartan blob with straps on a hanger. "When in doubt, Westwood. It's open in the back. What do you think Ana's going to have on?"

I shrugged, exhausted.

"How you hanging in there, doll? You look bloody tired."

"I'm knackered, as I guess you'd say over here. It's been all guns blazing. We haven't stopped for months."

"Babe, you either let the wave wash over you, or you ride it." He paused and checked his face in a mirror. "I say just ride the wave, love."

We were singing "Tits on the Radio" with Pete at Crash, and we rehearsed in a moldy East London space the night or two before. Pete showed up in a black jumpsuit with a plunging neckline and an orangutan-fur coat. I could sense he was nervous, but the band was so friendly and happy to have him, his nerves seemed to dissipate. "Can I warm up, doll?" He pulled out a CD, which I stuck in the boom box. I handed him a mic, and he started swaying to the intro. For the next twenty minutes, the band just sat cross-legged and slack-jawed, getting our very own private Dead or Alive set.

The next night, when we sang together at Crash, some guy must have been taunting him from the crowd. In the middle of the song, Pete leaned into the audience and pummeled the guy in the face. Usually if there was ever a fight, it would be reason to stop the show. But we kept on singing, giddy. The room was an electric stove: quick to cook, faster to burn. It felt like anything could happen.

When the set was done, Pete and I were on our way back to the dressing room with my friend Andy (who was living in London now) and Wolfgang Tillmans, when some very disheveled drunk teenager (could have been the same one in the crowd, who knows?) passed by with his chin tilted up. "Yeh, off ya go you fookin' tranny shite!"

Without missing a beat or changing his expression, Pete turned around, threw the fucker down the staircase, fixed a stray hair, and kept going as if nothing had happened. "Doll," he said, "definitely ready for a bloody cocktail."

The "Comfortably Numb" single debuted in the charts at No. 10, and the album landed just out of the Top Ten at No. 11, which was a little disappointing. But the chart position of the single meant that we got to go on *Top of the Pops*, a singular institution of British music. I sat in a café with Neil, our manager, and mused, "If all this goes to shit, at least someday we can look back and say we were *Top of the Pops.*" It was funny, there were so many of those "At least ifs." *At least if the album bombs, we can say that we made one. At least if no one buys tickets to this or that concert, we can say that we went on a tour.*

Being in the BBC studios for the first time felt monumental. The dressing rooms were fancy, and they treated us like we were stars. I had a brand-new hand-sewn pair of purple suede dungarees made by Fee. Derek had grown these huge muttonchops overnight that I thought made him look really different. When I found out we were going on *Top of the Pops*, I demanded that Derek shave them. I thought we should be consistent, mimic our album cover and promo shots, solidify the looks we had already established.

Scott agreed, but didn't think it was worth really harping on, just to keep friction low. But I hadn't figured out how to pick my battles yet, and I stuck with it, making Derek shave before we made our biggest television debut to date. It didn't make me feel good, but I rationalized it. Someone had to steer the ship. But Scott was right, I should have just let it slide.

Before we went on, Andy asked me if I was nervous. I lied and said no, but I was losing my mind with anticipation. Derek was too, having a meltdown that his guitar was detuned for some reason. And I was just scared. But we got on the stage, my nerves aflame. About halfway through the song three things occurred to me. My voice was sounding good, the audience all looked excited, and I was singing for thousands of people. Hundreds of thousands of people. This was what the word *broadcast* actually meant.

Joy shot up my spine and plastered itself on my face. It was a kind of connective pleasure I'd never felt before. There were eyes and ears, tons of them, watching us, listening, making judgments good or bad. I had people's attention and fuck, it felt good. The song ended. I leaped up and down on the stage and hugged anybody who was nearby. I was so happy. I wanted to feel more. We were right where we needed to be, doing exactly what we were supposed to be doing.

34

February 10, 2004

*As of this morning, I'm missing the States. Homesick for
California or Miami for some reason. My throat is fucked. I
feel like I'm destroying my voice every time I sing. Not getting
enough days off. Had to seriously yell at Neil on the phone
yesterday. He booked another show now, the day before the
Astoria gig, without Scott's and my permission. Scott and I have
to keep control of this stuff. We played a great gig last night at
the Charlotte in Leicester. Really sketchy, dodgy, dingy place.
Totally packed, with the crowd going crazy. It was so hot, the
clothes came off earlier than usual.*

*We played at the Scala in London last night. I woke up a little
more nervous than usual. Could be those stupid Madonna
rumors. Some radio station in an interview said that apparently
she and Guy Ritchie were coming to see us play. I thought it
was horseshit, but then later on in the day, Ana started to cry,
saying that she thought Madonna was going to come and take
Scott and me away, vampire us somehow.*

Had video and artwork meetings, and then Scott yelled at
me for running around in my underwear in front of the
merchandise people. I yelled back and got in his face. We made
it to the Scala, where David Ross, our new lighting guy, had his
rigs all set up and it looked fantastic. Lots of LED panels, etc. I
was pleased with our performance, though Paddy's drums could
have been a lot tighter. I wore deerskin trousers with fur, and
a brown cotton-ball genie boa. "Mary" for the first time went
really smoothly. Afterward, Mark Moore [DJ and founding
member of S'Express] *had a great after-show party, lots of*
champagne, very Wizard of Oz. *Lots of old friends and many*
new ones. I could hardly get across the room in under thirty
minutes.

June 2, 2004

In a good state of mind and it's the first day back in the US
on a bus. Just arrived two days ago from a five-day European
jaunt that included Lisbon: playing on the ocean outdoors,
Barcelona (4:30 a.m., of course), England for the Homelands
festival (about ten thousand people in the crowd). Then on to
Ireland for a little pub gig with a GQ shoot in the middle of
it. At one point at Heathrow I fell asleep facedown on the cold
floor right at British Airways ticketing. My body just shut down.
Before we left for those shows, we played two great ones at
Bowery Ballroom in NYC. Both sold out.

Everybody and their grandma's dog came and saw us in DC.
Turned out to be a great night because afterward there was
a really hot guy named Chris waiting there with a bucket of
meringues, obviously sent by Christoph.

I froze when I first saw Chris. He wore a busted black leather bomber, had thick curly black hair and a nose that looked like it should be on display at the Louvre. Ana pointed him my direction. "I think those are for Jake."

He handed a bag of puffy cookies to me. "These are from Christoph, not me, really," he said. Christoph was a sexy, burly friend of mine I knew from London. Before shows, he always brought me homemade meringues, delivering them personally to the dressing room. "He asked me to come and bring this for you," Chris said. "I told him I would. I just live down the street." He was soft-spoken—gentle, even.

I asked him how he knew Christoph. Apparently they'd met when he spent a semester in London last year. Chris was code-red hotness, I wasn't going to let him just walk away. I couldn't tell if he was gay, either. But fuck, he was so handsome.

"So . . . what are we doing tonight?" I blurted. "Where is the fun place to go?" A question I ask guys sometimes when I can't tell their sexual orientation.

"I don't know that much about tonight, but there's always JR's, where I bartend." *Okay, thank God, a gay bar*, I thought. I was heading to dinner with my family, but he and I agreed to meet up after.

When I found my mom a couple minutes later, I said, "I think I just met my husband."

I was correct.

35

IT FELT LIKE MONTHS SINCE WE'D HAD A PROPER DAY off. Life was all tracers, a blur of dirty club benches and vinyl uphol-stery, darkness. There could suddenly be swells of people crashing all around us at any given time. Record label folks, fans at shows, inter-viewers, photographers, radio people, festival security. There was no time for names. Hours seemed like they were coming from above and backward. No matter how tired I was, though, I kept eye contact. I refused to totally slip away.

We played an *Attitude* magazine party and Elton John showed up with his partner, David Furnish; George Michael; Emma Bunton; and Lulu. The band played in custom pajamas: I almost felt naked in my silky leopard-print set. Afterward they came backstage, and it felt as if the band had just won some kind of game show. I could see Elton out in the crowd while we played. Every time a song ended he would hold up his hand and wave like the queen instead of clapping. And now here suddenly were multiple legends in our dressing room. George was kind and complimentary. In moments like this I'd start to feel as if I were having a dream, the scenario was so illogical.

"How you doing? Really?" was the first thing Elton asked me.

I was tongue-tied, but I managed to tell him how excited I was, but overwhelmed with the pace.

He reached up and pinched both my cheeks. "Welcome to show business!"

During this visit to London, the record label Parlophone was doing a greatest-hits collection for Kylie Minogue and needed a couple of singles, so they put Scott and me together with her in a studio in London for a couple days to see what we came up with.

I was never a huge pop music fan, but Kylie was another story. While Scott and I were recording the first album, I'd just had this feeling that I really wanted to work with her. It was a hunch that we could make something really special together. Kylie and I talked on the phone the day before we met, and I ran some title ideas past her. I was unable to sleep that night.

The moment she walked in the room I was bowled over by her specific, delicious charm. We clicked right away, laughing and getting weird, doing interpretive dances, hooting when we wrote a good hook. It was like we'd known each other for a long time. We wrote two great songs in those two days. One was called "Everything I Know," and one was called "I Believe in You."

Kylie was fast family—someone I immediately cared about and wanted to spend time with, create with, and make memories with. She's a good person who loves what she does, a proper showgirl, effervescent and grounding at the same time. You'll never hear her say anything bad about anyone, and she sings supernaturally. When you record her voice, it has this automatic flange in it—you don't need to bathe it in any effects. My first thought when recording her was that the only voices I could compare hers to were Dolly Parton's and Kate Bush's. She's a woman whom I feel a very deep bond with. And on top of that, she and Scott and I turned out to be a great songwriting team.

Our day-to-day went haywire. I remember running through Heathrow in stage clothes with half my ass hanging out, entertaining everyone in airport security. I climbed up on a speaker in Glasgow and some drunk person in the audience tried to pull me down. I burnt my back on a hot stage light. Paddy started a fistfight, drunk at our bus door. We got shoved around by Eminem's security at our second *Top of the Pops* performance. I almost got arrested for smoking pot outside of a gig in Manchester. We played just about every small city in Britain twice. We shot the video for "Take Your Mama" on a couple hours' sleep, then left for a small tour of two-hundred-person senior college banquets with us and Amy Winehouse opening for Ash. I met up with Carly Simon in New York to write but we ended up pouring our hearts out to each other while we fiddled with chords on a piano. We did a whole UK tour opening up for Duran Duran in arenas. Elton had us come play some outdoor shows with him in the countryside. During one of those performances my pants busted and my balls popped out. DJ gigs were packed up against theater gigs and then we'd go back out the same night for a club gig. We played the Astoria in London and our whole guitar rig shorted out, so Ana had to sit on the stage for twenty minutes and tell stories to the audience while our tech guys tried to fix it. We took DJ Sammy Jo and Kiki and Herb on the road with us through England. I was so proud to be playing with friends who had brought me so much inspiration. After releasing the record in North America, we played *Saturday Night Live*, where I wore a backless Heatherette woman's pantsuit. John Cameron Mitchell directed the "Filthy/Gorgeous" video starring just about every drag queen in New York.

You realize they might be onto something when multiple journalists ask you: "What does it feel like to be the hardest-working band in the world right now?"

Since record releases were staggered around the world at that time, the album didn't come out in the United States until June. The band was just beginning to make some headway in America when the *New York Times* ran a small piece about us with the headline "Hot over there, cool over here." It wasn't a fair assessment. It had taken five months for us to break into the UK after our record was released there. We hadn't had that opportunity or time to do that yet in the States. But the general perception of us in the media was that it wasn't really working in America. I believe that this can be traced entirely back to that bogus *New York Times* sidebar. It's interesting how much it affected the band's story. But I didn't really care all that much, it didn't feel like any kind of failure from our perspective.

My face looked different: haggard, drawn, older. I had gotten so skinny you could count all my ribs. It was hard to keep any pants on, as I had gone past the last loop of every belt I had. I stopped wanting to eat. With all the adrenaline pumping through my veins each day, food didn't look very appetizing. The shows were marathons, and I was burning more calories than I was consuming. We'd take flights late and early. I'd fall asleep on airport floors. There were two-day periods when we wouldn't be able to go to bed, and would just have to wait for the next night to pass out. I couldn't escape anyone, not even on the toilet. There were doors being knocked on, questions being asked, decisions to be made, the hiring and firing of people to be attended to.

I had to wear an eye patch for a week with an eye infection as we went through freezing Scandinavia. It was at a tiny Stockholm gig where an owlish young man and his kind sister approached me with the album they'd just finished. They were called the Knife and the album was *Deep Cuts*.

Late nights were for talking strategy with Scott: We'd conjure arguments over small choices that were neither here nor there, but could feel like life-or-death to us at the time. The pressures were intense, and if someone in the band was in a bad mood it could color everyone else's day. There were some nasty little fights—I could explode easily. Afterward I would sit by myself in a parking lot, feeling ashamed that my fuse was so short.

All of this fell away when I stepped out to play. I would shed my thoughts, forget who I was, and relish the drug of the stage, which came in phases. I detonated at the first note, running in circles like a sheepdog, in a kind of frenzy, unable to stop moving and shaking. The first few songs were always scary, and for the first third of each show I was nothing if not a bundle of fright. My eyes bugged out. I was like a junkie getting sick after shooting up, but soon, bliss washed over me. The high flooded through me and took over, allowing me to stomp my feet and slam myself around the stage without feeling pain.

And when there was the rare quiet moment in the shower or a hotel room, by myself, I began to feel something new in my core. A sensation of the floor dropping out, or as though I were falling over the edge of a roller coaster. There was a voice that appeared, speaking to me in my head, circuitous negative thoughts that reminded me that I wasn't creating, being productive, or writing songs. The voice would tell me that maybe I wouldn't ever be able to write another song again with the magic that I'd found. I had reoccurring nightmares that we'd be playing a show and people would start leaving in droves, or that I couldn't remember the words of any of the songs. Or that Ana refused to perform because her horoscope told her to. My diary entries from this time are full of pleading, of me telling myself that I wasn't good enough or capable of doing better. I was suddenly terrified of failure. It was out of control. The abundance of adrenaline in my system was making me sick, and a little crazy.

In one of my journal entries during this time, I wrote: *I need to dispel this notion of myself. The sadness that I have somehow become creatively infertile, that somehow I have nothing left to say.*

I had various lovers in many different cities. This boy named James in Sheffield, who was stocky and hairy. There was Jan, whom I nick-

named Yawn, he was from Norway, dreadfully boring, really handsome, but a snooze in the sack. There was Sven in Brussels. Every time
I played there he would sneak away from his boyfriend and give me
head in an unused dressing room.

I was around so many people at every moment, but at the same
time felt so lonely. In a band, it's unnatural the way you're forced to
be together for insanely long stretches of time, all sleeping together
in a cubicle. I read a study about chimpanzees that said when they
were put in areas too small and crowded, they would begin to look
everywhere they could except at each other. Sometimes we just had
to pretend that we weren't even there.

I never got high or drunk before I went out onstage, and I still don't.
So many people over the years have said to me, "I've seen you onstage,
mate, you must have been off your face."

"No, that's just my face," I explain. When we first started, I enjoyed a drink to calm my nerves before I went on, but soon I realized
that even just a tiny bit of alcohol would make me feel like I was
chasing after my own dance moves. My control wouldn't be as tight.
Sometimes, a crew member would pour me a drink for the encore,
but the effects wouldn't hit while I was still onstage. Even offstage
I wasn't a big drinker. There was just no way to get as little sleep as
we did and feel hungover at the same time. I was also plagued with
constant colds and coughs.

In the mornings, my legs and feet would be in such pain, I would
wake up and barely be able to walk. I have big, flat feet that can give
me trouble if I'm on them too much in one day. But every night, I was
dancing and banging my feet on the stage in wood-soled shoes. Every
stomp sent a sick wave of agony up my leg that I knew I would pay for
the next morning. It would take me five full minutes to stop limping
and walk properly after I woke up.

Some nights I would sit at the front of the double-decker bus, on the second floor, after everyone had gone to bed, and sink into the relative silence, like when I rode the ferry at night as a kid, trying to forget the rehab centers or counselors we'd seen that day. Or seeing New York from the fire escape, enshrouded by an infinite nothing during the blackout. There was comfort in the darkness beyond the bus's headlights. I'd gaze at the street median and let it hypnotize me into a lull. It felt like we were building and climbing with no end in sight. Before some shows I'd feel like I had no energy to access. I would dread walking out and have to run the equivalent of a triathlon. It felt like there was no light to look forward to, no escape from the grind. But again, the moment I did step out on the stage, all that went away.

36

I WOKE UP VERY EARLY IN THE STALE PITCH-BLACK OF the bus. Falling sideways out of my windowless bunk, I could tell by the chorus of snores floating from every angle like buzzing bugs in the night that I was the first one up. I waded through the loamy, narrow hall, trying not to step on or touch any of the hair and hands hanging over the edges. Opening the door to the light of the sun was like being freshly born. It was a magnificent day at Glastonbury.

I'd never seen anything so big. Standing on the bus steps, I could see the renowned festival stretch to the horizon. Rainbows of plastic tarps and tents swept like a patchwork wave behind a huge pyramid stage in the distance. I slipped my shoes on and buttoned my small-waisted American-flag pants. I didn't bother looking in a mirror. I knew what I would see: someone who didn't even look like me anymore.

Scissors had been looking forward to Glastonbury, a festival we had only heard spoken of with reverence. We hadn't been exactly sure what to picture, but we knew it was a big fucking deal. Two days before, our drum tech, Nigel, in all seriousness, had made us gather around him and he'd given us a talk: "A band's career can be made at Glasto," he told us. "A good gig there can become stuff of legend. This one's yours for the taking."

I walked for what seemed like a mile and found Chris. He and

Christoph were setting up our tent for the weekend. I could see the surprise on Chris's face. I wasn't as handsome as I had been a month ago. He was seeing firsthand the toll of being on the road. He, on the other hand, looked just like the knockout I remembered. I hadn't expected to ever see him again, and I'd stopped thinking about him after our first night together. But he'd called me two whole weeks after. Sure, he was gorgeous and funny (the morning after we'd hooked up, I'd walked in on him in the shower, where he was nonchalantly wearing a pair of wax lips). But being as busy as I was, I had made a pact with myself to stop being so boy-crazy. Even though I was dazzled at first sight, I had talked myself out of getting hung up on him. I thought, *That guy sure would make an amazing boyfriend for somebody.* It just didn't cross my mind that it could actually be me.

When he finally called me, it turned out he was going to be in England, so I invited him and Christoph to come for the Glastonbury weekend as my guests. I still wasn't thinking it would be anything romantic. He and Christoph were both ridiculously hot; I just assumed that the three of us would have some great sex.

Chris wore an old Adidas hat that looked like it had gone down a garbage disposal, gotten covered in mud, and then dried in the sun. It was an oddly beautiful thing, and so was he. On that crisp day, I couldn't stop looking at him, at his strong features and frame. He didn't look like anyone I had ever seen. His body wasn't overcooked from too much gym—it was solid and hairy and real.

I had a couple hours free before we had to get ready for our afternoon show on the main stage. The three of us marched over to see some of PJ Harvey's set on the Pyramid stage. Chris and I were a little awkward. A picture of Paul McCartney flashed on the side screens: He'd be playing that night.

"Damn, he's looking old," Chris said.

"Have a little fucking respect," I snapped back. It was a strange moment. I know he must have thought, *Who the fuck is this guy? This is never going to work.*

At around 3 p.m., I had to say goodbye to Chris and go get my press drag on. But first there was a band meeting with Neil. It was outside by the buses; the day had become warm. The band sat in a circle, and the general feeling was one of excitement to be there, but a malaise and dissatisfaction with our reality had set in. It would continue for the next ten years. Everyone was exhausted, complaining about the amount of work, the lack of time off. The grousing was something I couldn't help but take personally. Scott and I were stoic about the fact that we were overdoing it. But he and I were aware of the work getting our music to people's ears was actually going to take. I refused to take that opportunity for granted.

Everyone was solemn, chastising Neil that we were going too hard. I felt guilty. Whenever people were upset, I thought it was my fault. "I'm not going to let this band affect my relationship," someone would say. "I don't want to lose my life." And here was the rub: I knew in my heart that we were losing our lives as we knew them, but I also knew that the trade-off was going to be a singular experience that few people get. It's like boarding a space shuttle for years. Your regularly scheduled existence is gone, but still you get to see the earth from an angle that no one else ever will.

Ana pointed at me and said through her tears that whether I liked it or not, this was my baby. I would carry these words with me. When the band was unhappy, the blame easily fell on my shoulders. I was the one dragging them through this circus. But still, no one was forcing anyone to do it. People could leave at any time.

These insecurities were tough. The band could be angry at each other after interviews, not approving of how we discussed our experiences or one another. Sometimes I'd yell, telling someone they were being ridiculous, then concede and apologize. When any of us got mad onstage in front of an audience, I'd be furious. Whatever was going on in our heads, my biggest stage rule was not to impart that to the audience. It wasn't their fault: Nobody in the audience cared or wanted to know if you'd had a bad day. If Derek's guitars were fucked-up, he would glower and not acknowledge the crowd. Ana would complain during the show about how tired she was, or how crappy the hotel we had been staying at was. I would explode afterward in the dressing room, in front of everybody.

I was no saint, with my big mouth. Onstage I would let jokes fly, certain ones just for shock value. Often I could be offensive and insensitive, crudely sexual or misogynist. I'm sure it made Ana feel like shit. I could be oblivious to these things for days, and the resentment would bubble over, me not understanding or realizing what I had done. It would pop out in little firecracker arguments. Even after I said I was sorry, I knew I hadn't changed the band view of me as bossy and callous. I could still act like that child, nicknamed so many years ago "The Little Dictator." They were right—I often was. My learning curve was steep, but over time, over years, I did change. I figured out that no one likes to be told what to do, and that some fights are more worth it than others.

By midnight at Glastonbury I was in a stupor, could barely feel myself walking on the wet grass. The second set had been a gorgeous assault on my own senses. Chris had stood there smiling with his camera in hand, waiting for me as I exited the side of the stage. It was all happening at once. We'd played on the main Pyramid stage in the afternoon, done hours of press afterward, and then played the Dance tent at eleven.

The daytime set on the Pyramid stage had been lighthearted: We'd played as the crowd was bathed in a gentle, temporary rain. Ana had some great lines like "If you holler loud enough, a big sunny rainbow is going to shoot out of Jake's ass!" There was nothing purer than us surprising one another with a quick joke or a look. Or sometimes we'd literally just fall on our asses, which was never not hilarious.

The Dance tent show had been almost the opposite. The crowd's simmer had quickly turned into a boil from the top of the set, creating an energy so boisterous and electric, it almost felt devilish. We ended with absolute chaos, all of our freak friends and creatures joining us onstage. I wore a catsuit printed with hundred-dollar bills. It was the first time we'd had an audience that large, teeming with an expectation that we were fulfilling in front of their eyes. It was like I'd harnessed a new level of control, and the sensation was overwhelmingly satisfying.

I got offstage and Chris and Christoph and I were ready to party. We met up with my friends Kat and Will, traipsed across the entire festival to head to Lost Vagueness, a section of the festival that was known for its jaw-dropping installations and debauchery. I had a pocketful of MDMA, and even though I was completely spent, the exhilaration from the shows had me floating. I'd walk along crowded trails sticking my hands out behind me for Chris to hold.

As though some switch had been thrown, suddenly everyone knew who I was. Strangers were happy to see me at every step, screaming and hugging me like long-lost friends. It was my first taste of this kind of thing. It's an incredible feeling, when people you've never met before are thrilled to just see you; when you walk into a party or stroll down the street and they just want to talk to you and hug you.

We ended up in some '50s-style diner playing oldies on the jukebox and didn't move from there the whole night. Little Richard screeched as salty waitresses walked around with pots of coffee. The place looked exactly like an old greasy spoon, down to the checkered floors and ketchup bottles. We danced well into the next day.

I fell in love with Chris that night. In a moment of absolute clarity and inspiration I asked him if he'd marry me. He said yes. It was our first date. I just inexplicably knew he was the one I would be spending my life with.

We sat in the grass by the stone circle monument, a popular gathering spot at Glastonbury with twenty standing stones, where people play drums and lie about in the grass. Fog rolled through, the silhouettes of festivalgoers just barely perceptible through the mist. I held Chris's hand and kissed him again, both of us knowing that our lives had just dramatically changed in a matter of hours.

I thought about being alone on that beach in Barcelona, years before, dressed as a mime, knowing this moment would arrive. And here it was. I don't know if I've ever experienced such pure, unadulterated happiness.

Our album went to No. 1 in the UK charts the following Tuesday and stayed there. It would be the highest-selling album in the country that year.

We were in New York for just one night. The band was performing at PS1 for a summer Warm Up party—the same party that had started when I lived at the Cake Factory, where I first saw Fischerspooner, where I spent so many wild and sweltering afternoons, slugging back beer and dancing. We were playing the steps of the museum. The turnout was in the thousands.

I asked Klaus Biesenbach, the director of the museum, if there was a place away from everyone that Chris and I could go spend a few minutes together. He took us to a sparsely furnished but airy room with a couch that overlooked the courtyard. We had a perfect view of the entire crowd.

It was the only time Chris and I would have alone that day. We put the hour to good use. Afterward I lay in his arms and gently dozed off. When I extracted myself from his naked limbs, my face bleary, I sat up on the couch. "I think it's time. I need to go down and start getting dressed," I said.

"Where's your mom?" He looked around us, as if we had lost her in the room. I laughed.

"Oh, I'm sure she's making new friends." I reached over to the window and pulled back the shade. The courtyard was jammed with people waiting for the show. They spotted us and started cheering. We were shirtless, with our arms around each other, smiling in our post-sex glow. It was as if they were celebrating the fact we'd just found the loves of our lives.

I got down to the dressing room and Bono was there, wearing his sunglasses and perusing our looks for the day's show. "There he is, the man of the hour." He reached out and hugged me. My mom's eyes bugged out as he gave her a hug as well.

"I didn't know you would be here," I said to him like an idiot.

"If you knew everything that was going to happen, then there would be no surprises," he replied.

We played a killer show that day. I wore Vivienne Westwood shorts that tied all the way up on the side, half obscene, making me look naked, thin black suspenders, a leather cap, and a giant feather brooch. The stage was set up at the top of the front museum stairs, but behind a railing, so I spent most of the performance climbing it and standing on the edge, singing. The crowd was a sea, and I felt like I was crossing over it on the bow of my own party boat.

Afterward, in a James Turrell room called Meeting with no ceiling, only an unobstructed blue sky above us, Bono gave a toast. "To these times that we will never forget, to pop music, to family. One day we will all look back at this and realize how truly blessed we all are to get to experience such beautiful moments." I sat holding Chris's hand. "May the journey be long and fruitful."

Bono then pulled me aside and gave me "the talk."

"Jake, you have a road in front of you, you do realize that, yes?" His voice was serious. "You have decisions to make. Hey." He splayed his hands. "This can be just a moment in time. And that's fine. But it can be more than that, you see. This—music—can be your life. There's two paths you can choose. One, you can go and get caught up in all the parties and attention, become *interested in art*. Or you can remain focused and just keep making music. Building something that lasts more than just now." I've since heard that he gives this talk to a lot of younger artists, but his words stuck with me.

That night, Chris, my mom, and I got to my apartment and it turned out the roommate I had at the time hadn't found another place to sleep, which he had agreed to do that night because he hadn't been paying rent. My mom, such a trooper, ended up sleeping in his bed with him. She could see how excited Chris and I were just to be able to spend a few more hours together. "For God's sake, please don't tell your father," she said. We were in such good spirits, someone could have robbed us at gunpoint and we would have thought it hilarious.

Chris and I got in bed together and laid our heads on the pillow, looked into each other's faces horizontally. We both actually squealed as we embraced. That moment was the most in love with anyone that I had ever been.

The summer heat had stuck around that following fall in New York City. I stepped into a sunset-kissed Union Square in destroyed black cowboy boots and a Heatherette tie-dyed hoodie with Amanda Lepore's face stenciled on the front. Waiting there to greet me was Chris, roses in hand.

We were playing Irving Plaza that night. It was a show I'd been looking forward to—a homecoming of sorts. We'd received sad news that day about a friend's child passing away. There was a dark pall over the dressing room. It turned out to be the first show in New York that we played where I looked out at the crowd and didn't recognize a soul. *Who are these people?* I thought. Where were our friends? For the first time I felt homesick in my own city. That night I just didn't connect with the audience.

After we said our final goodbye from the stage, I trod up the stairs back to the dressing room where Chris took my arm and said, "David Bowie watched the show."

"What?" All the bustle of the room quickly tuned out, and all I could hear was the ringing in my ears.

"He was up in the balcony."

"Which side?"

"Your left."

I suddenly started babbling. "Is he still here? Why didn't anybody say anything? How come no one told me? The show was fucking terrible! I was fucking terrible. . . ." I paced in a circle, feeling my throat closing up, trying to hold back tears. I stopped and pulled it together, put on a clean shirt, and prepared myself to meet him. He never came backstage. He was gone.

Growing up, no matter what I was doing—whether it was theater, tap dancing, or writing horror stories—his sounds and visions guided my way. And now he had seen my shitty show and left. I was inconsolable. They say never meet your idols. I guess the only thing worse than meeting your idols is not meeting them. The whole thing made me feel like a fraud.

Later that month, I received a somewhat cryptic email:

Hi. I came to your show a few weeks ago. It sounded very good from where I was sitting. db

I froze. What was this? As if I didn't know he'd been there? From where *he* was sitting? As opposed to where everyone else was sitting? This just exacerbated my pain. Why did he even bother to write me an email at all? The black type on white just read to me as: "Dear Jake, though you may think yourself a rock star, you will never be me. David Bowie."

My response took about three weeks to compose. I made sure that even if it was a little longer, at three sentences, I kept it equally terse:

Dear David Bowie,

You mean more to me than any artist on earth. My favorite song you've ever written is "Fantastic Voyage." Thank you so much for coming to my show, but I really hope at this point that we never cross paths. There's not a lot in this world I keep sacred, but I would rather you just stay imaginary.

Sincerely,
Jake Shears

Now I realize that it was my insecurities that made me prickle. I felt like I didn't deserve to be so close to what I knew to be greatness. David Bowie, the man who gave me the idea and inspiration to perform in the first place, sent me a note to just tell me he liked my show, and I couldn't just see that for what it was. I wish I'd just replied with a simple "Thank you."

That winter, I flew my parents and Mary over for a theater tour that we did in the UK with Le Tigre, which included a show at Royal Albert Hall. After having received so much support from my folks for so long, I was happy to have the money to fly them all over and put them up comfortably.

My mom and dad were beaming and it was touching to see my dad so fascinated with the operation. He couldn't get over the fact that we had a crew, and trucks! After the show he just wanted to linger and watch everyone pack up and load our gear. I think he finally saw something that we both had in common. He had always been a man who was able to make something out of nothing, fabricating and designing machines that he'd just dreamed up. We had now done the same thing, just in a different way. He had also painstakingly taught himself to make leather pants, many pairs of which I now wore onstage.

Mary was enchanted with the UK, a place that she'd never imagined she would actually see in person. We shared hotel rooms when we could and spent late nights watching infomercials with the sound off and dancing in our pajamas. Sometimes she would give me a little look in her eyes as if this was the last place she'd ever expected us to be. She was proud of me.

And "Mary," the song, was a proper radio hit. I had the money finally so that Mary could get her gastric-bypass surgery. Now, both of our lives would be changed.

37

BEAUTIFULLY LIT, STOCKED WITH GIFTS, STACKED WITH suitcases and steamers, the dressing rooms were buzzing. As I walked down the hallway, I passed names on each door: THE KILLERS, ROBBIE WILLIAMS, KEANE. It was the night of the Brit Awards, known as the Brits, the UK's equivalent of the Grammys. Though we had been nominated for three—Best New Act, Best International Album, and Best Live Act—I was on everybody's shit list.

About three weeks before, we were playing the University of Kansas and were caught in a snowstorm on our way to the gig. We arrived late and had to move the showtime to midnight. As the crew set up our equipment, Scott and I were scheduled for a couple of press interviews, one of which was with Victoria Newton from the *Sun* in the UK. She'd flown all the way in from London, and I knew in advance the conversation was going to be a minefield. She was a notoriously difficult interviewer, the reason being that she wrote for a gossip rag. I was seasoned enough by then to be careful of journalist traps. They coaxed you into confiding certain elements of your life, only to twist them around for any kind of salacious headline they could get.

"We've got to be super-careful," I told Scott on our way in. "This lady is going to try to get some dirt."

"We have to think before we answer anything," he agreed.

"Don't answer the question if it's a trap. If we say anything, one way or the other, she'll turn it into something."

I always wanted to give interesting interviews. I never saw the point of being a jerk or complaining to journalists. I even excused myself once in a whole-band interview that NME conducted because I felt like everyone was so negative and complaining. It gave me major anxiety. So I did my best to just be positive, and not talk shit about anybody.

Victoria Newton tried everything, even the most basic questions: "Would you ever work with Madonna?" I laughed and wouldn't answer. If I had answered no, she would say that I slagged her off. If I said yes, she would say that we were "desperate to work with Madonna." We finished the interview cordially and I hoped that I'd given her enough stuff to at least make her happy. After all, she had traveled all this way.

And today, the day of the Brits, the Sun interview had come out. And made the front page. The headline read: "SCISSORS SHOCKER: 'I KNOW ROBBIE WILLIAMS IS GAY.'" Neil stormed into the dressing room and slapped the newspaper down on the table in front of me as I drank my coffee.

"What the fuck is this?" Veins were popping out on his forehead. "Why would you say this, you fuckhead?"

My stomach dropped and the blood drained from my face. I was confused—how could this have happened? And today? And our dressing room was right next to Robbie's to boot. Scott sat in a chair in front of a makeup mirror rimmed with bulbs and glowered, shaking his head.

"I didn't say this!" I grabbed the paper and looked at it in disbelief. "I never said this, you guys. What the fuck?"

"Well, it sure looks like you fucking did." Neil chewed on a cinnamon stick like an anxious dog with a bone. He'd quit smoking a month before.

"Scott!" I looked at him to defend me; he had been in the interview, too. "Scott, you were there! We specifically avoided saying any-thing that could be misconstrued."

"I can't remember every word," he said. "You could have said something like that." I felt betrayed. How could he not remember? We had done the interview only three weeks before. I'd said nothing of the sort.

Suddenly I realized what it was. "No—wait! I did say it!" I stood up and held my hands out in front of me. "This is so fucked-up but I said this, like, two years ago. It was some band interview with this tiny gay zine." That had been back in the days when we'd say just about anything for a little attention. And now it had come back to bite me in the tits.

Neil and Scott acted like they didn't believe me, which floored me. I had never said it to the *Sun*, and I sure hadn't thought they'd go and dig up that quote from some interview we'd done two years ago.

During a quiet moment, when it seemed like no one else was around, I tapped on Robbie's door. He was at his dressing table, sitting and sipping tea.

"Hey." I reached out and we shook hands. He looked at me, amused. "I just want to say that I'm so sorry for what came out in the papers today. It's something I said, being flip. It was years ago. And totally stupid."

He gave me a hug, gripped my shoulders, and looked me in the eyes. "Jake. Even if people believed everything they read . . . it's no big deal. Seriously, don't worry about it."

That night when he gave his speech accepting a Lifetime Achieve-ment Award, he said he'd like to thank his "boyfriend, Jake Shears."

We opened the Brits, performing "Take Your Mama," which was to be the last official project for Jim Henson's Creature Shop in the UK. The number was intricate, with countless moving parts, and in-volved days of rehearsal with dozens of puppeteers. It was a meaning-ful experience for me, to get to spend time and be creative with these brilliant people I'd been fans of all my life. Most of them had worked for Henson and Frank Oz since they were young, and many of them had been a part of *The Dark Crystal* and *Labyrinth*. The actual baby Toby in *Labyrinth* was even one of the puppeteers. Our number took place in a barnyard. Ana and I were dressed like birds, me as some sort of turkey. There were dancing eggs, a singing barn, and a background chorus of watermelons. The performance was a triumph.

We all then went back to our table after we changed our clothes to wait for our award categories to be announced. We won the first, then the second. And when Siouxsie Sioux emerged from the wings of the stage to reveal the winners of the last award, I realized we were going to have won them all. When she called our name, we stood up from the table. I felt like I was going to pass out. A confusing feeling washed over me. It was a mixture of absolute accomplishment and finality. We began our walk to the stage and all I could think was *It's over*. I never want to watch the footage of that moment. I imagine that I must have looked so sad.

This was a peak, and it felt like the end. We had reached the top in the UK. We had the best-selling record of the year, moved over three million copies in that country alone. We'd won all the awards we possibly could that night. There was nowhere to go from here but down. This was the moment I had wished for when we had first arrived in London. I had wanted it, whatever the price. As I approached the stage, it dawned on me that I'd never quite known what form that would take. And now I saw it very clearly. The price was the comedown, and it was time to pay the piper.

Our last night of the tour was a few weeks later in February, and we performed at the Elton John AIDS Foundation Oscar party. My mom and dad and Jennifer Lebert, my former guardian from Arizona, all came into town. The band was in high spirits, ready for a break. I ran out of clothes to wear, though, and was dressed like Blanche from *The Golden Girls*. I sat next to Elton and Mary J. Blige at dinner. Elton turned to me at one point: "You want to come to Vegas, you big homo?"

I said that yes, of course I would. He was going to be at Caesars for a couple weeks the following month and invited Scott and me to come write with him. We could work on the stage at the Colosseum in the daytime. He grabbed a marker from someone and reached over to me and wrote his phone number on my shirt collar in Sharpie.

The evening continued in this surreal vein. Elton introduced me to Liz Taylor a few minutes later, her eyes and diamonds sparkling. I asked her how her night had been so far and with a kind smile she said, "It's great. I just wish the music wasn't so loud."

38

I LUGGED MY TWO SUITCASES UP THE FIVE-FLOOR walk-up to my tiny little place. The stairs had always been crooked, but now it was hard to ascend them without falling into the wall. The paint was peeling on the banister and I could see sandy bits of broken glass and dirt in the cracks of every corner. I lugged one case up a flight at a time, and then trod back down and grabbed the other one—they were too big to round the corners with both at once. It reminded me of heaving my luggage up the Penn Station steps so many years ago.

I finally reached my door, slipped the key in the lock, and pushed it open. The place was still, frozen and foreign, as if it were waiting for someone who wasn't me. I pulled my cases in and they filled a third of the kitchen. It was silent. As I walked forward, I passed the tiny room that my roommate had moved out of. I saw it had been completely redecorated. I realized that Chris had turned it into a glamorous little dressing room closet space for me. He had been here and organized everything, gone through all my things piece by piece, imagining where all these objects and weird clothing had come from. Chris had been going to grad school at Yale, studying sculpture and video art, but had spent quite a bit of time at the apartment since I left.

I stepped into the living room/bedroom and sat down on a worn footstool. The sun licked at my face. Everything around me looked like a relic of some other time. It was all my stuff—my stereo and CDs, my posters on the wall of *The Muppet Movie* and *The Last Unicorn*—but now it felt like someone else's.

When I stepped out onto Twelfth Street, at first glance it didn't look like much had changed. Ciao for Now, the café right under me that I had eaten at every day, was still bustling. The owners, Kevin and Amy, greeted me with open arms and a grilled sandwich. I then walked around the block and saw that the Cock had moved, and the old space was being renovated into some kind of restaurant. *Gross,* I thought. It seemed unholy that anyone could be cooking or eating food in there. I walked farther down Avenue A. Leshko's was gone and had turned into a Mexican margarita joint. I walked down still farther, thinking of ringing Mark Tusk's doorbell to see if he was around to get stoned and listen to some Tina Turner records, but I realized he had moved from the city. I strolled to the Bowery, dialing Matthew Delgado's number to see if he was around to catch up. I just got his voice-mail, and when I reached the building, I could see from the street that all of his plants were gone from the penthouse deck. It looked like he had moved too.

I'd thought for some reason that when I got home from tour, from this seemingly endless journey around the world, I would experience some kind of celebratory feeling, a sense of homecoming. Now, I realized that there would be no ticker-tape parade, nobody calling me much for a while. Everyone had just assumed that I was gone anyway. New York had simply moved on without me. As I climbed each stair back up to my place, I could feel my stomach sinking with every step. I quietly paper-toweled the dust off of my TV, and I heard the voice starting, as if on cue, waiting to pipe up in this very moment. *What are you going to do now?* it said. *Better come up with something fast.* I ordered some weed from a delivery service and smoked. A few more voices chimed in. *Everyone's waiting.* And then another. *What do you even think you're going to write about anyway?*

Chris and I took a much-needed vacation to Maui. I felt like I was in shock, some kind of cracked shell made of dead leaves. We stayed at a little gay hotel and went to a hippieish nude beach every day. Chris was driving us around for the first time, after having just received his driver's license. I had lost the ability to drive, living in New York for so long, and hadn't been behind the wheel in many years. One day we took the Road to Hana, this incredibly windy, steep one-lane trail with only sheer cliffs beyond the edges. I gripped the dashboard, petrified we were going to go sailing off the side.

I called Scott, who informed me that GLAAD wanted us to perform at a function, and that somehow this was related to MTV, and they might start playing our videos. I completely lost my mind. "When does this shit end?" I remember screaming into the phone. "We're supposed to be fucking done! Why are there more gigs coming in? Fuck if I'm going to do it. And basically fuck you. And Neil." Chris could hear me screaming out on our room's porch.

Even when my temper would flare, or I'd get so preoccupied putting out fires, Chris never acted bothered by it. He accepted where I was at that moment of my life, becoming a refuge from outside pressures and pulls. He stayed even-keeled in the face of my pandemonium. I'm sure it wasn't an easy task. I was drawn to the consistency of his presence and patience, two things I needed so badly. Also, for the first time, after years of being unapologetically slutty, I was in a monogamous relationship. The dependence on him emotionally and sexually was a relief from the scattered world around me.

One day at the hotel I called my dentist's office to make an appointment with the lovely lady who had worked on my teeth for years. I needed a checkup when we got back. Her husband answered awkwardly. "Hey, Jason, I'm sorry to be the one to tell you this, but she passed away recently." I didn't ask why, but said I was sorry and hung up the phone. It didn't seem possible. She was so young and sweet and was the only dentist I'd ever looked forward to seeing.

Chris and I went to a liquor store, where I got a small bottle of rum and drank it on the beach. The waves were pretty big, but I decided to wade in just to my waist and play in them. I had a buzz on, and was feeling sad about my dentist. I'd spent a lot of time with her in that chair.

The waves crashed over me. I closed my eyes and allowed them to slap at my chest. But suddenly my feet weren't touching the bottom. I started to swim back to solid ground, but I wasn't making any headway. Another wave smacked over me, and then another. I got my head above water and thought to swim sideways, because that's what they tell you to do in a riptide. But the waves kept pulling me out farther. Now I was underwater more than I was above it and I began to panic: The ocean was sucking me into it and I was losing my strength. I got my head above water. "Chris!" I yelled, and as I went back down I saw him waving at me. I struggled to get above one more time and just yelled, "Help!"

A plain inner voice spoke. It was myself, checking in, saying that this might be it. I couldn't breathe. Every one of my limbs was cramping just trying to get my head up for one more breath. *I guess I'm drowning*, I thought as Chris's hand reached under me and placed my arm around the boogie board he'd grabbed to haul me back to shore. I was amazed that he had gotten to me so quick, that I hadn't been irretrievable.

On the sand I lay on my back and felt sucked dry. I was shaken, had almost disappeared. Everything seemed wrong. Was I even supposed to be here? Why wasn't I working? I didn't deserve a vacation.

"Honey." Chris took my hand and smiled. "Someone wants to say hi. I think he's waving at us." I looked to where he was pointing and there was a humpback whale that had surfaced in the distance and was waving a flipper up and down.

We got some pot brownies on Little Beach and ate them back in our room at sunset. I got super high, and we made love in a fiery yellow, orange, purple, and red light. It barely made sense to me that I had someone in my life now who could love me so much, could save me from drowning in the ocean. As the sun dipped below the horizon we listened to "I Am a Bird Now" by Antony and the Johnsons and held each other.

So much had changed so quickly.

39

THE COLOSSEUM AT CAESARS PALACE FELT LIKE A HUGE ornate salad bowl. I was standing on the edge of the stage, right at the lip, with a mic in my hand and singing at the top of my lungs. What was coming out of my mouth was nonsense, and there was no one in the audience. Elton sat at his red piano behind me, just banging away, while Scott gripped a bass and plucked along.

"What about that?" Elton looked at me and reached for a sip of his Diet Coke. "It's got a very New Orleans vibe to it, no?"

"Let's try it with the chorus thing coming a little earlier."

"Don't bore us, queen. Get to the chorus." He played a few more chords and glanced up again. "You need a name."

"I have a name," I said.

"No, your drag name. I give everybody a drag name. . . ." Elton studied my face for a second as if he were just looking at me for the first time. "Britney."

"Britney?" I was mildly offended. "Really?"

"Britney Shears. All right, done." He began to play again. I wasn't crazy about "Britney," but I guessed I had no choice at this point. We'd been at it for a few days: Elton would play his show at night, and then in the day we'd set up a studio onstage and just have fun playing around. After the show each night we had dinner together with various people, including Robin Hurlstone, a very debonair British art dealer with a dry sense of humor who had been married to Joan Collins years ago.

"Tell Robin about your Bette Midler obsession," Elton said.

"I'm not obsessed with Bette Midler," I lied.

"Obsession is relative, darling." Robin leaned in.

"'Oh Industry' from *Beaches* is just one of my favorite songs," I explained, rolling my eyes.

"This is what I love about you," Elton said, glancing at Robin. "He's a fucking weirdo."

We ate late and spent the evenings laughing harder than I'd laughed in a long time. Every step I took wandering around on the carpets at Caesars, it was like I was wearing someone else's shoes. I was reminded, as I breezed through the smoky casino, watching the wrinkled and the seeking, sinking their coins into the slots, how just ten years before I had been only a few blocks away, telling my parents I was gay. Would I ever have imagined, staring at that Dorothy diorama, that I would actually be back in Vegas, writing songs with Elton John?

One night I watched Elton's show by myself. I sat in one of the boxes and realized I recognized Paul Shaffer and his family sitting next to me. Elton took the stage and began to sing, his iconic voice heavy with experience and deep sadness.

He dedicated "Rocket Man" to me that night. And as he played the song, I began to weep into my hands. It was so cathartic and confusing and painful and exquisite. I've never cried so hard before or since. I had been sent to Mars, had come back and didn't know who I was anymore. There had been another seismic shift inside my heart. I had attacked stages when I felt like there was nothing left; I had screamed until my voice was hoarse at people when things didn't go right; I had fallen in love with the man who was to be my life partner; I had made enough money that I didn't need to work for years if I didn't want to. There were now so many people counting on me, from the record label to the fans themselves. And in that moment, when Elton called out my name, I truly did not know if I could carry the weight. The future looked terrifying.

40

I LAY IN MY SMALL DOUBLE BED WITH CHRIS SNORING softly next to me. It was 5 a.m. and it was still dark. I was wide-awake, my heart racing in my chest. The moment when my eyes opened and I registered that first note of consciousness, when I realized I was alive and human, was now the worst part of every day. There was nothing to do other than quietly get out of bed and face it, which meant immediately putting pen to notebook. I was filling them up, with endless scribbles and scratches of words that didn't mean anything. Broken melodies plagued every waking minute. I tried to pluck them from the air, saying to myself, *That one? Or what about that one?* My brain would obsessively try to turn into a song every word or phrase that I saw on a sign or read in a book. It was as though I were scratching at the wall of a room with no doors.

I was usually going to bed at around 7 p.m. now. I would take any chance I could get to retreat to my dark room and sleep. Being awake was miserable. I was getting adrenaline rushes now almost every minute, that feeling of flying down a dip in a roller coaster. I didn't want to see people or hang out with anyone or go to parties. Every five fucking minutes it seemed like someone was saying, "How are you?" "How's the record coming?" "I can't wait to hear what you do next."

The parties in New York had changed, too. A lot of places had shut down. Even Luxx in Williamsburg wasn't there anymore, much less any remnants of the electroclash scene. It had died the death. Now most of the party invitations were for four-course dinners hosted by one magazine or another. I did have a good time at these glamorous occasions. But often, I sat in my chair, thinking, *Don't get used to this. They're going to realize pretty soon that you don't belong here.*

The designers Heatherette put me in their fashion show and I was embarrassed to walk down the runway. Why would anybody even know who the hell I was? I would end up on a red carpet and I'd just want to hide somewhere, go back behind the filing cabinets in the teacher's lounge, like when I was fifteen. They put me and Ana in the front row of a Marc Jacobs show and I almost panicked.

This isn't to say I wasn't having fun, because I was. Especially getting to meet so many incredible people whom I'd looked up to all my life. Like being pushed by Ingrid Sischy into the back of a car with Iman. Or sitting across from Lou Reed as he gazed at a menu, watching him flip his clip-on sunglasses up with a scowl on his face, listening to him order his food in his deep voice. Rehearsing a song with Norah Jones and David Byrne in David's studio. Chris and I spent many evenings now with Michael Stipe and his boyfriend, Thomas Dozol, eating delicious food and listening to music into the wee hours of the morning. Patti Smith sang us a new song one night while we sat around the dinner table for Michael's birthday. David Furnish took me to Paris for a Dior show where I got to talk to Mick Jagger. Scott and I tracked down Paul Williams and began writing songs with him, as well as with Carlos Alomar, who'd been Bowie's guitar player since *Young Americans*. Bryan Ferry spent a week with Scott and me in the studio in New York recording songs for a possible new Roxy Music album; then we went with him to London and recorded with the rest of the band. Every day, it felt like one outlandish rock-and-roll fantasy after another was being lovingly fulfilled.

Chris and I had just returned from a week at Elton and David's summer house in Nice. It was like being in some luxurious palace, sunbathing all day and then going to elaborate dinners at night, with everyone from Mikhail Gorbachev to Rod Stewart, whom I witnessed one night sitting next to Elton, the pair of them catching up like two gossipy women at bridge club. That week we were staying at the Nice house with Susannah Constantine, a UK TV personality who would become one of my most unlikely best friends. George Michael was also there with his then-boyfriend, Kenny Goss. George and I went on walks through the elaborate gardens and talked songwriting and his love of soul and R&B. He said he had a song for me to sing, kept mentioning it for years, but sadly he never sent it or played it for me.

One night, a bunch of us were hanging out by the pool late at night, swimming and laughing. I wondered where George and Kenny were, so I dried off with some loud Versace-print towel and went to tell them we were by the pool, and that they should come hang. My hand rapped on the door once before it was flung open by Kenny and I walked in.

"What're you guys doing? You should come outside, it's super fun—" I stopped in my tracks as I looked down to see George naked on the bed, facedown, spread-eagled. He'd just been lounging as I barged in. He was looking back at me and laughing.

"Uh—yeah, it's fun, you guys," I said. "You should . . . come out and hang?" I turned and ran out, blushing. I have to say, seeing George Michael's bare ass on that bed was like seeing the *Mona Lisa* in person. It was perfection.

And then here Chris and I were, back at my tiny, grimy Twelfth Street walk-up, a visible contrast to everything else in our life. Nothing was fitting. The lady below me who made knitted hats would still bang on my floor anytime she thought the music was too loud. My clothes were haphazard. I wasn't used to having money now to spend on things that seemed as frivolous as everyday clothes. I wore either what was given to me, or old clothes from years before. The whole past winter I hadn't even had a proper coat. I'd just put on layers upon layers underneath a boxy Levi's corduroy jacket.

I got up and stepped into the bathroom, reminded of the prank Chris had pulled on me a few days before. I'd come home and opened the bathroom door to a huge silhouette of an alien man sitting on the toilet in the dark. For a split second, my brain had short-circuited: I'd thought I was having a waking nightmare. But it was just a silly scarecrow he'd made. I was so startled, instead of laughing and thinking it was funny, I burst into tears.

I showered and combed my hair in the steamy mirror, looking a little better than I had a few months before on the road. But now I'd let my hair grow longer. It would get greasy and stringy, made me feel unattractive. I grabbed my notebooks and left for the café downstairs so I could write until it was time to meet Scott at the studio.

I didn't understand it at the time, but I was grieving my loss of freedom. No longer was anything just for fun. When I wrote a song now, I felt the weight of expectation. It seemed like everyone was drumming their fingers on the table waiting for "hits." No longer could I go out and party at the gay bars without knowing I was being watched to some degree. And, if hypothetically I was having a bad day and just wanted to go find some random hot guy and get laid, I couldn't do that, either. I was happy being monogamous with Chris, but it had been a swift change. I was captive to a new set of guidelines, having so much now to lose.

Scott and I had moved to our own proper studio space on Fifth Avenue and Twenty-Second Street, right across from the Flatiron Building. It was spacious, and we painted it purple and silver, calling it Discoball Jazzfest, after the names of the colors on the cans. Our hours were from Monday through Friday, eleven or so to seven, religiously. We talked, fiddled around, and played, trying to come up with decent tunes. But so much of the time I felt incapable of melodies anymore. My voice, both speaking and singing, had become quieter. It was almost as if I was embarrassed to hear myself sing. Scott and I could get frustrated with each other, when we were out of ideas, when neither of us seemed to have any mojo.

There was no question that he and I were both depressed. But the studio was inescapable. We had nothing else to do. Anytime I wasn't in there, trying to create something, was a day that I knew I could be writing that one special song. We would try to take days off, but I would end up just pacing around the city on my phone, trying to make sense of it with anyone.

I remember taking a call from Roger Daltrey one afternoon. He wanted Scissors to play his yearly Teenage Cancer Trust fund-raiser. I was walking through Washington Square Park with my phone glued to my ear. I had never met the guy and here I was pouring my heart out. "I think I'm depressed."

"Over here in the UK," he said, kindly, "we call that the black dog. Sometimes it comes to hang out for a while."

I had lunch with Anohni one day, and we had a conversation about antidepressants. "What would you say if we were living in some tribe somewhere, and the village shaman said, 'Here, I have this root and if you eat it, it will make you feel better'? You would take it, wouldn't you?" We finished the afternoon by going back to her flat, painted white, with nothing but a white piano in the middle of the room, and talking about writing. She balked at my process, going into the studio to write every day. "Writing songs for me takes a long time. It's almost like laying an egg."

Elton would get on the phone and tell me he was concerned about the way I was acting. "You don't sound like yourself," he'd say. "I'm worried about you. You're usually like a shot of B_{12} wherever you go. This is not you."

He and David went above and beyond to cheer me up. Once, when my mom was in town, they took us to Dior Homme, had the whole store shut down, and bought me the entire men's collection. I'll never forget the look on my mom's face. If anyone knows how a wild shopping spree can make you feel better for at least a day, it's Elton.

I might have been depressed, but it was nice to hear a new cheer in Mary's voice every time I talked to her. She'd been going to surgery seminars and had found a hospital in Seattle that would perform the gastric-bypass operation in a couple months' time. I'm not sure if it was the new excitement in her life, but she had actually started dating somebody for the first time in the entire time I'd known her. She sounded genuinely happy. The surgery was scheduled for the spring.

One afternoon Elton came over to meet Scott and me at our studio. He brought us shopping bags of Y-3 winter clothing, which I sorely needed, and then sat down at the keyboard and got down to business. "I was thinking something kind of Bo Diddley, like this. . . ." And he played a cool riff. Scott and I gathered around him, the three of us chiming in on chord changes and timing. Within minutes we had a structure with multiple sections. Scott put down a rhythm track and started building on the progression. "Have at it," Elton said, standing up abruptly. "I'll see you guys later this week." He chipped off, and then it was just me and Scott again. My heart sank.

Here we suddenly had a potential song, right in front of us, straight from Elton John's fingertips, and I was immediately convinced that I didn't have melodies or lyrics for it. But I began singing around it anyway. "Maybe this is a song about dancing or something?" It was a pretty bland start of an idea.

I kept playing with it, but nothing great was coming. I wanted to give up, go home and go to bed. But then suddenly the words "I don't feel like dancing" fell out of my mouth. They were true. I didn't. Didn't feel like doing anything—writing, singing, exercising, anything. We wrote the whole song that evening, and when we left the studio, I still wasn't sure if it was any good.

The next day I went to the therapist I had been seeing for a couple months. She was on the Upper East Side, was a big doctor at Columbia

University Medical Center. Her office was tranquil, and she had an empathetic nature about her. We both decided that we would try talking my problems out. I really didn't want to go on antidepressants.

"I feel paralyzed," I said. "Every second, somehow I'm reminded that I'm going to fail."

"Well, when you tell me you're reading sites called Metacritic and Pitchfork five times a day, that doesn't surprise me." She had me on a regimen of fish oil and concoctions that would hopefully help me. It all felt like a placebo, though.

On my way out of the office I called Neil. "We wrote a song yesterday. . . . I'm not sure, but it may be good." You never really know until you do the day-two test. What was sounding amazing could be revisited the next day and sound like hell. But every once in a while, you can return and realize you have something exceptional.

41

I ASKED CHRIS TO KIND OF MARRY ME (AGAIN), OR AT least be my partner for life, while we were getting ready to head to David and Elton's bachelor party in London the following holiday season. We were in our hotel room primping and making ourselves look handsome, I didn't have pants on, but I pulled out the rings I'd chosen with my friend Aimee Phillips. They were simple platinum bands. Chris was taken aback, I think. I popped a boner when I pulled them out.

He never wanted to actually get married, but he committed to being my partner. I knew it was a challenge to be with me, not the easiest life. But he was secure, handling all my quirks with a kind of grace. I'm sure it would have given anyone a complex, constantly being introduced to others not as who you are, but as whose boyfriend you are. Chris was stoic when I left home for extended periods. He gave me hugs and made me food when I was fretting and downcast. Sometimes I couldn't figure out what he saw in me.

That night, when the bachelor party show was over, in which I sang "I Am What I Am" with the Pet Shop Boys, I got on a stripper pole for old times' sake and pulled my clothes off. I was pretty drunk. Some psycho Justin Bond brought ended up ripping my underwear off while I was dancing. I remember just looking down at Ozzy Osbourne's face, gaping up at me, confused. But "Lust for Life" was playing, and even though I was now completely naked in front of a roomful of people, I decided to finish what I'd started. Chris handed me a bowler hat that I had worn for my number. I used it to cover my dick and just kept boogying until the song ended. It's a wonder I didn't get thrown out.

The next day I took a train to Paris to visit Kylie, who was living there while recovering from chemo treatments. She'd been diagnosed with cancer the previous summer and had canceled a run of touring. On the phone she was positive, but you could hear the pain in her sweet voice.

I was so excited to see her, but my heart broke when I did. She was really sick. We spent the day going on walks and talking. Her mood was up, and we talked about her recovery. I had no doubt that she was going to beat it, but still I was scared. This was very serious. When we rode in the back of a car with the windows down, the Eiffel Tower sparkling in the distance, I looked at her across from me, so beautiful in her turban. I prayed right there to God in my heart that she would get better. Kylie, and the bright, luminous light she gave to the world, had a lot left to do on this planet.

It was Elton who finally had the talk with me about going on antidepressants. I was despondent, and it felt like there was nothing I could do about it. I think the last couple of years had been so hard on my body: Lack of proper food, not drinking enough water, sleep deprivation, had led to pure exhaustion. I feel like once I put my body through that, it never really came out the other end the same. I have no doubt that those crazy years did some damage. Strangely, it wasn't a story of a downward spiral of drugs and alcohol; it was just too much work.

"I'm just going to say this, and you need to listen to me. You've got to take something. You need to just try it. David and I are very worried about you. If you don't like them, then just get off of them. But you have to at least try it."

I got a bottle of Lexapro from my shrink, and Chris and I planned a trip to Disney World for the week I started. It was the only thing I could think of that could get my mind off of things, and why not go to the happiest place on earth when you were feeling like total crap?

We were there for about five days and rode everything. After about forty-eight hours, I started feeling the brain zaps of the pills beginning to enter my system. Every twenty minutes or so, I would feel this unpleasant rush that felt like a laser show was going off in my head. It wasn't unlike the feeling of coming down off ecstasy. Splash Mountain and Roger Rabbit kept my mind off it, and we just lived like that, in this demented Disney limbo.

From Florida I flew down to Belize to meet Scott at this little resort where we'd set up a makeshift studio space. Though the beach was beautiful, I was completely unable to write anything.

When we were planning the trip, Scott and I got in this huge fight about the fact that he wanted to bring some guy he had just started seeing. He didn't really know the guy all that well, and I was just pissed off because I didn't want to be the third wheel on one of Scott's dates. Of course this devolved into a huge row that culminated in our studio with Neil witnessing it. I remember Neil said afterward, "I've barely ever heard two people talk like that to each other. I've never even gotten in a fight with my wife or ex-girlfriends that was that intense."

So we decided that the last half of the trip we'd have two of our best friends, Aimee and Sammy Jo, come down and hang with us. They jokingly called it "the suicide watch." Scott and I barely got any work done. I was borderline catatonic a lot of the time. I read Murakami books, but mostly I sat on my bed and stared at the wall. This was the worst and the deepest part of the depression I'd ever experienced. Any stimulation was too much, whether it was speech or music, a movie or a suggestion. I just wanted to sit and stare at a blank white wall. That was the only way I could manage the static in my head, the voices that had become so loud and overbearing. At least when I looked at a wall, it gave them space to have their say.

At the end of the trip, we were gathering our bags to bring to the boat to leave the remote spot. It was the day we were going home. That's when I felt it. Something like a tickle, a tingle in my core. A kind of small relief, a brief sensation of contentment that I hadn't felt for a long time. Some small internal whisper that said simply: *Everything's going to be okay.*

I would continue to wake up in the middle of the night, see the vague outlines of my surroundings, and try to figure out exactly what I had gotten myself into. But it was time to learn how to inhabit the life I had created for myself, and accept the person I had become. I wasn't and would never be that same kid anymore, wondering how far you could take a daydream.

42

THE WARHOL SHOW WAS AT SOME GALLERY IN MIDTOWN, a series of party snapshots he had taken over the years that were being sold individually. All the images, in black-and-white, lined the walls like a timeline of New York royalty. I now had the money to buy such things every once in a while. I walked the length of the gallery, trying different photos on, figuring out what would be fun to look at every day. Instead of choosing a glamorous shot of Liza or Mick, I decided on one of Caroline Skelly, an elderly New York socialite heiress who had gained most of her fame from being robbed multiple times. In the picture she looks very old, almost grotesque, and is wearing what looks like a sombrero and muted sequins.

Scott and our friend Aimee had accompanied me, and the three of us decided to take a cab down to my apartment on Twelfth Street. Scott usually didn't hang out at my place, so I welcomed the rare occasion to have him over. My CDs were stacked in individual mountains: I'd run out of shelves. *Liza with a Z*, the soundtrack of Liza Minnelli's eponymous 1972 television special, had just been reissued, so I threw it on and puttered around, offering them drinks. "Cabaret" came on after a few minutes, and I sang along to some of the words. Scott and Aimee were staring at me, which was strange.

"Jason, there's something we need to talk to you about," Scott said. Something was very off.

"Are you kicking me out of the band?" I laughed. "What the hell is going on?"

"Mary is dead. Your mom called an hour ago."

Liza responded, exactly that moment:

> *But when I saw her laid out like a queen*
> *She was the happiest corpse I've ever seen.*

"I just want to say this, and I don't want it to sound stupid," Mary had said, a few weeks before on the phone.

"Oh God." I rolled my eyes. "What?"

"If anything happens—"

"Nothing is going to happen!"

"*If anything* happens," she continued, "I want you to know that this surgery is entirely my decision. This is something I've always wanted to do."

"You're being ridiculous. Nothing bad is going to happen."

"Just in case," she said.

Liza was now singing that song about everyone getting her name wrong. It sounded truly macabre. I stared at the floor for twenty minutes, with Scott and Aimee just sitting, then excused myself to buy a pack of cigarettes. When I walked out of the deli, Chris was standing on the sidewalk. He had heard the news and had come back from Yale to be with me. We didn't say anything and he embraced me without speaking.

I put on a nature DVD about fish and sat on the couch, watching the huge schools move in unison. I should have been there when she had the operation. Her boyfriend, Jim, had been with her, and we'd been talking every few hours. I should have been there. I looked at the black phone on the floor that only she had the number to. It would never ring again.

Jennifer traveled from Arizona to Seattle for the funeral. My mom met Chris and me there as well. I was in charge of putting together elements of the service, enlarging some of my favorite photos of her and making a playlist of her favorite hair metal on a CD. Ratt, Warrant, and Skid Row blasted through the church, at first confounding the mourners as they entered. The music was wholly inappropriate, which I knew would have at least made her laugh. When I spoke, I didn't have anything written down, and I didn't have much to say. I think I was still in shock.

My sister Sheryl hosted the wake at her family's house. It was somber. Mary's brother was unable to stop sobbing into his hands. Her mom sat in a corner and held conversations quietly. I couldn't help but feel that every time they looked at me, they saw the reason for Mary's death. I wasn't able to cry.

Jim and I had picked up her ashes at the crematorium. The vase sat in my lap as we drove in silence with the windows down. When we stood on the end of a pier and scattered the chalky dust into Puget Sound, the ashes undulated beneath the surface, at first appearing like a cloud. I leaned against the railing and watched as the form shifted shape, turned into a gray, symmetrical creature with wing-like fins, crystalline. I said some kind of goodbye under my breath as it swam away.

I still think about Mary and me when we met, two disoriented souls looking for the understanding of a friend. When we'd first talked on that chat line, how could she or I have known the extent that our fates would intertwine? We had a seemingly random connection, but we were both outsiders, and shamed by others for who we were.

I wish I had something more eloquent to say about it. I wish there was some uplifting truth that I've gleaned from her death. If there is, I'm still waiting for it. I can hear her voice speaking somewhere, but not to me. There's still the reflex to call her when good things happen, or to share some ridiculous story or gossip. She would probably be alive now if we hadn't met. I know it's stupid to think that, but I do.

I could say she's still with me, but she only remains in my life as a memory and a tattoo on my arm. Mary's gone. When she left, rather than sticking around, she took a part of me with her. I hope that wherever she is now, she knows it's in her possession.

43

I WAS WALKING THROUGH CENTRAL PARK, ON MY WAY to band rehearsal with the Warhol photo under my arm, the one I'd bought on the day of Mary's death. I had just picked it up from the gallery. It was an easy stop after my visit to my shrink.

I spotted Lou Reed, dressed in black, taking a stroll. I said hello and we walked together.

"You making the record?" he asked in his low voice.

"It's done. Just finished mixing in those studios behind Hammerstein Ballroom."

"You happy?"

"You mean—happy with life or happy with the record?"

"Both." He looked straight ahead. I felt like we were spies, meeting in the park to have a secret conversation.

"I guess so. I got really depressed."

"Happens."

"I think the ride wore me out."

"Drugs?"

"Nah, there doesn't seem to be much time for them anymore."

" All the people I knew that used to keep ducking into bathrooms at parties . . . one day, they just stopped coming out."

"Didn't happen to you," I said.

"Could have. Easily."

"Well, you're alive and can tell the tale. You're a fucking hero, Lou."

"I'm not a hero," he said. "I'm just here."

Ana and Scott were intensely inspecting a T-shirt design on his laptop screen when I entered the rehearsal space. John Garden, our keyboard player, and Paddy were taking naps on the couch while Derek was crouched down futzing with his guitar pedals. It was our first rehearsal for the first shows for the second album, which I'd named *Ta-dah*, a sardonic title given the strains of expectation that had been foisted upon it.

The band gave me hugs. It was the first time I'd seen everyone since Mary's funeral. But there was a grim sense in the air, a distrust among all of us that we'd be able to survive an onslaught anything like the last one. But we were all there, together. We had defied common logic and made it far enough to be starting again, even if we were still a little broken.

Ana took my hand. There were tears welling in her eyes. "This is gonna hurt for a long time," she said. "It's never going to go away." She would know. Her father passed away when she was a teenager.

Everyone roused themselves to prepare for the painful first plays of the new songs; they could really sound like shit at the start of rehearsals. There was never much for me to do except warm up my voice, no analog synths to look after, no guitars to tune. But this whole thing was one big instrument, one that I was still learning to play and maintain. It wasn't going to be easy to master, but God, I was so truly glad to have it. To have them.

Guitars were strapped on, Ana and I stood across from each other in front of our mic stands, our sound guy gave us the thumbs-up. I glanced around the room, doing a lazy spin.

"Everybody ready?"

ACKNOWLEDGMENTS

First of all, this wasn't even my idea. I got an email one day from Rakesh Satyal, who thought it would be neat if I wrote a book about my life. At first, I didn't take him very seriously. But after hanging out a couple times and talking about our mutual love of books, I realized he meant business. Rakesh has kept a steadfast belief in me and in this book, without which I wouldn't have had the confidence to create it. Thank you, Rakesh, and everyone at Atria, for making this possible. I will forever be grateful for this awesome opportunity.

Writing it has taken exactly two years and has been a strange, difficult, but ultimately rewarding experience. It's always been a dream of mine, except I always thought I would start with fiction, and that a memoir would come later. The main reason being, I really wanted to wait for my parents to have moved on from this planet, so they wouldn't have to suffer through reading about all my shenanigans. There are lots of gruesome details you never really want your mom and dad to know about your life. That said, they have been so supportive with this whole thing. So, thank you, Mom and Dad. And the rest of my family: Windi, Sheryl, Montana, Caleb, Sophie, Sonya, Avery, and Kathleen. All the Sellards and the Rectors.

Two years ago, I had a big life transition moment and I bought a one-way ticket to New Orleans. It was always a dream to move down there. I went, not knowing a soul, and started a new chapter. I felt the city's embrace immediately: Suzie Jagger Richards, never having even met me, took me in like one of her stray cats and told me, the moment I arrived, that New Orleans was my new home. She was correct. Though I split my time now between there and LA, that's exactly what it feels like down there. Home. Other amazing people who I owe huge gratitude to are Megan Few, Diogo Lima, Chris Alfieri, Mac Warren, Kyan Douglas, Granite, Stacey Hoover, Carrie Estes, Heather Hansen, Adam Skidmore, Caroline Bozier, Jody Day, Huzefa Dossaji, David Schulman, Dan Burton, Dan Davis, and Chance van Meter.

A big thank-you to my dear pals who read drafts and really helped me reconstruct and reconsider. Andy Slaught, Martin Pousson, Michael Warner, Craig MacNeil, Tim Kvanofsky, Deanne Reynolds, and Lex Gjurasic. Thank you for being such great, loving friends.

Eve Barlow really helped at a crucial time, and brought her music-writing brain, and asked me when I needed to hear it: "What the fuck are you even talking about?" Her feedback was crucial in turning what was a blob into a book.

To Scissor Sisters: I hope I did us some kind of justice. Ana, Scott, Del, Paddy, JJ, I miss and love you. I'm so proud of what we all accomplished. We made a lot of people very happy.

The Consuelos family: Kelly, Mark, Lola, Michael Joaquin, and Chewie. You all bring me so many lols, so much love. Your Gruncle treasures you.

The Homme family: Josh, Brody, Jason, TR, Mommie Homme, Big Mike, Camille, Ryder, Wolf, and of course Bob. Thank you for bringing this Domesticated Animal in years ago, even though I wasn't exactly housebroken at first. You all mean so much to me.

Caleb Barclay, I wouldn't trade our friendship for anything. We've had a couple really fun fucking years. And son, get ready. You're next.

To my favorite band, Queens of the Stone Age. You treat your stalkers very very well.

Carrie Brownstein: I've never had the pleasure to meet you. But *Hunger Makes Me a Modern Girl* was released soon after I started this thing. It's had a huge influence on this book, structurally and spiritually. Thank you for writing it.

Chris Moukarbel, thank you for all those years of love and support. I'll always cherish the good times and memories.

To my manager, Neil Harris: I'm so happy the gang's back together. We're gonna slay it.

Justina Heckard, you are a joy and I feel very lucky to work with you every day. Thank you for all that you do.

Sammy Jo, Texxx, and Jeremy Lingvall: Please never contact me again.

Amber Martin: Mummaahhhhh.

Justin Vivian Bond: Thank you for injecting the juice into this world. You are one of my life's greatest inspirations.

Kevin Ratterman: Someone saved my life tonight.

Elton, David, Zachary, and Elijah: Thank you for always always *always* being there. Britney doesn't know what she'd have done without your love and support all these years.

Tom Donaghy: I will always be your puppet man.

Lance Horne: Round 2, please.

I know I'm forgetting a million people, and if you don't see your name here, just know I love you. . . .

Larry Mark, Eric Polito, Alex Rhida, Nadine Blesses, Cody Critcheloe, Jacob Glass, Angela Becker, and Stuart Price, Ned Atkins, Taylor Brechtel, Jennifer and Mat Lebert and fam, Aram Kirakosian, Andy Towle, Mario Diaz, the Miccelli family, Michael Cunningham, Darren Dryden, Mike Doyle, Lucy Blackburn, Texxxx, DJ King Atlas, Michael Stipe and Thomas Dozal, Luke Gilford, Kim Hastreiter and David Hershkovits, Drew Elliot, Jackie Sue Netherton, Raphael Chatelain, Sean Belman, Hush, Jeff Whitty, Mitchell Kulkin, Tommie Sunshine and Tiny Daniela, Sandra Bernhard, James O'Neill and Bryan O'Sullivan, Kylie Minogue, Leanne Buckham, Leo Herrera, Blythe Russo, Adam Dugas, Anne-Marie Hess, Seth Sharp, Christine and Paul Waring, Christine Ronan, Oliver Daley, Aimee Phillips, Rod Thomas, Andy Cohen, Mr. Turk and Trina Turk, Dan Savage and Terry Miller, Adam Lambert, Lara Schoenhals, Nick Willox, Tim Hailand, Elton John and

David Furnish, Suzannah Constantine, Ben Hudson, Darren Criss and Mia Swier, Drew Straus, Travis Greisler, Jason Moore, Richard and Laurie Stark, Craig Pfunder, Dave Givan, Anderson Cooper, Benjamin Maisani, Nashom Wooden, Daniel Nardicio, Orla Lee, Rachael Harris and Christian Hebel (and Henry), Ed Droste and Simon Renggli, Sam Sparro and Zion Lennox, Charlie Carver, Larry Mark, Alex Miller, Max Hershenow, Casey Spooner, Adam DiCarlo, Suzanne Geiss, Mike Jackson, Justin Kelly, JB Ghuman, Julie Knowles, Gail Solod, Amaryllis Knight and Ian Barry, Thed Jewel, Matty Pipes, Moises Kaufman, Sam Marionni, Chris Cruse, Brian Emrich, Rio and Libby Hackford, and of course the O'Keefes at Queensdale (love you, Tara).

And Adam. You are my dreamiest dream. I love you so much.

ABOUT THE AUTHOR

Jake Shears is the lead singer of the multiplatinum-selling glam rock band Scissor Sisters. Born in Arizona, he grew up in the Seattle area before moving to New York City, where he studied fiction writing at The New School. He wrote the music for *Tales of the City*, a 2011 stage musical based on Armistead Maupin's best-selling book series of the same name. He divides his time between Los Angeles and New Orleans.